THE
GOLDEN
THIRTEEN

THE
GOLDEN
THIRTEEN

How Black Men Won the
Right to Wear Navy Gold

DAN C. GOLDBERG

BEACON PRESS
Boston

BEACON PRESS
Boston, Massachusetts
www.beacon.org

Beacon Press books
are published under the auspices of
the Unitarian Universalist Association of Congregations.

23 22 21 20   8 7 6 5 4 3 2 1

This book is printed on acid-free paper that meets the uncoated paper
ANSI/NISO specifications for permanence as revised in 1992.

Text design and composition by Kim Arney

All photographs are from the U.S. Navy, located in the
National Archives Record Group 80-G.

Library of Congress Cataloging-in-Publication Data
Names: Goldberg, Dan C., author.
Title: The golden thirteen : how Black men won the right to wear
Navy gold / Dan C. Goldberg.
Description: Boston : Beacon Press, [2020] | Includes bibliographical
references and index.
Identifiers: LCCN 2019059058 (print) | LCCN 2019059059 (ebook) |
ISBN 9780807021583 (hardcover) | ISBN 9780807021897 (ebook)
Subjects: LCSH: United States. Navy—African Americans. | United States. Navy—
Officers—Biography. | United States—Armed Forces—African American officers—
History—20th century. | United States—History, Naval—20th century.
Classification: LCC VB324.A47 G64 2020 (print) | LCC VB324.A47 (ebook) |
DDC 359.0092/396073—dc23
LC record available at https://lccn.loc.gov/2019059058
LC ebook record available at https://lccn.loc.gov/2019059059

To everyone who has been told,
"No, your idea isn't worth a book."

CONTENTS

CHAPTER 1

"WE'RE SENDING YOU UP TO GREAT LAKES."

Jesse Arbor, a cheeky and irreverent twenty-eight-year-old, was sweeping for mines off the coast of New England and helping direct ships to their berths in the fall of 1943 when he learned he'd been selected to serve aboard the USS *Mason*.

The *Mason*, an Evarts-class destroyer escort, was going to be the first warship in US history to boast a black crew. He would finally see real action on the open sea, not just operate off the coast.

"My chest flew wide open because I was so proud," Arbor recalled.[1]

Arbor was just a tad over six feet tall, with broad shoulders and powerful thighs that gave the two-hundred-pound football stud surprising agility. He had enlisted in the Navy the year before, only a few months after it was announced that black men could try for a general-service rating, the first time the Navy allowed them to do more than cook, clean, and serve white men aboard ship. Black men could now train as gunner's mates, machinist's mates, quartermasters, and electricians.

After twelve weeks of boot camp, where Navy customs and regulations were so drilled into his consciousness that they became second nature, Arbor had spent sixteen weeks at quartermaster school. He studied navigation, flashing-light communications, sextants, compasses, steering, and other nautical skills at Great Lakes Naval Training Station, in Great Lakes, Illinois, close to where his parents lived, in Chicago.

1

He was a middling student at Great Lakes, graduating in April 1943 as a quartermaster third class, the lowest rating for new navigation experts. His first assignment was at a receiving station in Boston, where he spent August and September aboard the USS *Bulwark*, an Accentor-class coastal minesweeper, a relatively small ship designed for protecting harbors and bays. The crew left between five-thirty and six every morning and spent eight hours sweeping for mines in the cold, choppy waters off New England.

This could be dull work, but it was still considered a plum gig for a black man at the time. Many black sailors with the same training spent their days waxing floors in the barracks, washing pants, and cleaning toilets, a reminder of the racism that governed social relations in twentieth-century America as it fought for democracy abroad.[2] Though black men had been training for the general-service ratings for more than a year, the Navy had thus far limited their assignments to shore establishments or guarding the coast.

But the *Mason* was no minesweeper. This was a warship that would patrol the Atlantic, fending off German U-boats.

This was where the action was.

By the end of 1942, U-boats had sunk nearly 1,200 US merchant vessels attempting to supply Great Britain with military equipment, food, and fuel. The supply lines were key to winning the war, and the Navy developed destroyer escorts such as the *Mason* to combat German submarines. The destroyers carried depth charges and antisubmarine weapons known as hedgehogs. They had mounted three-inch, fifty-caliber guns, as well as anti-aircraft guns. They had sophisticated tracking equipment that used high-frequency radio, radar, and sonar.[3]

No black man had ever worked as a quartermaster on a ship like this.

The height of Arbor's ambition was to be a quartermaster aboard the *Mason*, where he could play an active role in defending his country. Maybe, one day, he could even earn a promotion to chief quartermaster.[4] That he would help break a color barrier by serving on the first warship with a black crew only added to his excitement.

Arbor's bags were already packed when orders suddenly changed. He was told that he would not be going aboard the *Mason*. He wasn't told why.

He could barely contain his rage, and the news that he had been given leave for Christmas did little to assuage his disappointment.

When Arbor returned to Boston from a trip home to Chicago, the first thing he did was wash his clothes. To pass the time, he started playing poker with some of his Navy buddies. Sitting in his skivvies, Arbor heard someone say that he needed to report to the officer of the deck. Annoyed, he didn't even look up.

"Hell, I just left there," he said.

No answer.

When Arbor finally raised his head, he realized he was addressing a commander.

He stood at attention.

"Sir, I don't have anything to put on. In a few minutes, it will all be out of the washing machine, and then I've got to dry something."

The officer turned and left.

Arbor sat down, but before the next hand was dealt, another officer appeared.

"Jesse Arbor, you're wanted by the officer of the deck on the double." Arbor realized no one was interested in his laundry. He borrowed a uniform and rushed out. On the steps, he was met by a captain who handed him a sealed brown envelope.

"You have ten minutes to get your seabag lashed up," he said. "There's a car sitting down below to take you to Back Bay Station. In thirty-five minutes, you're going back to Chicago."

That wasn't enough time to pack so Arbor didn't bother. He grabbed, borrowed, and stole what he could—bell-bottom trousers, an undress blue jumper, and a peacoat that didn't quite fit.

His mind was racing. Why was he being sent back to Chicago? Was he in trouble? He remembered that he had once been in a car accident on the corner of Fifty-First and South Park. He had been driving an old Pontiac and he wrecked a doctor's Packard. Maybe he was being sent back to answer for that.

When Arbor arrived at Chicago's Union Station, a Beaux Arts masterpiece near the Loop, a sailor greeted him and the two drove thirty-five miles north, to Great Lakes, the headquarters of the Ninth Naval District.

Arbor was shown to a barracks, where a couple other black men were waiting.[5]

———

John Reagan also had hopes that he would finally see some action. He had been in the Navy for eighteen months, an electrician's mate of some repute who had impressed his superiors at Hampton Institute in Virginia, home to a segregated training station led by Lieutenant Commander Edwin Hall Downes.

Reagan had spent 1943 aboard the USS *Firefly*, an auxiliary minesweeper stationed out of Naval Base Point Loma, California. At the end of the year, he was ordered to Norfolk Naval Operating Base, in Virginia, so he could be an electrician aboard the *Mason*.

Back in Virginia and brimming with excitement, Reagan ran into his old boss, Downes, who by then had been promoted to commander. Downes asked Reagan what he was doing back in Virginia. Reagan stuck out his chest and declared, "I'm going aboard this DE [destroyer escort] as an AC electrician's mate. I'm going to get a ship at last."

"The hell you are," Downes replied. "Come over here to the personnel office and get your orders changed. You come over to my quarters at the school this afternoon or this evening, and I'll tell you a little bit about what's going on."

Reagan followed up with Downes, but the commander was coy.

"We're sending you up to Great Lakes for a special class and it's something that you'll like. You'll be glad you're going. It might lead to something you never suspected."[6]

———

James Hair suspected little when he was told to report to Great Lakes. He had been working out of the Brooklyn Navy Yard as a quartermaster on a tugboat, the USS *Penobscot*, and enjoying the life of a young, single sailor in New York City.

A shore-to-ship call came: "Transfer James Hair to 90 Church Street immediately upon docking." The massive building between Vesey and

Barclay streets near New York's City Hall served as the headquarters for the Third Naval District.

Hair reported and announced himself. He was given little regard, just a large brown envelope sealed with red wax, a train ticket, and no explanation. He was told to proceed immediately to Great Lakes Naval Training Station and report to Commander Daniel W. Armstrong, a white officer in charge of the segregated Camp Robert Smalls. The camp had been designated for black men almost two years before, to accommodate the Navy's new enlistees after Pearl Harbor.

Hair hustled uptown to Penn Station and, exhausted, fell asleep while waiting at the gate. The next sound he heard was a porter yelling, "All aboard!"

Hair grabbed his gear and ran along the narrow platform toward the departing train, which was beginning to pull away. He screamed at the porter, at anyone who could help, as he tried to jump aboard the moving train before he ran out of platform. Just before he did, he threw on his bags and climbed inside. Breathless, Hair found a seat as the train headed west under the Hudson River and into New Jersey before making its way through Pennsylvania, Ohio, Indiana, and Illinois.

The train pulled into Chicago after midnight, and Hair arrived at Great Lakes at around 1 a.m. The officers there didn't know what to make of this young man. Hair couldn't provide much help. All he knew was that he had orders to see Commander Armstrong. But Armstrong was asleep, and no one was going to wake the commander for a confused black man clutching a brown envelope. Hair was sent to sick bay, the only area where there was a bed available, and was told he could see Armstrong in the morning.[7]

═══════

When the sun rose the next morning, Sam Barnes was given an order he did not understand: Armstrong had ordered him to the main side— the white side of the station, where senior officers worked. The only time African Americans were ordered to the main side was when they were in trouble. Barnes racked his brain wondering what he might have done wrong. Nothing came. Barnes, a petty officer third class stationed at Great Lakes, was popular with his superiors and appreciated by his peers. He had never been disciplined. Why, he wondered, was Armstrong ordering him to the main side?

Barnes arrived to find several other black men waiting. He knew a few from Camp Robert Smalls. He recognized Reginald Goodwin and Lewis "Mummy" Williams (Williams got the nickname because of a grammar school book report on King Tut; it suited him because of his quiet nature). They were standouts, same as he was. He didn't recognize the other black men, and judging by the looks on their faces, they had no more idea than he as to why they had all been summoned.

Armstrong, a tall, handsome, aristocratic-looking man with an upright gait and an immaculate uniform, looked the men over.

"Do you know why you are here?" he asked.

Silence.

"Well, the Navy has decided to commission Negroes as officers in the United States Navy, and you have been selected to attend an officer indoctrination school."

The statement was matter-of-fact, unemotional.

No allotment was made for the weight of history it carried, no moment spared to mark its significance. There were no kind words of congratulations, no expressions of encouragement.

Along with Arbor, Reagan, Hair, Sam Barnes, Goodwin, and Williams, ten other black sailors had been summoned from training schools and shore installations across the United States to be informed, coldly, that they had been chosen to break the Navy's most rigid color barrier.

Phil Barnes, Dalton Baugh, and George Cooper had worked at Hampton Institute.

Augustus Alves, J. B. Pinkney, Charles Lear, Graham Martin, and William Sylvester White had been stationed at Great Lakes.

Frank Sublett had been at Naval Section Base, Lockwood Basin, in Boston, and Dennis Nelson had been at a recruiting station in Nashville, Tennessee.

The men stared at one another, wondering whether Armstrong had lost his mind.

But no one said a word.

Armstrong ordered the men to return to Camp Robert Smalls and head to Barracks 202, where they would meet their executive officer and instructors.

"But before you go," Armstrong said, "in order to be considered for officer candidate, you must be at least a chief petty officer or a petty officer first class. So, all of those who are neither as of this moment are first class."[8] There was a moment of elation. The sudden promotion meant an instant boost in pay. But the giddiness was brief. Whatever illusion any of these sixteen men might have had about the Navy entering some new era of racial harmony was shattered the moment the door to Barracks 202 swung open.

When the men peered inside, they saw sixteen cots, sixteen foot lockers, and one long table with sixteen chairs—the kind men sat around at chow. The spartan setting made plain just how the Navy intended to integrate the officer corps.

A white officer looked from the room to the men and said, "This is it."

"What do you mean?" asked George Cooper, a Hampton man and sheet-metal whiz who had worked with Commander Downes for nearly two years.[9]

"This barracks in which you are now sitting is going to be your school."

The men's hearts sank in their chests. Great Lakes was home to an elite service school with plenty of equipment that could aid their training. But they'd see almost none of that. They would train separately, drill apart, and eat alone, essentially under house arrest for the crime of being black. The officer corps was ready to be integrated. Great Lakes Naval Training Station was not. This experiment was a secret. They were to tell no one. They were to have no contact with anyone, white or black, save for their instructors and family members.

"That was sort of a letdown off the bat," Cooper remembered.

The sixteen men sat together that first night, a wintry Saturday, inside a cold barracks, contemplating the weeks ahead and the magnitude of their responsibility.

CHAPTER 2

"DON'T PUT YOUR TIME IN NEGROES."

It was January 1944. There were nearly 100,000 black men in the Navy. If any of them were ever to rise above the rate of petty officer, if any were ever to command a ship or graduate from the Naval Academy, if any were ever to lead white men in battle, then this radical experiment with these sixteen officer candidates would have to succeed.

This training program was the culmination of a four-year campaign to have the Navy live up to the democratic ideals the United States was preaching and defending around the globe. Men and women of all races, from all over the country, were demanding a better, freer, more democratic world, not only for allies in Europe and Asia, but for themselves and their children in America. Thousands had marched and protested, written letters and signed petitions, beseeched their congressmen, and begged the president, all so that black men could serve equally in the US Navy, a branch that had historically been so hostile to people of color. Those men and women were met at every turn by an intransigent bureaucracy that was far more concerned with efficiency than with equality, by a Navy secretary who was certain that integration would bring disaster, and by admirals who were adamant that worthy black men could not be found in the whole of the United States.

Because of that history, many in this first group remained cynical and kept up their guard, not yet willing to believe the Navy would really allow black officers. But each man swore he'd give it his all—for his own sake, for the countless souls whose sacrifice made this moment possible, and for all the black men yet to come.

"We believed there were people who hoped we'd fail," Sam Barnes recalled. "We were determined to succeed in spite of the burden that was being placed on our shoulders."[1]

Barnes wasn't wrong to distrust the Navy. Less than two years before, Navy Secretary Frank Knox had threatened to resign before so much as integrating the sleeping quarters aboard a ship or allowing black men into the Navy's general service, where they would work alongside white men. Knox and his admirals insisted that African Americans should only serve as messmen, servants derided as little more than "seagoing bellhops."[2]

It had been less than a year since Knox told President Franklin Roosevelt that he opposed accepting black men from the draft, fearing that doing so would force the Navy to resort to mixed crews aboard a ship, an outcome he deemed foolish in the face of a two-ocean war.

And it had been only two decades since an Army War College report had concluded that black men could hold no position that required leadership, courage, or intelligence. A generation of military policy was based on this so-called exhaustive study of how black men had performed during World War I. Released in 1925, *The Use of Negro Manpower in War* asserted that black men were genetically ill equipped to serve. "In the process of evolution, the American Negro has not progressed as far as other subspecies of the human family," wrote Major General Hanson Edward Ely in the War College report.[3]

In reality, black men had displayed a courage that heartened allies and terrified enemies. So successful was the 369th Infantry Regiment, the Black Rattlers of the New York Army National Guard, that the French referred to them as Men of Bronze.

The Germans knew them by another name: Hellfighters. They were on the front line for 191 days and never had a single soldier taken prisoner nor had they surrendered a single foot of ground to the enemy.[4]

But acts of heroism and bravery by African Americans were forever anomalies in the eyes of the military's leaders, mere exceptions to the self-evident truth that black men were inferior.

The same year that Ely released his report, 1925, Major General Robert Lee Bullard, commander of the Second Army during World War I, published his memoir, in which he wrote, "If you need combat soldiers, and especially if you need them in a hurry, don't put your time in Negroes."[5]

Ely and Bullard, American heroes in contemporary eyes, were writing on paper what most military men felt in their hearts.

Of course, those feelings were simply a reflection of American society. Ely's and Bullard's works coincided with the second flowering of the Ku Klux Klan, which boasted more than four million members at the time and included governors, congressmen, and a future Supreme Court justice.

It also coincided with the founding of the American Eugenics Society, which popularized anthropometry, which equated physical measurements with mental capabilities and purported to demonstrate the superiority of certain races and ethnicities. By 1928, there were 376 separate university courses on eugenics in many of the United States' leading colleges and universities.[6]

Civil rights leaders such as W. E. B. Du Bois had hoped and argued that a courageous performance during the fight in Europe would win black men respect when they returned to the United States. But after the war, black soldiers and sailors were accorded little respect. Patriotism was a currency of no value to black men, particularly in the South.[7]

During World War I, black men in the Navy mostly served as coal-passers and firemen on coal-burning ships. Anything more than menial work was a rarity. Only a handful of black men were promoted into petty officer ratings. Those who were served as water tenders, assigned to manage the fire in a boiler, or, occasionally, as gunners' mates, who were nearly always in charge of the armory, working alone, away from white men.[8] But even that much responsibility was considered distasteful, an encroachment acceptable only because of the necessities of a world war.

When the war ended, the US Navy, no longer needing as many men, suspended new enlistments of black men entirely. The chores they had performed would be handled by Filipinos, considered better suited than African Americans for a servant's role.[9] By 1932, when Franklin Roosevelt was elected president, the Navy had 81,000 men, only 441 of whom were black, the lowest percentage in American history—considerably fewer than at the end of the nineteenth century, when African Americans made up between 20 and 30 percent of men serving in the Navy.[10]

It might have remained that way had Japan not invaded Manchuria in 1931, which prompted Captain Abram Claude, the Navy's director of enlisted personnel, to suggest phasing out Filipinos, who had come to dominate the servants' ranks. Claude thought it unwise to have so many East Asians employed on US ships when Japan might advance on American interests in the Pacific. He proposed opening the messman branch to African Americans again, telling his superiors that it "would enable us to answer the criticism that Negro citizens are not allowed to enlist in our Navy."

Claude's memorandum garnered quick condemnation—had it been written by a less well-credentialed officer, the suggestion might have been dismissed altogether. But Claude was an American hero. He had earned the Navy Cross for saving his ship, the USS *Cassin*, during a widely publicized clash with the German submarine *U-61* in 1917. He was a scion of a prominent and influential Maryland family that had once owned slaves.

Claude was no radical, but his heroism, prestige, and lineage were not enough to push forward as revolutionary an idea as reshaping the messman branch of the United States Navy with men born in the United States.

The day after Claude sent his suggestion, Commander Robert R. M. Emmet, then the head of enlisted personnel training, railed against the idea. "As an officer of considerable experience with Officer's Messes, using both Colored and Filipino servants, I feel we ought to hang on to the Filipinos till the last," he wrote. "They are cleaner, more efficient and eat much less than Negros [sic]. Negros are capable of being better cooks though even the best require very close supervision or you will find yourself drenched with grease in the cooking. . . . Going back to colored men would be a distinct step backward."[11]

Claude persisted, arguing that black men had never received adequate training for those tasks. He promised he "could get a high type of Negro and train him in his duties before sending him out to the service and the result would eventually be improvement in officers' servants."

A compromise was reached. The Navy would "maintain a nucleus of Negro messmen without dispensing with the services of Filipinos until necessary."

Claude was warned not to accept the "wrong" kind of black man. Northern blacks were undesirable because they were "apt to be independent, insolent, and over-educated," and therefore unsuitable to play the "lackey."[12]

The Navy wanted African Americans from the South because "by training and environment the Southern colored man has inherited a servant's point of view and is usually contented and happy in that position," Commander D. A. Weaver wrote to Claude.

In the South, the Navy believed, it would find the "unspoiled young Negro."[13]

———

While the Navy debated changing its policy on black messmen, a meeting was taking place in Pittsburgh that would forever alter black politics and have a far more profound impact on integration in the military than anyone at the time could have possibly imagined.

Michael Benedum, the head of the Pittsburgh-based Benedum-Trees Oil Company, who was known as the man who "uncork[ed] more oil than anyone else in the world," sought out Robert Lee Vann, the esteemed publisher of the *Pittsburgh Courier*, one of the most influential black newspapers in the country, to make an outlandish request.

He wanted Vann, the son of slaves, to abandon the party of Abraham Lincoln, endorse the Democrat, Franklin Roosevelt, and use his paper to encourage the 181,000 black registered Republicans in western Pennsylvania to vote for FDR in the 1932 election.

Look how African Americans were faring under President Herbert Hoover, Benedum pondered aloud. More than 40 percent of Pittsburgh's blacks were unemployed and living in squalor as the Great Depression cast a pall over American life.

"What had the Negro ever gotten by voting the Republican ticket?" Benedum asked when the two met.

"Nothing," Vann conceded.

Benedum told Vann that he admired African Americans' loyalty to the GOP but felt that they owed no further debt to the party simply because of what Lincoln had done seventy years earlier. By 1932, Benedum said, blacks "had already paid this debt many times over and with plenty of interest."[14]

Vann agreed.

The *Pittsburgh Courier* became relentless in its criticisms of Republicans and prolific in its praise for the Democratic nominee, reminding its readers—in articles and editorials—of the Republican government's unequal treatment of black Americans in the midst of the Depression. The Republicans were not paying attention, Vann told his audience. A wakeup call was needed and the voting booth was the alarm clock.

Vann sympathized with those who hesitated to leave the party that had freed the slaves and join one so beholden to Southern racists. But, in a speech titled "The Patriot and the Partisan," he argued that if black people desired change from their politicians, they needed to be willing to change their politics.

The marriage between African Americans and the Republican Party had gone stale. The thrill was gone. Vann intended to convince his fellow African Americans that the time had come to sue for divorce.

"So long as the Republican party could use the photograph of Abraham Lincoln to entice Negroes to vote a Republican ticket they condescended to accord Negroes some degree of political recognition," Vann said in his speech. "The Republican party under Harding absolutely deserted us. The Republican Party under Mr. Coolidge was a lifeless, voiceless thing. The Republican Party under Mr. Hoover has been the saddest failure known to political history. . . . I see millions of Negroes turning the pictures of Abraham Lincoln to the wall."[15]

Vann's speech was reprinted in the *Pittsburgh Courier* and other black newspapers, and also was circulated nationally as a pamphlet. Vann could not swing Pennsylvania, which gave Hoover 36 of his paltry 59 electoral votes in the election that swept FDR to power, but the margin was exceedingly close. Allegheny County, where Vann's influence was strongest, went for Roosevelt by 37,000 votes.[16]

Roosevelt named Vann special assistant to the attorney general. But before Vann accepted the appointment, he sounded a warning. The black vote, to have any meaning, would have to remain in play, and never again be wedded to one party.

"I came to the Democratic Party because the Republican Party no longer serves the interest of the people," Vann said shortly after Roosevelt's inauguration. "When this party gets to where they no longer offer my people any service I'll either go back to the Republican Party or to some other party."[17] Vann called it "loose leaf politics."

The man who could shape black opinion throughout the country with a single story became one of the most powerful and most feared black men in America.[18] When his newspaper reported that black men in the Tenth Cavalry at West Point were assigned to groom officers' mounts and shovel manure or when it informed readers that blacks at Fort Benning were working as orderlies or on routine garrison duty, other black newspapers chased the story and amplified the outrage.

Roughly one-third of all African American families in cities regularly subscribed to a black newspaper and then shared them with families who could not afford a subscription. Porters on Pullman railroad carriages would haul copies of the *Pittsburgh Courier* and *Chicago Defender* to the rural South.[19] They were read aloud to those who could not read themselves. They were available in barbershops, churches, lodges, and pool halls.[20]

By 1936, the *Courier*'s circulation had reached 174,000, and Vann's reach was as undeniable as his influence.[21]

After helping Roosevelt win reelection and become the first Democrat to win Pennsylvania since James Buchanan, Vann felt that the president and the Democratic Party owed African Americans something tangible, something audacious, something commensurate with the size of the electoral victory.

Vann chose equality in the military. "Although colored citizens have participated with honor and distinction in every war the United States has fought and died in the thousands that this grand Republic might live, they are today barred from virtually all service in our Army and Navy which they help support," Vann wrote in a letter he published in the *Courier* and sent to college presidents and US senators. "In the Navy they are rigidly restricted to service as mess attendants. . . . We do not believe that the thinking white people of this country are acquainted with this situation or would approve of it if they were. We are trying to have all branches of the Army and Navy opened to colored youth that our nation may be certain of a trained reservoir of loyal, intelligent and dependable men."[22]

Vann wrote an open letter to President Roosevelt outlining ten reasons why black men deserved equality in the Army and Navy, one of several articles that appeared month after month demanding fairer treatment in the armed services.[23] "I feel, and my people feel, that this is the psychological moment to strike for our rightful place in our National Defense," Vann wrote Roosevelt in 1939. "I need not tell you we are expecting a more dignified place in our armed forces during the next war than we occupied during the World War."[24]

———————

James Hair became acquainted with politics and civil rights struggles in a shoe shop in Fort Pierce, Florida. He was a high school student who wanted the owner, Ronald Warrick, to teach him the secrets of fishing, but while hanging out there Hair was just another kid listening to older black men discuss the day's news: Roosevelt's New Deal, Adolf Hitler's rise abroad, and the push for greater equality at home. The shoe shop was filled with books, and although Warrick himself had never made it past the eighth grade, he operated an unofficial library and open forum for black men to discuss current events, social politics, and world affairs. They discussed the station of African Americans, how it had improved, how it had not, and how education could be the great equalizer.[25]

At the time Hair was so much more interested in fishing, but what he heard stuck and remained with him throughout his life. Education, dignity, respect—they were the qualities that would a decade later help make this son of a slave one of the first black naval officers.

Hair was not from Fort Pierce. He had been born in Blackville, a part of South Carolina known as the Backcountry.

Blackville, like so many little hamlets across the United States, owed its existence to the railroad. In the early nineteenth century, businessmen seeking a way to keep Charleston competitive with the growing port of

Savannah, Georgia, founded the South Carolina Canal and Railroad Company in the hopes of connecting Charleston with Hamburg, near Augusta.

John Alexander Black, one of the company's founders, chose where the train would stop for the night, and that location became the village of Blackville, which was incorporated in 1833. Hotels and shops sprouted up in town to cater to the passengers making their way across the 126 miles of track. Demand for crops in Blackville soared. Cucumbers, asparagus, and watermelon became staples of the surrounding farms.

It was on one of these farms that James Edward Hair was brought into the world in 1915 when Blackville had about a thousand residents. He was the twentieth of twenty-one children born to the Reverend Alfred Hair and Rosa Nix, each of whom had children from previous marriages. Reverend Hair, a Baptist minister whose sermons were more fire and brimstone than "love thy neighbor," was nearly sixty years old when his son James was born, and many of his other children were already married with families of their own. Reverend Hair had been born a slave in South Carolina, likely the product of his mother and her master. When he was still a boy, his mother and her husband had been sold and he was raised by his white owner, reuniting with his mother only after the Civil War.[26]

Reverend Hair's children were expected to work the farm before and after school. James was barely out of diapers when he was in the field picking cotton. The family also grew corn, peas, rice, sugarcane, and other vegetables, enough to provide for the large brood.

Blackville was a bit peculiar for a Southern town in that wealth was more divisive than race. Poor sharecroppers helped one another, regardless of skin color. Children of both races played together in the cotton fields alongside their laboring parents.

James, a good student, loved Blackville. He was content even with the rigorous schedule and strict religious upbringing. He was enamored with his old man. His father seemed to know everything, to have an answer to every question. It was a short relationship. James was only eight years old when his father died. His mother, unable to manage the large farm by herself, moved the younger children to Fort Pierce, Florida, where some of her older children were already living.

Rosa tried to shield her son from the day-to-day racism, but it was harder to do so in Fort Pierce than it had been in Blackville.

In Fort Pierce there was a black section of town, a segregated ghetto in the northwest part of the city bordered by Seventh Street to the east and a canal to the south. African Americans were not supposed to be outside those boundaries after dark. There were "colored" signs above water fountains and tacked to restroom doors. African Americans walked through the back door at a restaurant. They sat in the balcony when they went to a movie. If they worked in the white section of town, they made sure they were back in the black section by sundown.

Follow the rules and there was no trouble.

As a kid, Hair didn't think too much about segregation. It was just the way things were, and he had plenty to keep him busy in the black section of town. Avenue D, the center of what was known as "colored town," "black town," or "nigger town," was lined with juke joints. There was a pharmacy, an ice house, and the Lincoln Theater. The bar was on the corner; so was Warrick's shoe shop.

Hair attended Lincoln Park Academy, which Jean Ellen Wilson, a historian and librarian, said was arguably the best black high school in Florida, attracting families from all parts of the South. After his father died, Hair's male role model became Estes Wright, who had married his older sister Margaret. Wright became even more important to Hair in 1933 when his mother, Rosa, died.

Wright, a fruit picker by trade, was dynamic and charismatic and Hair became his shadow, learning and emulating.[27] Wright was one of the few men Hair knew who did not stand for any kind of racism or segregation. When local authorities set up two lines for the government surplus food that was handed out during the Great Depression—one for whites and one for blacks—Wright ignored the signs. The policy was that all the white families had to be served first, and if there was any food left over, the black people could take.

Wright never waited. He and Hair would walk right in, fill their burlap bags with the food on the shelves, throw the sacks over their shoulders, and walk away.

No one said anything. Perhaps it was because Wright was known to carry a .38 revolver wherever he went and had on more than one occasion pointed it in the face of a man he felt had done him wrong.

One night, Wright and Hair were fishing off a bridge, violating local mores that held black men were not allowed to fish after dark.

Three white men approached and asked why "two niggers" thought they could be on that bridge.

Wright whipped out his revolver.

"Because we want to," he said. "I'll give you ten seconds to get off this bridge. If I ever see you again, I'll kill you."

Hair never saw the men again.

And so while the black press talked of ending segregation in the military and breathlessly reported the works of a new generation of civil rights heroes—A. Philip Randolph, Walter White, William H. Hastie, Charles Hamilton Houston, Thurgood Marshall, Mary McLeod Bethune—Estes Wright, who by age thirty had fathered five children and had a sixth on the way, was doing his own, unheralded part to live a life free of racism.

His death in September 1935 remains shrouded in mystery, and, more than eighty years later, relatives dispute a few of the details. There was no obituary and there is no gravestone.

Lynchings aren't recorded like that.

"A black man would get 'uppity' and he would just disappear," said Jean Ellen Wilson.

Wright's final moments appear to have begun when he tried to help a black man named Frank Ricks, who had gotten into a car accident with a white driver at the corner of Avenue D and Seventh Street while making a delivery run for Sid's Dry Cleaners. A group of white men gathered threateningly around Ricks.

Wright intervened.

Ricks ran.

Wright could not get away.

The mob had him.

Hair's sister Carrie was the first to hear and ran screaming for her brother.

"James! James! They're killing Estes. They're killing him."

Hair grabbed his bicycle and together the two pedaled downtown toward the jailhouse. They arrived in time to see Wright's bloodied body, gasping for a few last agonizing breaths.

Wright lay on a bench—surrounded by about six hundred white men.

"All he could do was give these death sounds, the death rattle in his throat—what a hurting sound," Hair remembered.

Hair and Carrie took a handkerchief and started wiping the blood from their brother-in-law's battered and bruised face. Wright's skull was as soft as the cotton Hair had grown up picking—"Nothing hard about it."

Sheriff Robert Brown spotted the pair tending to Wright.

"What in the hell you doing here?" he shouted.

"We're here to take care of our brother."

"Get the hell out of here right now!" Brown screamed at the two. "Get out!"

The two started to leave when Carrie, almost under her breath, said, "Look like they would let us do something for him."

Brown grabbed her arm and spun her around.

"What in the hell did you say?"

Hair lowered his shoulder and charged into the sheriff, knocking him back.

There was a moment of absolute stillness as the crowd, thirsty for blood, stared at their sheriff on his heels, waiting to see what would happen next.

Brown walked over to Hair and patted him on the head. "Son, go on about your business."[28]

That night the mob brought Wright's near-lifeless body back to his home at 713 North Thirteenth Street. His whole family, even his pregnant wife, was forced out of the house while the body was placed in bed. A line of cars drove up in front of the narrow, rectangular, shotgun-style home. A man dressed in a white shirt and white pants and carrying a shotgun got out of the lead car. Another man, similarly dressed, got out of the second car and stood at attention. Then a third and a fourth. Maybe a dozen men in all got out of their cars and stood silently. No one moved until the last man exited his car. The white men formed a line and marched through the Wright front door to the bed on which Wright lay dying, out the back door and around the house. They stood again by their cars. They stared at the African Americans who had gathered to watch this curious procession.

The message was clear: this is what happens to a black man who doesn't follow the rules.

Then they got back in their cars and drove away.

The next afternoon, Estes Wright died in his bed, never having re-gained consciousness.

The only contemporary mention of his death can be found in the *Fort Pierce News Tribune*, which reported that Wright had died after falling and hitting his head on the sidewalk.

On his death certificate, Dr. C. C. Benton attested that Wright's death had been caused by a "blow on head" resulting in a "fractured skull and compression." The coroner's jury found Wright "came to his death by in-terfering with [a] legal arrest and through his own negligence when he fell and struck his head against a street curb."

As far as anyone could remember, that particular street had no curb.

CHAPTER 3

"I JUST DON'T BELIEVE YOU CAN DO THE JOB."

Jesse Arbor dropped out of Arkansas AM&N College, a black land-grant college, in March 1937, a few months shy and $38 short of a diploma. He returned home to Chicago and found work at the Chicago Beach Hotel, one of the premier establishments in the city. The gig paid well, $70 per month—more than most other jobs in an economy still reeling from the Great Depression. Arbor may not have been rubbing elbows with the city's elite, but he was opening doors for them, and for an African American kid with no college diploma that seemed pretty good.

Arbor wasn't originally from Chicago. He had been born the day after Christmas, 1914, in Cotton Plant, Arkansas, in the Mississippi Delta, on land deeded to his family after the Civil War. He was the grandchild of slaves—his maternal grandmother, who lived until the age of 105, often told stories that began with, "My master said . . ."

He was one of twelve children born to Alexander and Tecora Arbor in the farm-dominated town, about sixty-five miles west of Memphis. At the time of his birth, Cotton Plant was in the midst of a population boom, growing from 458 people in 1900 to nearly 1,700 by 1920.

By then, Cotton Plant had a post office, two banks, three cotton gins, a sawmill, and a factory that made shirts for the Army. The town boasted a Masonic lodge and an opera house. There were two "white" churches and three "colored" churches.

Arbor attended Cotton Plant Academy, a Presbyterian school three miles away, and the religious principles taught there were reinforced at home. There was a rule against playing ball or shooting marbles on Sunday. That was the Lord's Day. If a commandment was violated, Jesse's father, a soft-spoken, devout Christian, wouldn't whip his sons on Sunday because, well, that was the Lord's Day, but first thing Monday morning, before breakfast, the commandment breaker would receive his righteous punishment.

Mr. Arbor was a carpenter, able to provide both a reasonable living and plenty of wooden toys for his children. He was slight, dwarfed by his nearly-two-hundred-pound wife, Tecora. The couple believed in God and education with equal fervor.

At night, Mr. Arbor insisted that his ten boys and two girls sit near the fireplace with a book and read aloud. Alexander Arbor, a first-generation freeman, had never made it beyond the fourth grade. It wasn't long before his children had a better vocabulary than he did—and that was the point. They needed to know more to become more. If his children stumbled on a word—it didn't matter whether Mr. Arbor understood what the word was—he made them repeat it until they could read the word smooth and proper.

The Arbors moved to Chicago when Jesse was fifteen years old, part of the Great Migration that brought hundreds of thousands of African Americans from the fields and farms in the South to cities and factories in the North. Few places were as affected as Chicago, where the black population grew from 2 percent of the city in 1910 to 33 percent by 1970.

Boll-weevil infestations and emerging technology were sending cotton farmers the way of horse-and-buggy drivers. And the Immigration Act of 1924 closed the borders to southern and eastern Europeans, a factor that, when combined with the many white men lost in World War I, meant job openings in factories and mills in the nation's urban centers.[1] Arbor's maternal uncles had already moved to Chicago and insisted that better opportunities for prosperity existed there.

The Windy City was far more tolerant of black families than Arkansas, but it was no Shangri La. White Chicagoans passed zoning laws and used violence to keep black families from moving into white neighborhoods.[2]

That kept African Americans on the South Side of Chicago, which is where the Arbors found themselves in the early 1930s.

Arbor's skill as a right tackle earned him a football scholarship back in Arkansas, but he struggled academically and lost his financial support. That forced him home and then to a Chicago resort on the shore of Lake Michigan, where he worked first as a waiter and later as a doorman. At the age of twenty-two, Arbor, an unremarkable thread in the tapestry of a fast-growing city, found himself at the entranceway to a life far beyond his means, ushering people into luxuries he could only imagine.

He worked at that hotel for nearly four years, until one day a familiar face opened a door for him.

"What are you doing standing up on this door?" asked Mr. McMannen. He was the father of a high school classmate of Arbor's and a vice president at the famed Pullman Car Company.

"Why aren't you doing something commensurate with your education?"

"Mr. McMannen," Arbor replied, "I need not tell you why I'm on this door. The jobs that I can get commensurate with my education do not pay as much as this."

McMannen suggested that Arbor look into the railroad, which would give him a chance to see the country and earn a living.

"They are not hiring anybody," Arbor said.

McMannen smiled and handed Arbor his card. He said, "Go down to 18th and L," and ask George Bulow about being a Pullman porter.

Arbor politely took the card but made no follow-up. He was a smart-ass who liked to run his mouth and hated taking orders. Besides, he liked his job and was concerned about taking another without any seniority. Seemed risky.

McMannen returned a few weeks later, incredulous that Arbor hadn't taken his advice. A job as a Pullman porter was a ticket to the middle class, and porters had one of the strongest unions in the country.

"Didn't I tell you to get off this door?" he asked. "Where's that card?"

Arbor lied and said he had lost it. McMannen handed him another and again instructed him to go down to 18th and L. This time McMannen called the office and told them to expect the young man, making it plain he would not take no for an answer.[3]

Arbor took the hint and the help. He spent much of the next two years riding the rails, cleaning the cars and taking care of passengers, but he never warmed to the life. He came home to Chicago and found a job at Kuppenheimer (B.) & Co., a leading manufacturer of men's clothing. Still preferring to give orders, not take them, he opened up his own tailor shop and soon hired three employees, not bad for a C-student who had flunked Introduction to Economics.[4]

Arbor was earning good money, and life in Chicago was grand, but the prosperity was short-lived. In the spring of 1940, the Germans invaded Belgium, the Netherlands, Luxembourg, and France, and were on their way to take Paris. The war in Europe, which Arbor had heretofore given little thought to, would soon demand another career change.

———

In Washington, President Franklin Roosevelt was building his "arsenal of democracy," and his call to defend democratic ideals gave civil rights leaders a new argument for an old fight.

By the summer of 1940, discrimination in the Army and Navy "cut deeper into Negro feelings than employment discrimination," and had replaced lynching as the chief political priority for the black community.[5]

The NAACP released a statement saying that it was "sorry for brutality, blood, and death among the peoples of Europe, just as we were sorry for China and Ethiopia. But the hysterical cries of the preachers of democracy for Europe leave us cold. We want democracy in Alabama, Arkansas, in Mississippi and Michigan, in the District of Columbia, in the Senate of the United States."[6]

Robert Lee Vann, editor of the *Pittsburgh Courier*, surveyed the political landscape and surmised that black Americans may never have a better opportunity than 1940 to pressure the White House for equality in the military.

Roosevelt was running for an unprecedented third term, and the black vote, he knew, could swing the election. It seemed to Vann that the nation could ill afford to rely on Major General Ely's report from fifteen years prior and ask African Americans to contribute to a military that insisted they were inferior. Vann told his readers to flood Congress with letters protesting "military taxation without representation."[7]

The response was overwhelming. Congressmen from northern and border states—commanding plenty of electoral votes—were suddenly championing the *Courier's* call on Capitol Hill.

Vann organized the Committee on Participation of Negroes in the National Defense Program and chose as its head Rayford Logan, a history professor at Howard University, an elite black university in Washington, DC. Logan lobbied Congress to add antidiscrimination language to the Selective Training and Service Act. He was successful, but only to a point.

When the bill reached the president's desk on September 16, 1940, it contained an antidiscrimination clause but also said that "no man shall be inducted . . . until he is acceptable to the land or naval forces." This gave both the Army and Navy plenty of ways to limit African American opportunity without technically discriminating under the law.[8]

Navy Secretary Frank Knox immediately announced he would take advantage of the loophole. The Navy would not accept black men from the draft. Instead, the branch would rely on volunteer enlistments, which would allow the Navy to limit the number of black inductees.

Black men who were accepted would be messmen, as they had been since 1933—nothing more. Their work would be limited to serving white men: preparing their meals, making their beds, and shining their shoes. Aboard ship, they'd sleep separately in messmen's quarters. They'd eat separately—after serving meals to white sailors and officers. The general-service ratings—gunner's mates, electrician's mates, quartermasters, shipfitters—would be reserved for whites only, and vessels would be strictly segregated so that whites would not have to share a room or a table with blacks.

The *Crisis*, the official magazine of the NAACP, impressed upon its readers the insidiousness of Knox's stance. "There is more to all this than standing on the deck of a warship in a white uniform," the editorial said. "To be stigmatized by being denied the opportunity of serving one's country in full combat service in the Navy is humiliating enough. But the real danger and greater injustice is to deny a tenth of the citizens of this country any benefit whatsoever from the billions of dollars spent on our Navy."

Picking up on Vann's taxation-without-representation argument, the editorial pointed out that taxes from black households maintained the US Naval Academy at Annapolis, which black boys could not attend. They paid for naval bases, navy yards, and naval air bases from which black men were excluded. They paid for the training of thousands of white boys, who would learn skills valuable long after their service ended, but black men were offered no such training or career paths.

"The health care, the character building, the training in efficiency, the travel and education—all at the expense of the taxpayers—are for whites only! This is the price we pay for being classified as a race, as mess attendants only! At the same time we are supposed to be able to appreciate what our white fellow citizens declare to be the 'vast difference' between American Democracy and Hitlerism."[9]

———

The same evening that President Roosevelt signed the Selective Training and Service Act into law, First Lady Eleanor Roosevelt was in New York City speaking before two thousand delegates and their families at a biennial dinner for the Brotherhood of Sleeping Car Porters. The dinner was held at the Shriners' resplendent Mecca Temple, an ornate structure in the Moorish style on West Fifty-Fifth Street in Manhattan, two blocks south of Carnegie Hall.[10]

Looking out at a sea of black faces, the First Lady told the crowd that there was a growing understanding that they had plenty to contribute to the defense effort.

"People are beginning to realize that we can't let any one group suffer because it then becomes a menace to the whole group," she said. "You know that we have many difficulties still to overcome. I happen to be tremendously interested in the young people of your race and I know their difficulties."[11]

The audience roared with appreciation, and the *New York Age*, a black newspaper, said it was one of the most "inspiring boosts of support" for Roosevelt's third term.[12]

But the jubilation for Eleanor, a champion of civil rights, masked the growing frustration with her husband's intransigence on integration of the military.

Vann, fed up, endorsed Wendell Willkie, the Republican nominee, making good on his threat to desert the Democratic Party if it stalled on civil rights. He told his readers to abandon the president because of Roosevelt's refusal to prohibit segregation in the Army and Navy.[13]

Walter White, executive secretary of the NAACP, and A. Philip Randolph, the president of the Brotherhood of Sleeping Car Porters, were equally distressed. They had been asking the White House for a meeting to discuss how black men would be used in the armed forces and the fact that the Army and Navy were hell-bent on segregation, even in the face of a coming war.

Their repeated requests were ignored, so they petitioned Eleanor Roosevelt, who, just before she took the podium, had promised to help.

With the long evening over, the First Lady retired to her Greenwich Village apartment and wrote her husband to complain that no meeting had been scheduled.

"There is a growing feeling amongst the colored people, [that] they should be allowed to participate in any training that is going on, in the aviation, Army, Navy. . . . This is going to be very bad politically besides being intrinsically wrong and I think you should ask a meeting be held."

Eleanor returned to Washington two days later, determined to make her case in person. She bypassed the staff—to their great annoyance—and went straight to her husband to demand that he meet with the civil rights leaders.[14]

She arrived during a particularly low point for the president's reelection campaign. The *New York Times* was about to endorse Wendell Willkie.[15]

Roosevelt decided his wife was right. He needed to take that meeting—and fast.

The following Friday morning, Randolph, White, and T. Arnold Hill, an assistant director with the National Youth Administration, were ushered into the Oval Office. The president, a former assistant secretary of the Navy, had given the august room a nautical theme. Prints of Navy ships and Hudson River landscapes, reminding Roosevelt of his Hyde

Park home, dotted the walls. What drew the eye, however, was the president's desk, always cluttered with knickknacks: lighters, paperweights, cigarettes, assorted toys and dispatches and reports spilling out of wire in-baskets.

Walter White, a Southerner with fair skin, blue eyes, and blond hair, who had led the NAACP for nearly a decade, was no stranger to the president. He had visited the White House in 1934 and 1938 in a doomed effort to have Roosevelt support an antilynching bill. The majority of White's ancestors were white, and although the physical traits of his African ancestors were not visible, he devoted his life to championing the cause of black America.

He took his seat across from Frank Knox and Robert Patterson, assistant secretary of war and a former federal judge in New York. Secretary of War Henry Stimson, Patterson's boss, thought integration so absurd that he boycotted the meeting. That left Patterson, a small bundle of nervous energy who was constantly chewing gum, with little to say and even less to offer.[16]

Knox, for his part, thought little of White, dismissing the NAACP chief as a man "constantly agitating for greater Negro recognition in the Navy" and one who should not be considered as speaking for "the Negro race in America, by any means."[17]

Randolph opened the meeting by saying black men "feel they are not wanted in the armed forces of the country, and they feel they have earned the right to participate . . . by virtue of their record in past wars since the time of the Revolution."

Randolph's Shakespearean diction and melodic voice, a stirring basso profundo, lent gravitas to every syllable. He spoke slowly, enunciating each syllable so there could be no mistake in his meaning. In 1940, Randolph was at the height of his organizing and oratorical powers. Wartime demands for rail service had made his 35,000-member union indispensable.

He would not be charmed by Roosevelt, the master politician, and he even interrupted the commander-in-chief when he felt the president obfuscate or digress, which took no small amount of courage for a black man sitting in the Oval Office.

"The Negroes as a unit, they are feeling that they are being shunted aside, that they are being discriminated against, and that they are not wanted now," he thundered.

There were only two black combat officers in the half-million-man Army and none in the Navy. There was not a single black soldier in the Marine Corps, Tank Corps, or Army Air Corps.

Roosevelt, who needed to assuage the civil rights leaders without alienating his military, promised Randolph that black men would make up a proportional share of the various Army units. He didn't oppose integrating the Army, he said, and the nature of war would solve the problem without the need for proclamations from the White House.

"Now suppose you have a Negro regiment . . . here, and right over here on my right line, would be a white regiment," the president said. "Now what happens after a while, in case of war? Those people would get shifted from one to the other. The thing gets sort of backed into."

The Navy, however, would not be so easy.

Knox told the group that men live in close quarters aboard ships and taking "Negroes into a ship's company . . . won't do."

"If you could have a Northern ship and a Southern ship it'd be different," Roosevelt said. The president chuckled at his own joke.

No one else laughed.

Randolph asked Knox if there was single Negro officer in the Navy.

"There are 4,007 Negroes out of a total force at the beginning of 1940 of 139,000," Knox said matter-of-factly. "They are all messman's rank."

Roosevelt, needing to break the tension, said he had recently been toying with the idea of having a "colored band" on ships "because they're darn good at it."

That way white men could become used to living with black men, and it would "increase the opportunity," Roosevelt said. "The more of those we can get, a little opportunity here, a little opportunity there."[18]

To Roosevelt, it was an attempt to crack open the door, if only a little. But the idea was paid little regard.

Stimson, writing in his diary that night, bemoaned the president's attempts "to satisfy the Negro politicians who are trying to get the Army committed to colored officers and various other things which they ought not to do. . . . Leadership is not embedded in the Negro race yet," Stimson wrote, "and to try to make commissioned officers to lead the men into battle is only to work disaster to both. Colored troops do very well under white officers but every time we try to lift them a little beyond where they can go, disaster and confusion follow. . . . I hope for heaven's sake they won't mix the white and colored troops together in the same units for then we shall certainly have trouble."[19]

Knox was even more blunt. He told the president that if he were asked to desegregate the Navy, he would resign.[20]

––––––––––

Knox, the sixty-six-year-old former publisher of the *Chicago Daily News*, had been on the job only three months when the Oval Office meeting took place, but he harbored zero doubts that disaster would ensue if Randolph and White got their way.

From the moment he was sworn in, Knox was determined to make the Navy more efficient, and that meant finding out what his admirals wanted and ensuring that it got done. And when it came to integrating the Navy, Knox knew his admirals wanted nothing to do with it and he saw no reason to question their wisdom.

Less than two weeks after Knox's confirmation, the Bureau of Navigation, responsible for personnel matters, prepared for him a letter explaining to New York's lieutenant governor, Charles Poletti, that black men were incapable of discipline and that to integrate ships was to invite discord.

Knox accepted these assertions without protest, and quickly warmed to the reasoning. "It is no kindness to Negroes to thrust them upon men of the white race," he told Senator Arthur Capper, a stolid seventy-five-year-old Republican from Kansas, just a few weeks after his appointment. Black men, he suggested, could contribute to the defense effort in the Army.[21]

Knox was so reliant on his admirals' judgment and experience because he had so little of his own. He had never served in the Navy and knew nothing about fighting a naval war. He wasn't even much of sailor.[22] He was easily impressed by officers who whispered the mathematical secrets of gunnery, romanticized life on the high seas, and explained the latest technological innovations aboard modern ships.[23]

But despite his inexperience, Knox established an easy rapport with the top brass. He invited them to golf and he cursed like a sailor.[24] He called admirals by their first names, or nicknames, a habit from his newspaper days, as was his tendency to call the Navy Department "the shop."[25] The husky, deep-voiced, and usually even-tempered Knox was intelligent without being intellectual, and had a much-admired common-man touch born of his humble upbringing and his days as a newsman.[26]

He did not look his age, and his vitality and dynamism betrayed no secrets. The only sign that this man was midway through his seventh decade was the wispy strands of thinning hair that clung to his fleshy head. Full faced with a prominent nose, the bespectacled secretary earned his admirals' admiration by keeping a "sharp division" between administrative tasks and military functions, and he let it be known that he thought the worst secretaries made the mistake of assuming their appointment endowed them with "professional skill in the strategy of war."

"Any layman would be a damn fool to get himself mixed up in the professional business of trying to fight a naval war," Knox told friends. "My job is to find out what the top admirals want to put across, talk it over with them and then do my damnedest to see that the job gets done as economically and efficiently as possible."[27]

—————

Knox's lack of naval experience was only the second-most surprising fact about his nomination. Far more dumbfounding to the political class was that Knox had been the vice-presidential nominee on the Republican ticket in 1936, a campaign he had spent berating Roosevelt. A hagiographic biography, intended to introduce Knox to the country, had declared that he "was the first great editor in the nation to point out the hidden menace in the New Deal."[28]

He was also early to realize the dangers of Hitler's aggression, which is why he was tapped to replace the dimmer-witted Charles Edison, who had infuriated Roosevelt when he refused a direct order to send needed supplies to England and France.[29]

Roosevelt needed a Navy secretary who not only appreciated the Nazi threat but also could help ready a woefully unprepared nation for war. In Knox, the president found an eloquent defender of democracy, and a man whose lack of Navy know-how was more than made up for by his managerial acumen.

Knox's knack was put to quick use. Among his very first moves, he pressured the Civil Service Commission to hire 2,200 additional clerks who could process requests from the scattered fleet and bases. No longer were pleas left lingering on desks. Knox ordered that every person's desk must be clear before he or she left for home at night.[30]

Following the advice of Edwin G. Booz, a shaggy, slow-speaking, efficiency expert with the business consulting firm Booz, Fry, Allen & Hamilton, Knox also put in separate switchboards for the Army and the Navy so phone calls meant for admirals were no longer sent to generals. He placed receptionists at the entrance to the Navy's headquarters so tourists couldn't roam the halls while the nation prepared for war.

"We must become intolerant of delay," he told his staff. "We must tear our way through red tape. We must pillory bureaucrats who stupidly sacrifice time in the pursuit of an impossible perfection."[31]

It was a role perfectly suited to Knox, who, while working for William Randolph Hearst, had earned a reputation as a boss who could pinch pennies—or find efficiencies, as it is often called. He removed the free Kotex from the newspaper's ladies' rooms and decreed that before any reporter received a new pencil, he had to turn in the stub of the old one.[32]

The papers profited.

Knox was on the golf course on June 20, 1940, pivoting his "beefy buttocks into powerful drives" and cursing himself as "yellow" for being short on his putts, as he habitually was, when his nomination as Navy secretary was announced.

Publicly, Knox made the case that his decision to accept the nomination was about patriotism, not politics: "I am an old soldier [who] has fought in two wars and if my Commander in Chief gave me a rifle and told me to start out again as a buck private, I'd do it," he said. "I am an American first and a Republican after that."[33]

Privately, Knox was wary, admitting to his new boss that he was "one of the most active, and I fear sometimes cantankerous, critics of your domestic program."[34]

No worries, said Roosevelt. They were aligned on Europe and that's what mattered. "You and I will wish many times that we could eat some of the things we said about each other in 1936."[35]

The nation's new Navy secretary began his days with a deep breath of fresh air, which he gulped next to the open window in his suite at Washington's Wardman Park Hotel, where he made his home. Then he did squats in his pajamas, stretched his torso, and circled his arms before taking a "relaxed trot" around the apartment.[36]

He was in the office by 9 a.m., sitting behind an always orderly desk holding few trinkets save for a bust of Teddy Roosevelt, his commanding officer when he served with the Rough Riders and a lifelong hero. Knox required all bureau chiefs and heads of offices who needed his signature to come to his office personally and be prepared to explain the document's significance. In this way he became acquainted with high-ranking officers and their problems.[37]

So even though he had been on the job only three months by late September, when he met with Randolph and White in the Oval Office, he knew well how the men under his command felt about integration, and he would defend their interests.

Burdening the Navy when it had such a monumental task ahead would be an inefficient use of time and resources, and Knox was, if nothing else, all about efficiency.

———

Knox's efforts to head off opportunity for African Americans were deliberate; meanwhile, however, the march toward war was having a less intended but no less deleterious effect on opportunities for thousands across the country, including a twenty-four-year-old sheet-metal worker living in Washington, North Carolina, named George Clinton Cooper.

By the end of 1940, Cooper was struggling to find work. Metal was available for defense contractors but not for maintenance and upkeep of homes, which was Cooper's livelihood.

He had a new bride to provide for and needed steady employment, so when he read in the newspaper that a National Youth Administration facility had opened in Ohio and was in need of a sheet-metal instructor, he sent his application. That the facility was at Wilberforce University, the alma mater of his wife, Peg, made the prospect seem like destiny. He was invited to interview for a position as senior foreman, teaching aircraft sheet-metal work. Cooper, excited for his future, made the six-hundred-mile trek.

When he arrived, the supervisor looked at the young man quizzically.

"Somebody made a mistake," he said.

"What do you mean?" Cooper replied.

"I'm going to be perfectly honest with you. We thought you were white."

"I thought you were looking for a sheet-metal instructor," Cooper said.

"We are. I am going to be honest with you again. I've never seen a colored sheet-metal worker. I just don't believe you can do the job."

Cooper was pragmatic and congenial by nature. He insisted his credentials were solid and told the supervisor that he had traveled all the way from North Carolina.

"You have, in fact, come a long way," said the supervisor. "I'll tell you what I'll do. I don't really believe you can do this job, but we have a fully equipped shop here. I will give you a set of blueprints for a simple thing like a metal locker, and if you can make one in a week, I'll give you the job."

Cooper thought that unfair but accepted the offer.

Two days later, he presented his locker, which he had built with the help of three students.

"I thought you were going to take a week," the supervisor said.

"No, that was your suggestion. I didn't say how long it was going to take me to do it."

The job was his.[38]

Cooper was unfazed by the supervisor because he was used to that kind of attitude. Racism and even violence had been as much a part of his North Carolina upbringing as the Pamlico and Tar Rivers, which bordered the southern part of Washington, the small town where he was born on September 7, 1916.

Washington, like so many Southern cities and towns, was strictly segregated. Cooper first became aware of race when he was in kindergarten. His class had only black children. He knew there were white children in town. He had even, on occasion, played with them in the tobacco fields.[39] Where were they now, he wondered.

His father, Edward Cooper, owned a successful sheet-metal shop and earned a reasonable living. His mother, Laura Jane Johnson, tended to the home, which included several gardens whose produce supplemented the diet of their eleven children.

Edward Cooper was considered "one of the most outstanding Black citizens [who] ever lived in Washington." When electricity came to Washington, he made the tin ornaments and stars for the town's very first illuminated Christmas tree.[40] The Coopers were one of the first black families in town to own a radio, and many nights were passed sitting around this miracle machine that brought the sounds of professional baseball, the comedy of Amos 'n' Andy, and the voice of the president of the United States into their very own home.

The elder Cooper, who had moved to Washington from Pactolus, North Carolina, in 1890, never made it past the fourth grade, but he became an avid reader. He was a stern, formal man who kept a library in his home; in its center there was a piano, which he insisted all his children learn to play.[41]

Cooper's mother had never made it past the third grade and never learned to read, but Miss Laura, as everyone in the neighborhood called her, was a savvy businesswoman who boosted the family's income selling milk, vegetables, and occasionally a chicken. During the Great Depression, Miss Laura, a rotund, solemn-looking woman, would often tell her son to drop in on a neighbor with a package of food. "I know she needs it," she would say. "Just tell her Miss Laura sent it."[42]

She was also the disciplinarian. Backtalk or disobedience was cured with a wet dishcloth across the face. If one of the Cooper children did something wrong at school, he or she would be whipped by a teacher. And if word got home that they had been whipped at school, they could expect another whipping at home.

Washington, which the Coopers always referred to as "little Washington" to distinguish it from the more prestigious city on the Potomac, was a fairly typical small town. A horse-drawn cart would bring wood already cut to fit the stove. In a woodhouse beside the kitchen surplus wood was laid and could be axed down to smaller chips when needed. Behind the Cooper home was a four-holer outhouse, which had different size holes to accommodate growing children. The homes in town were built on stilts and pilasters because of the tides—high enough for kids to crawl under and hide when they were playing games, looking for shade on a hot day, or running from a whipping. Teenage boys and girls, feeling the pull of innocent love or, more often, the pangs of irrepressible lust, would walk back and forth across the three-quarter-mile-long bridge that spanned the Pamlico River and, perhaps, share an ice cream cone from the drug store.

Like the Arbors and countless other African American parents who were the children of slaves, the Coopers wanted more for the next generation than they had had for themselves, and that meant insisting on their children's education. All of the Cooper children graduated from college.

"You've got to have something upstairs to make it," his parents would say.

Also like the Arbors, the Coopers reserved Sunday for God.

Breakfast was not served until the family prayed together.[43] Edward Cooper was a trustee at the African Methodist Episcopal Zion Church, a modest structure that had expanded over the decades. It became a symbol for the black community and a source of pride. It had grown as they did. It had thrived along with them. It was their own, amid a culture that afforded them little to claim as their own.

Sunday after church was the week's big meal. The Coopers picked vegetables from their garden and always had the freshest fried chicken, seeing as how it was "just a matter of going out in the yard and wringing the neck of the next meal."

Miss Laura, despite never having encountered a cookbook, knew how to make a feast without spending a fortune. One of her specialties, the hog haslet, was made from the heart, tongue, and other internal organs of the pig. Farmers and butchers would throw the offal away, but the staff who helped butchers, usually African Americans, would bring it home. Miss Laura would take these organs and cut them into small pieces and cook them on the back of a wood-burning stove for hours.

"Man, that was good eating," Cooper remembered decades later. "When you put that stuff in your mouth, it was as tender as a baby's bottom—delicious food."

After graduating from high school, Cooper worked as a bellhop. He made decent money handling bags, though not as much as he made hustling whores.

There were always a few white girls hanging around the hotel, and traveling salesmen, called drummers, would come looking for a good time. Cooper played the middleman.

The going price for the girl was a couple of bucks, and Cooper got to keep twenty-five cents. The salesmen would also want liquor. Washington was in a dry county, so Cooper would keep four or five pints of Craven County Corn whiskey—pretty good moonshine—in his private closet at the hotel.

He called himself the customer service representative.

It wasn't all fun and games, however. Anything that angered a white customer could mean the loss of employment, no matter who was at fault, and these customers could unload on black bellhops without any fear of consequence.

One time Cooper was showing a patron to his room. He placed the bags in the elevator but did not hold the elevator door open. "I thought the man was going to hit me, really," Cooper remembered. "He called me everything he could think of, everything derogatory that came to his mind. . . . That kind of thing was just a part of living, just a part of being there."[44]

Despite all the charms of rural life—the family meals, church, playing in tobacco fields, and hiding under houses—there was always a lurking fear, a terrifying thought that life could end or be upended at any moment, just as it had been for Hair's family in Florida. Two men had been lynched near Cooper's home when he was a child, and there were always stories of black men who had been beaten because they had done something, seemed like it could be anything—maybe just for looking the wrong way, or saying the wrong word, or maybe they hadn't said or done anything at all. Maybe they were just black. That could be enough.

Edward and Laura Cooper begged their son to leave Washington. Get out, they said, before you are beaten, or worse.[45]

"You had to feel intimidated by it," Cooper later said. "First of all, that it was done simply on the basis of prejudice, for the most part; secondly, there wasn't a hell of a lot you could do about it; and thirdly, because I think at that point in time, there was no groundswell from the majority community to try to do anything about it."[46]

That was changing in ways Cooper would have found hard to fathom as the 1940 election approached.

———

Vann's desertion of the Democrats opened a floodgate of critical editorials from the rest of the black press, which, by 1940, had a hold over its readers rivaled only by the church. The Office of War Information estimated that four million black citizens were reading black newspapers each week, providing publishers with enormous opportunity to shape public opinion.[47]

And Vann was arguably the most powerful voice in a powerful chorus, for the *Pittsburgh Courier* had, since 1938, become, according to historian Richard Miller, "the single most influential force in the drawn-out quest for racial justice preceding the climactic civil rights movement of the 1950s—the role of the NAACP notwithstanding."[48]

The week after the president promised Randolph and White that he'd work to find more opportunity for black men in the Army and Navy, the *Courier* printed a letter from fifteen black messmen aboard the light cruiser USS *Philadelphia* in which they detailed their shabby and prejudicial treatment. "We sincerely hope to discourage any other colored boys who might have planned to join the Navy and make the same mistake we did," the letter said. "All they would become is seagoing bellhops, chambermaids and dishwashers."

Vann was by now dying from abdominal cancer; with only days left to live, he used his outlet to turn the "Philadelphia Fifteen" from a story

other ratings . . . the Negro youth of America will cease to enlist in the U.S. Navy."[57]

It was quite a condemnation to a nation headed for war, but if any of these complaints reached Knox's desk, they were swept aside, a nuisance to be dealt with during a less pressing time. If his admirals did not want black men serving as anything other than messmen, then that was how it would be. The political pressure that moved Roosevelt could not sway Knox—not yet.

William H. Hastie, Stimson's new civilian aide, recounted an apocry-phal tale of a White House meeting during which the president, sitting with top staff from the Army and Navy, asked what the branches were doing about the increasing black protests. The Navy man responded, "We file them in the wastebasket."[58]

CHAPTER 4

"WE ARE DISCRIMINATED AGAINST IN EVERY WAY."

John Reagan exited a movie theater on a Sunday night in Missoula, Montana, to find the streets alive with the shouts of newsies selling extra editions. The Japanese had attacked Pearl Harbor. The world, Reagan knew, would never be the same.

Reagan, only twenty-one years old, had not yet made it home when he decided he would not be drafted. No one need compel him to defend his country. He dropped out of college, intent on enlisting in the US Army Air Forces, the precursor to the Air Force, which had recently opened up a training program for black pilots in Tuskegee, Alabama.

He wanted to be in the Air Forces as much as he'd ever wanted anything.

But the Air Forces did not want Reagan—not yet.

He'd have to find another way to serve.

John Walter Reagan was in Montana because of his prowess on the football field. He had been a nationally acclaimed high school athlete in Chicago, where his family had moved from Texas by way of Louisiana.

His parents, John Llewellyn and Bernice Bonita Ector Reagan, had a fitful marriage. John Sr. did not want his wife to work. Bernice was not interested in being a homemaker. She had married when she was only fifteen and wanted more than "wife" and "mother" on her résumé. Their fights were persistent, and the couple frequently broke up and got back together, splitting for the final time when Reagan was nineteen.

The loving but broken home meant two things for Reagan: he often had to help raise his two siblings—Johnetta, a year younger, and William, nine years younger—and he often lacked the presence of a male role model. In lieu of his father, Reagan hung around older boys on Prairie Avenue and Indiana Avenue on Chicago's Southeast Side. He was young to be in a gang, only about ten, but large for his age. No real harm was ever committed—mostly petty theft from idling ice cream trucks, or sweet potatoes from vegetable vendors.

But his mother worried her boy was falling in with the wrong crowd, so she moved the family to 6141 South Throop Street, a small, two-story bungalow-style home in Englewood, on the city's southwest side, about three miles from where the Arbors had settled.

The middle-class neighborhood was booming, thanks to the construction of new apartment buildings, which gave life to a popular shopping district.[1] It was a family-centered community with sports and Boy Scout troops, and Reagan thrived. He read anything he could get his hands on, including material that was well above his grade. Still at Copernicus Grammar School, he'd open books on the economy and even astrology. He'd stare at pictures and try to decipher what he could.

He was a dreamer.

His father, who came in and out of his life, was a hardened realist. He wasn't the kind of dad who threw the ball or took his son fishing. He preferred to discuss politics and current events.

The differences between the two men—the one who saw the world as it was and his boy, who saw the world as it could be—mirrored the generational divide that was shaping black discourse.

Du Bois, who had said during World War I that black men must "forget our special grievances and close our ranks," and other voices of his era were giving way to a new generation of civil rights leaders, men who would pressure a president and proclaim that victory for democracy would not come unless it happened both in Europe and at home.[2]

Reagan Sr., who washed and repaired trucks for the John F. Jelke margarine company, was a Republican who related to management, not labor, and thought unkindly of welfare programs. A man ought to work hard, earn his own way, he told his son. And he lived by those principles. He had no formal education but was always working two or three jobs, even during the Great Depression.

Reagan Jr. favored the New Deal's social programs and thought his father was overlooking the structural problems that tended to keep people, especially African Americans, from achieving their potential. The United States was a great country, he said, but "I'd just like to be more a part of it."

Reagan entered the Robert Lindblom Technical High School in the fall of 1935, the same month Estes Wright was lynched in Florida and two years before Arbor landed at the Chicago Beach Hotel.

The school, an enormous three-story Beaux Arts building, was integrated and catered mostly to the children of European immigrants. The culture focused on assimilation and the melting pot, so racism was not often in the foreground of Reagan's life.

By his senior year, Reagan had grown to six feet, two inches and filled out to 195 pounds. He lettered in several sports, including football, wrestling, boxing, and track and was voted Lindblom's all-around athlete in 1938. Known as Silent John, he was lean, muscular, athletic, and intelligent, a specimen who made one imagine that God was in a particularly generous mood the day Reagan was born. He won city and state wrestling championships and finished high school with a string of opponents shaking their heads and a string of girlfriends clutching their hearts.[3]

His football teammates were receiving offers from Big Ten schools and the whole backfield was thinking of attending the University of Michigan. But Reagan's wrestling coach was friends with the football coach in Montana and convinced Reagan to head to Missoula.[4]

He started college in September 1939, and by his sophomore year he was known as the Montana Grizzly, whose halfback and quarterback play were talked about in black communities across the country.[5] A game-winning eighty-yard touchdown pass against Gonzaga cemented him as one of the most popular students on campus, and the *Chicago Defender* reported that he was "a hero, a boy whose name is on the tip of every fellow student's tongue."[6]

Japan's surprise attack on Pearl Harbor came during Reagan's junior year. He knew from press reports that the Army was training black fighter pilots for a segregated squadron, and he imagined himself among

America's real heroes, fending off Japanese bombers over the Pacific or Germans over Europe.

What the newspapers had not told him was that the Army Air Forces command remained resistant to black fighter pilots, accepting very few into their ranks.[7] Reagan had no way of knowing that Major General Henry "Hap" Arnold had said that "the Air Corps was a club where negras would be out of place" and that white enlisted men "would never service an aircraft flown by a negra officer."[8]

When the anxious and patriotic Reagan went to enlist in the Army Air Forces he was told to go home and wait to see if he was needed.

———

The day after Pearl Harbor, twenty African American editors, publishers, and columnists met with Army leadership at the Munitions Building in Washington, DC, where the secretary of war had moved his offices two years prior.[9] The 841,000-square-foot complex, adjacent to the Navy Building on Constitution Avenue, had been expanding since World War I and would continue to be the War Department's primary headquarters until the Pentagon was completed the following year.

The meeting had been scheduled more than a month before by Truman K. Gibson, who had been a member of the so-called black cabinet since 1940.

Gibson, twenty-nine, worked for William H. Hastie, civilian aide to the secretary of war. Hastie was a big-picture man, and Gibson's job was to handle the more mundane tasks of his high office.[10] Among Gibson's duties was to bring to the attention of Hastie and the War Department cases of black soldiers who were treated violently or unjustly, of which there were plenty, but in 1941 he found few sympathetic ears, despite the myriad horrors that occurred.

In April of that year, Private Felix Hall had been found hanging from a tree in the woods behind Fort Benning in Georgia. The nineteen-year-old volunteer had been strung up in a jackknife position in a shallow ravine. His feet were bound with baling wire. His body had been suspended for six weeks, and when he was finally cut down maggots had already consumed chunks of his decaying flesh.

He was still wearing his Army uniform.[11]

A military physician ruled it a homicide, and that's what was recorded on Hall's death certificate. But the military insisted to the public that Private Hall had committed suicide, which raised eyebrows in the black community because his hands were tied behind his back.

Hastie brought Hall's case to Stimson, but the War Department did little to investigate.[12]

Gibson knew that "rancor and bitterness . . . were rife among black men to a degree whites couldn't appreciate."[13] He needed to make the War Department aware of what this type of treatment was doing to black morale and what that might mean for the nation's nascent defense efforts, so he brought men from the *Pittsburgh Courier*, the *Chicago Defender*, and the *Baltimore Afro-American* to Washington for roundtable discussions with representatives from the adjutant general's office, the Bureau of Public Relations, the Morale Operations branch, and other military agencies.[14]

That the meeting took place December 8, one day after the Japanese attack, seemed fortuitous. Emotions were running high and the black pressmen arrived that morning assuming they would be welcomed, their complaints considered, and their grievances addressed. With the nation fighting a two-ocean war and in need of every man's effort, surely, they thought, the segregation, humiliation, and violence would be a top concern.

They were wrong.

General George Marshall, the Army chief of staff, was scheduled to give opening remarks but could only meet for a few moments and said only that an African American unit might be formed.

The military's official position was delivered by Colonel Eugene R. Householder, representing the adjutant general's office. The military, he said, was a reflection of society. Segregation in the latter demanded segregation in the former.

"The Army cannot change civilian ideas on the Negro," he told the black pressmen. "The Army is not a sociological laboratory. . . . Experiments, to meet the wishes and demands of the champions of every race and creed for the solution of their problems are a danger to efficiency, discipline and morale and would result in ultimate defeat."[15]

The editors and publishers were horrified and told their readers that the insistence on segregation was "close to treason."[16]

If black America was going to be asked to buy war bonds and sacrifice its boys on the battlefield, then it must "be a sacrifice for a new world which not only shall not contain Hitler, but no Hitlerism. And to thirteen millions of American Negroes that means a fight for a world in which lynching, brutality, terror, humiliation, and degradation through segregation and discrimination, shall have no place—either here or there."

The military as it stood in December 1941 could not defend the world for democracy because it was so undemocratic. "A lilywhite Navy cannot fight for a free world. A Jim Crow Army cannot fight for a free world," the editors of the *Crisis* said. "Jim Crow strategy, no matter on how grand a scale, cannot build a free world."[17]

One month later, *Crisis* editors wrote that military regulations with regards to black men appeared little changed over the last century. "It will take more than the pat Army remark that it is not a 'sociological laboratory' to remedy this situation. The 1942 Negro resents and rebels against 1842 regulations. These must be rooted out whether they reside in the *Mein Kampf* of a Hitler or in a memorandum in the adjutant general's office of the American Army."[18]

The editorials both mirrored and reinforced the sentiment already pervasive in the black community during the first days of the war.

A survey of black residents in Harlem found that "resentment at Negro discrimination is fairly widespread throughout the Negro population." Most of those surveyed said they'd be treated better or the same under Japanese rule than they would under the United States government, while only 11 percent believed conditions would improve for blacks if the United States won the war.[19]

Secretary Knox did not bother to attend the meeting at the Munitions Building. He spent that morning in a state of despair, horrified over what had happened at Pearl Harbor the day before, and feeling personally responsible. For Knox, the attacks on the base were not only a national disaster but a "personal tragedy gallingly flavored with failure."[20]

Racial questions could not have been further from his mind.

He had already left Washington for what was to be a three-day trip to Hawaii, where he would personally conduct the first federal inquiry into the disaster at Pearl Harbor, when a telegram from the NAACP arrived asking whether "in view of the intensive recruiting campaign then under-way, the Navy would accept colored recruits for other than the messman's branch." The Bureau of Navigation replied that "there had been no change in policy and that none was contemplated."[21]

The day before Japan attacked, December 6, 1941, a committee that Knox had appointed six months earlier, tasked with investigating the Na-vy's racial policies, advanced several reasons why black men must remain limited to the messman branch.

The report cited the "existence of racial prejudice ... that cannot be ig-nored" and said "the close and intimate conditions under which men must live and work on board ship would make difficult, if not impossible, the maintenance of a high morale if the racial problem were injected into it."[22]

It concluded, without any real evidence, that black men have lower health, educational, and intelligence ratings than white men, so in order to get 1,000 qualified black enlisted men, it was necessary to process 40,000, whereas 1,000 qualified white men could be obtained by processing 4,500.

Walter White, executive secretary of the NAACP, protested directly to the president, demanding that the Navy "abandon its Jim Crow policy."[23]

The president turned the matter over to the newly created Fair Employ-ment Practices Committee and its chairman, Mark Ethridge, a liberal-leaning journalist icon from Mississippi—a short, round-faced, pink-cheeked man with a lyrical Southern accent.[24] Ethridge had already been speaking with Ralph Bard, assistant secretary of the Navy, about what could be done for the thousands of African Americans such as John Reagan who were eager to defend their country but were wary of how the Navy treated black men because of the stories they read in the black press such as those told by the men on the *Philadelphia*, the *Davis*, and the *Sampson*.

Ethridge was getting nowhere with Bard, who described the black press as "resentful with occasional vitriolic outbursts."[25]

The NAACP then turned to Lieutenant Edward Hayes, Knox's special assistant and the man who had managed his 1936 campaign for vice president. They begged him to "use your influence to secure better treatment for Negroes who wish to enter the United States Navy in any department."

"We are discriminated against in every way," they wrote Hayes in a letter. "The government of this country expects all citizens to be loyal and the Negroes are loyal but underneath that loyalty there is a hurt. . . . Why should Negroes be relegated to menial labor in their allottment [sic] of tasks? Why should our Army and Navy officials follow Hitler in his racial prejudices?"

They had chosen to approach Hayes not only because he was close to Knox but because he had lived in Illinois "long enough to know that Negroes are the same as other people." Hayes promised he'd try, but he had no more luck with Knox than Ethridge had had with Bard.[26]

Tensions were so high and black morale so low that Hastie, the highest-ranking African American in the War Department, proposed that black America's leading lights gather in New York to discuss how they should respond to Japan's attack, the military's insistence on segregation, and the very real possibility that black Americans would be fighting to save Europe for a democratic ideal that did not exist in the United States.

Dozens of delegates representing seventeen leading African American social and professional organizations met on January 10, 1942, at the Harlem YMCA on 135th Street, a site that had profound meaning to the black community. This YMCA, completed a decade earlier, was the largest and best-equipped YMCA in the nation; it had been built because so many other YMCAs were for whites only. The C-shaped building was eleven stories of red brick set in Flemish bond, with neo-Georgian-style details. Considered one of the architect James C. Mackenzie's finest achievements, it was a refutation of white privilege and was symbolic of the increasing wealth and social status black men and women felt they deserved.

The delegates arrived on Saturday afternoon, walking up cast-stone steps, flanked by metal handrails and through ornate double doors.

The night before, Joe Louis had defended his heavyweight title only a few miles south, at Madison Square Garden, easily defeating the much larger Buddy Baer. Louis, who knocked out Baer in the first round, donated his $47,000 purse from the fight to the Navy Relief Fund.[27] It wasn't lost on any of the delegates that if Louis wanted to fight for the Navy in a uniform he'd only be allowed as a messman, whereas Baer, a white man, could serve in any capacity. Yet the Navy Relief Fund offered no objections to accepting a black champion's check.

The delegates convened at 2:30 p.m. and met for more than seven hours. There was no disagreement—except on one point.[28]

The lone controversy was stirred by Hastie, one of the most famous men in the room. By the age of thirty-seven he had amassed a lifetime's worth of accomplishments. He had made history as the first African American appointed to the federal bench, serving as a district court judge for the US Virgin Islands, a position he relinquished to become dean of Howard University.[29] He had already served a stint in the Roosevelt administration, working as the assistant solicitor for the Department of the Interior. When he spoke, most knew to listen and consider his words well, but no one was quite prepared for what he was about to say.

"I believe today the American Negro is not wholeheartedly, unreservedly and all-out in support of the American war effort," he told the crowd. "I think we should settle in our own minds whether the Negro is one-hundred percent for the war effort or whether he isn't. If he is, we have one job. If he isn't, we have another."

Hastie, lowering his voice, then asked for a vote to see whether others shared his opinion.[30]

The conference was thrown into confusion "as if by a bomb shell."[31] Many sought to block the vote. Revealing black apathy might be seen as disloyal; antipathy could be seen as treason. And what would the Germans and Japanese think? Dissension would aid and comfort the enemy.

What Hastie was trying to do, he argued, was make the federal government aware of a very real problem, which it had created and perpetuated with policies conducive to neither morale nor battle efficiency. It was the very same effort Gibson had made one month earlier, to no avail, but whereas Gibson's meeting had taken place without public scrutiny in a Washington government building, this gathering was public and would be reported to the nation.

After much shouting, Walter White convinced the delegates that more was to be gained from the truth than from cowardly silence. The nation needed to know what segregation had done to the morale of thirteen million black men and women.

The vote on Hastie's question showed thirty-six delegates believed African Americans were not behind the war effort, five said they were, and fifteen remained silent. A reporter for the *Chicago Defender*, the most widely read black newspaper in the South, reported that those who abstained in fact sided with the majority.

The "incipient discrimination and segregation in all phases of the war, and the arrogant apathy of Washington officials have chilled the patriotic ardor of the Negro people," the *Defender* told its one million readers. "When an enthusiastic black youth, thinking himself an American citizen, presents himself at the recruiting office, he is quickly turned down and often met with humiliation."[32]

The conclusions reached in New York were by no means uniform, and plenty of prominent black voices felt it was wrong to equate Hitler's Europe with Jim Crow's South.

"It is true that we may have many internal grievances such as the infamous discrimination in the Navy and other departments," wrote members of the National Voters' League, the United Benevolent Society, Howard University's Mu-So-Lit Club, and the Washington Bar Association. "We emphasize that these are internal or family differences, but the colored people of this country are now as they have always been, one-hundred percent in the defense and protection of their common country and it is unfair and a misstatement of facts for them to be pictured as a group of Achilles sulking while our country is being assailed."[33]

But the conference had revealed that for most black Americans the calls to defend democracy rang hollow, while the German talk of a superior race sounded strikingly familiar.

This meeting succeeded where Gibson's had not. The Roosevelt administration was both shocked and alarmed, having assumed it could count on every American to recognize the German and Japanese threats.

The administration might have been less surprised had those in power listened to civil rights leaders, the black press, or even Eleanor Roosevelt. All had been warning that the maintenance of morale among American blacks would be a problem.

The day before the Harlem gathering, Eleanor Roosevelt spoke to the women of the Rector's Aid Society at St. Thomas' Parish, the Episcopal church where she and the president sometimes worshiped. Standing in one of the capital's most fashionable churches, she told the women that "the nation cannot expect the colored people to feel that the U.S. is worth defending if they continue to be treated as they are treated now."[34]

Eleanor, who often functioned "as an unofficial ombudsman for blacks," understood better than most how stories of casual racism told a thousand times in a thousand cities were damaging the war effort.[35]

And nowhere was the unjust treatment more profound, she believed, than in the Navy, which continued to treat black enlistees as little more than the seagoing bellhops that the Philadelphia Fifteen had described in their letter.[36]

In the days following Pearl Harbor, the Navy embarked upon an aggressive recruiting campaign with newspapers, radios, and sound trucks on the streets calling for "patriotic, red-blooded young men to join the Navy and help Uncle Sam to hit back."

But not black men.

In just one day some three hundred black men were refused enlistment in New York City. Some would return repeatedly to the recruiting office, hoping that the rules had changed, that the Navy had finally come to its senses. A forty-year-old pharmacist with a master's degree from Columbia University applied six times, to no avail.

Often, men would call the recruiting office, list their educational achievements, and be told of the ranks and ratings open to them. But when it was discovered they were black, the recruiting officer would have to start all over again.[37] These men wanted to fight, but the Navy let it be known that it wanted black men only as cooks, waiters, and valets.[38]

Ethridge, the chair of the Fair Employment Practices Committee, had told Knox that even if the Navy insisted on remaining segregated, the branch could still find more for black men to do—in the Caribbean or on harbor craft. But Ethridge had no real power. He could merely make suggestions.

Any change would have to be ordered from the top, and with war now raging and morale in the black community dangerously low, the president pushed. The same day that Eleanor spoke to the women at St. Thomas' Parish, the president wrote to Knox insisting that the Navy "might invent something that colored enlistees could do in addition to the rating of messman."[39]

Knox, still reliant on his admirals, turned the matter over to the Navy General Board, made up of admirals who acted in an advisory role, and asked for a plan to recruit five thousand African Americans for the general service.

When the General Board met on January 23 to discuss Knox's request, high-ranking officers from various branches tried to outdo one another in describing the calamity that would certainly follow if black men were allowed to do more than serve breakfast, make beds, and clean toilets aboard a ship.

Major General Thomas Holcomb, commandant of the Marine Corps, which was the only branch of the military that had remained completely segregated, told the board that if he had to choose to fight with 5,000 whites or 250,000 blacks, he would rather have the whites.

Holcomb called the enlistment of black men "absolutely tragic," and told the General Board that African Americans had every opportunity "to satisfy their aspiration to serve in the Army." Their desire to enter the naval service was largely an effort "to break into a club that doesn't want them."

"If we are defeated," he said, "we must not close our eyes to the fact that once in they will be strengthened in their effort to force themselves into every activity we have. If they are not satisfied to be messmen, they will not be satisfied to go into the construction or labor battalions. Don't forget the colleges are turning out a large number of well-educated Negroes. I don't know how long we will be able to keep them out of the V-7 [officer training] class. I think not very long."

Similar testimony was given by officers from the Bureau of Aeronautics, the Bureau of Yards and Docks, and the US Coast Guard.

One of the direst warnings came from Captain Kenneth Whiting, a sixty-year-old Massachusetts-born World War I hero who had trained with the Wright brothers in Ohio and was known as "the father of the aircraft carrier." Whiting was responsible for the tenets of naval carrier aviation and told his colleagues that if black men were allowed to be more than servants, then one day soon they'd demand to be officers. "The sponsors of the program desire full equality on the part of the Negro and will not rest content until they obtain it," he warned.

The lone voice of support for opening the general-service ratings to black sailors came from Rear Admiral Charles P. Snyder, the Navy's inspector general, who thought his colleagues were being a bit hyperbolic. He conceded the need for a segregated training facility and acknowledged that this would be "troublesome and require tact, patience and tolerance," but "we have so many difficulties to surmount anyhow that one more possibly wouldn't swell the total very much."

Snyder suggested that black men could play in the ship's band, pointing out that "the colored race is very musical and they are versed in all forms of rhythm." Snyder also suggested that black men might serve in the aviation branch, where the Army had reported some success, or on auxiliaries and other minor vessels such as transports. Besides, he said, this would allow the Navy to answer the criticisms coming from the black press.

Though Snyder's plan was almost identical to what the president had proposed fifteen months earlier, during his meeting with Randolph and White, the General Board paid it no mind.[40]

And Knox was just fine with that. The same day that the General Board met, Knox explained how and why he had already reached a similar conclusion as the board's members.

Leonard Farber, a New York realtor, had asked Knox to allow black men to serve alongside white men and "erase this blot on the American concept of Democracy." Knox told Farber that he had given a lot of thought to this problem, but it just wasn't possible. He harbored no prejudice, he explained, but he couldn't figure out how to integrate the Navy without impairing efficiency.

"Of course, you will understand that during the progress of a great war, we must not interject into the personnel situation of the Navy any new factors that might militate against the smooth functioning of the crews of our war ships," Knox said. "It is not through any lack of appreciation of the rights of colored citizens that the Navy hesitates to recruit Negroes generally to serve the Navy, but because we have not yet found a satisfactory way in which to handle the problem of race prejudice so that it will not impair efficiency."[41]

African Americans, Knox said, must remain messmen.

CHAPTER 5

"WOULD IT BE DEMANDING TOO MUCH TO DEMAND FULL CITIZENSHIP?"

The General Board's machinations and Frank Knox's stubborn insistence that black men remain limited to the messman branch did not mean a whole lot to Reginald Ernest Goodwin, who, in the winter of 1942 was preoccupied with his own home front.

Goodwin was about to turn thirty-five, and his relationship with the beautiful Emmita Cardoza was failing. The war tearing apart the world was an apt metaphor for the final embers of a tumultuous marriage that had once shined as bright as any light in the New York City skyline.

Cardoza was one of the famous Ziegfeld Girls, "a lace and chiffon vision of glamour" whose performances in the Follies, the revue staged by Florenz Ziegfeld in a lavish Broadway theater, helped define New York City during the Jazz Age. Ziegfeld had produced the musical *Show Boat*, but he was better known for his glorification of the American woman. The Ziegfeld Girls' enormous glittering, feathered headdresses and sultry strides were a magnet for men, from regular Joes to Babe Ruth, Will Rogers, and President Woodrow Wilson.[1]

And of all these beauties, few had the magnetic power of Cardoza, whose stage name was Emmita Casanova. Walter Winchell called her the most exotic of all the girls, with dark eyes that had the "sensuousness of the lotus flower."[2]

Goodwin appeared, at least physically, a suitable match for Cardoza. He was nearly six feet tall, 160 pounds of lean muscle, with expressive brown eyes, fair skin, and a neatly trimmed Clark Gable–style mustache.

He was charming, the kind of man who commanded attention the moment he walked into a room. And he was well educated, having attended Howard University and New York University before taking leadership courses at Columbia University.

Their 1936 wedding, held at the Plaza Hotel in New York City, was the talk of the town, and Goodwin and Cardoza were regularly referred to as "one of the most popular and attractive couples in Harlem social circles."[3]

But troubles were quickly apparent. By 1939 they were living apart, and although they denied a marital rift—"Reggie and I are as much in love with each other as ever"—the rumors were persistent.

In March 1940, Goodwin, who had been the physical director of the Harlem Children's Center, accepted a job as the director of the first unit of the Ninth Street Boys' Club of Cincinnati, and left for Ohio.

Emmita followed, and the pair moved to a two-bedroom, one-bathroom house on Beecher Street, but the marriage did not last. After two years she was on her way back to New York, alone, and Goodwin was left at the Ninth Street Boys' Club, contemplating bachelorhood and a possible future in the military.[4]

One of his friends, Sam Barnes, who worked a block away at the Ninth Street YMCA, was having more luck with love. He was engaged to Olga Lash, one of the most desirable bachelorettes in her home state of North Carolina, but, like Goodwin, he was apprehensive about a future in the military and the dangers of war. Barnes was born and raised in Oberlin, Ohio. Home was only two hundred miles from Cincinnati, but it might as well have been on another planet. Oberlin was a bastion of racial tolerance, whereas Cincinnati, just across the Ohio River from Kentucky, was a city where African Americans were required to enter through the back door of any restaurant that even bothered to serve them.[5]

Barnes had handled segregated environments before. After graduating from Oberlin College with a bachelor's degree in physical education, he accepted a job at Livingstone College, a small historically black school, in

Salisbury, North Carolina, with 250 students and 16 faculty members. When Barnes boarded the train in Oberlin, he could sit where he pleased. At Columbus, he would need to switch to the segregated coach, which was behind the fetid coal car.

At Livingstone he had held several positions, including the director of health, physical education, and athletics; head basketball coach; director of intramural sports; supervisor of the men's dormitory; and assistant to the dean. He also taught biology and mathematics, although he always preferred coaching.

Barnes had no assistant coaches—no help, really, of any kind. Before home games, he would wake early to mark the lines on the field. Then he'd come back and tape the players, issue the game equipment, and haul water to the sidelines.[6] For road games, he made sure the boys packed lunches so they wouldn't waste time looking for a restaurant to serve them. He found them school dormitories to stay in so they wouldn't waste time looking for hotels to house them.

It was at Livingstone, during a faculty banquet, that he first saw Olga Lash.

Decades later, Barnes would still tell the story of that moment. The chatter around him ceased, he would say with a smile, as his mind was transfixed by this beautiful creature before him. Olga was dressed all in black with a small black hat and veil that came to her nose. Her hair was parted down the middle and held with a Spanish comb. A foxtail stole was draped over her shoulder. She had a simple and well-tailored suit that accentuated her small waist.

Breathtaking.

"Who is that?" he asked a friend.

As Olga Lash walked by, Barnes stood up.

"Good afternoon, Miss Lash," he tried.

She turned her head but did not respond. She just kept on walking, with the air of a woman used to stealing men's hearts. She already had a list of suitors.

Barnes was smitten, but Miss Lash was no easy prize. She hailed from one of the most prominent African American families in the state. Her father, the Reverend Wiley Hezekiah Lash, was among the first African

Americans to graduate from Concordia College. A distinguished orator and preacher, he had founded three Lutheran churches in North Carolina.

Her mother, Mayzonetta "Mary" Grundy Lash, ran a neighborhood grocery on West Innes Street and was fluent in several languages. Her brother would become the town's first black mayor, and a plaque was unveiled in his honor in 2008.

With Olga's means, legacy, and beauty, she could have had almost any man in town, but Barnes won her over with his charm, intellect, and wicked sense of humor. He was fun to be around, and he made her laugh. She could take him anywhere, be it a high-brow function or something much less formal.

Barnes loved poetry, and one of his favorite lines, a verse he tried to live by, was from Rudyard Kipling's "If": "If you can talk with crowds and keep your virtue, / Or walk with Kings—nor lose the common touch."

"My husband was a very outgoing person with lots of personality," Olga later said.[7] "A people person, very popular with men and ladies, very friendly, just a very warm person. Very intelligent, interesting, animated always, very gifted in sports, a very well-rounded person. He seemed to draw people to him. He was the kind of person who would do whatever he could for whomever."

During his time at Livingstone, Barnes avoided white people as much as he could.

Samuel Edward Barnes would introduce himself in the South as S. E. Barnes. If white people asked what the S stood for, he would say, "It stands for nothing." When they asked what the E stood for, he'd just say, "My parents named me S. E. Barnes."[8]

The ruse was designed to avoid the indignity of having a white person call him by his first name, a common way to denigrate black men that Barnes would not abide. It was a small gesture, but his parents had taught him never to compromise his dignity, and he never would.

Barnes was the grandson of Kentucky slaves and the fifth and final child for James and Margaret Barnes, born January 25, 1915.

They had left the South in the hopes of finding a more tolerant environment in which to raise their own children. They settled on Oberlin, a small city about thirty-five miles southwest of Cleveland that had been founded in 1833 by two Presbyterian ministers who had grown upset with the decidedly un-Christian values that characterized the nation's new frontier. They built the college and named the town after a French pastor, John Frederick Oberlin, who established schools and taught trades to poor Frenchmen. Two years after it opened, Oberlin College admitted its first black students and two years after that its first black women; it became a stop along the Underground Railroad and a hotbed of abolitionist thinking.

It was Oberlin residents who helped John Price, a fugitive slave, find refuge in Canada. This violated the Fugitive Slave Act and caused a national uproar on the eve of the 1860 election, the contest that brought Abraham Lincoln into office.

By the time the budding Barnes brood made their way north, Oberlin had a long history of racial tolerance, and Margaret soon became a prominent member of the community. She was a trustee at Mount Zion Baptist Church, a member of the Order of the Eastern Star in the local Masonic lodge, a member of the board of trustees at Wilberforce University, where George Cooper would land a job, and a prominent Ohio Republican who served as an alternate delegate to the 1936 Republican convention in Chicago, where Alf Landon and Frank Knox were nominated.

At the church, Margaret worked with the Reverend Homer J. Tucker and the Phillis Wheatley Association to push Oberlin to hire the city's first African American public-school teacher.

The town that Barnes grew up in had a Norman Rockwell vibe. Everyone knew everyone else. When it snowed, kids pulled each other on sleighs and went ice skating. When it was warm, they hiked and fished. When it was hot, they could play kick-the-can for hours.[9] A ticket to the movies cost a dime. Popcorn was a nickel.

On Saturday nights, houses would empty and folks would gather in the center of town to listen to concerts. Children of every color played in the grass as ice cream drizzled down their chins while the grownups smoked cigarettes and drank Coke.[10]

James Barnes, who had not finished high school, was a chef at the Oberlin College dormitories. Margaret Barnes, a college graduate, operated a laundry out of her home, which allowed her to spend time with the children, who helped wash, fold, and deliver. The family was never rich, but thanks to the businesses of food and clothing, Barnes's parents were always able to provide food and clothing.

Like the Coopers, the Barnes family supplemented their diet with what they grew on their own. Sam Barnes and his older brother James Jr. weeded and harvested the garden in which the family grew apples and berries. Beans were picked, canned, and stored in the basement for winter.

Barnes's three sisters did most of the household chores, but Margaret made sure her boys learned how to do all the housework. After all, she told them, "You don't know who you may marry. I don't know whether they can cook or not, whether they can sew and iron, so you learn to do for yourself."[11]

The church also played an important role in the children's lives, acting almost like a third parent and a second school. Mr. Barnes had to work most Sundays, so the children went with their mother. They sat according to their age, which meant Barnes was farthest from his mother, but not out of reach. As a child, he assumed his mother had the longest arms in the whole world, because if he ever misbehaved, she could reach across four other children and smack him upside the head, without ever taking her eyes off the minister. And she wasn't afraid to take her kids outside church for a formal whipping and then sit them right back in the pew for the end of the sermon.[12]

Barnes, a mischievous child who occasionally got caught stealing apples, grapes, and other fruits and vegetables from carts or vendors, was often disciplined. That meant a whipping from parents or neighbors, and neighbors were worse, because that meant a second whipping at home for besmirching the family name.

As Barnes grew older, he learned that Oberlin's values and tolerance were rare, even for Ohio. On the football field, where he showed early promise as an end, opponents regularly goaded him with racial epithets. Playing in Fremont, Lorain, Norwalk, or even Elyria, only nine miles from Oberlin, meant enduring a barrage of slurs. Places such as Marietta, just across the Ohio River from West Virginia, were particularly hard because

Barnes might be one of the few black people in the whole stadium and the insults would rain down.[13]

Barnes also excelled at track. He could run the hundred-yard dash in less than ten seconds and once raced against, and lost to, Jesse Owens, with whom he developed a lifelong friendship.[14]

Barnes was on the football field and competed in track meets because of his older brother James Jr., a world-class athlete and track star, who tried out for the 1928 Olympics. James was captain of both the football and basketball teams at Oberlin, where he earned the moniker "Sunny Jim."

Barnes worshiped his older brother and took his word as gospel. Sunny Jim always encouraged his younger brother to do more than he thought he was capable of, and thanks to his confidence, he often succeeded beyond his own expectations.

James Jr. took a job coaching at Virginia State College and said he'd hire Sam, whom he always referred to as "kid."

"When you get your degree, you're coming down here with me," he said.[15]

Barnes couldn't wait.

He was one year short of taking his brother up on that offer when James contracted meningitis. His parents and brother made it to his bedside just in time to say their goodbyes and bring the body home to Oberlin.

James left behind a young bride, a six-month-old son, and a devastated younger brother, who, determined to honor his brother's memory, went into coaching and teaching, just like his hero.[16]

Barnes worked at Livingstone for five years, until 1941, at which point he was engaged to Olga Lash and saving for a wedding. The Reverend Homer Tucker, the man who had worked with Barnes's mother to see that Oberlin hired a black teacher, had taken a job at the Ninth Street YMCA in Cincinnati and offered a job there to Barnes.

Goodwin's Ninth Street Boys' Club often ran programs with the YMCA, and he and Barnes began running in the same social circles.[17]

By 1942, Barnes was accustomed to the racism that permeated Cincinnati, and he dealt with it by doing his best to ignore the white social structure that would keep him down. He was no more interested in so-cializing with whites than they were with him.

He could never fully accept the indignities he faced, but he dared not protest "because there's only one end to that problem," he later said, and "there was nothing to be said or done about it because doing so would have brought a very, very unhappy circumstance.... You had no opportunities for redress, so you just didn't get involved."[18]

＝＝＝

That helplessness was what a lot of young black men felt, which is why so many were conflicted about the war. Black men in Detroit were tearing up their draft cards, saying that if they must fight, they'd prefer to die in their home town fighting the Ku Klux Klan. "The Negro has been psychologically demobilized," Roy Wilkins of the NAACP told men from the Office of Facts and Figures (later the Office of War Information) as he tried to help federal officials wrap their minds around why black men might feel disinclined to serve.[19]

When the meeting ended, a despondent Wilkins told his boss, Walter White, "It is a plain fact that no Negro leader with a constituency can face his members today and ask full support for the war in the light of the atmosphere the government has created."[20]

The frustration was personified in the winter of 1942 when James G. Thompson, a twenty-six-year-old black cafeteria worker at the Cessna Aircraft Corporation in Wichita, Kansas, wrote a letter to the *Pittsburgh Courier* asking whether he should sacrifice his life to live half American and wondering whether life would be better for his children in the peace that followed victory, and, if not, was the present America worth defending.

"Would it be demanding too much to demand full citizenship rights in exchange for the sacrificing of my life?" he asked.

Thompson referred to the "V for Victory" sign on display in countries fighting tyranny. "If this V sign means that to those now engaged in this great conflict, then let we colored Americans adopt the double VV for a double victory," he said. "The first 'V' for victory over our enemies from without, the second 'V' for victory over our enemies from within. For surely those who perpetuate these ugly prejudices here are seeking to destroy our democratic form of government just as surely as the Axis forces."[21]

Three days after that letter appeared, on February 3, 1942, the Navy General Board issued a report saying it could not comply with Knox's request to open the general-service ratings to five thousand black men. They must stay in the messman branch as a means of promoting efficiency. Men aboard ship live in such close proximity that segregation was the only reasonable course, they said. "How many white men would choose, of their own accord, that their closest associates in sleeping quarters, at mess, and in a gun's crew should be of another race? ... General Board believes that the answer is few if any and further believes that if the issue were forced, there would be a lowering of contentment, teamwork and discipline in the service."

If restriction of blacks to the messman branch was discrimination, the board added, "it was but part and parcel of a similar discrimination throughout the United States."

The memo then offered three reasons why racism existed in the nation and must be replicated in the Navy: a white man will not accept a black in a position of authority over him; a white man considers that he is of a superior race and will not admit the black man as an equal; and a white man refuses to allow the black man intimate family relationships leading to marriage. "These concepts may not be truly democratic, but it is doubted if the most ardent lovers of democracy will dispute them, particularly in regard to intermarriage."

That no one had suggested, hinted, or even mentioned marriage seems not to have bothered the authors of the report, though it is indicative of the pervasive fear of miscegenation that permeated the military and society at large.

Although the board strongly recommended that the current policy stand, and based that recommendation on expert testimony, it also stated that "the negro problem is political" and an outgrowth of the need to "gain the support of the negro vote." "If, in the opinion of higher authority, political pressure is such as to require the enlistment of these people for general service, let it be for that."[22]

Even Knox had to laugh at the arrogance of that last line, a "prize sentence," he told Roosevelt.[23]

It was a shot at the president, who, in defying the General Board's recommendation, would be putting political considerations over military objections.

Roosevelt's feelings about the report, its racial undertones, its treatise on mankind's flaws, and its implicit threat, were made obvious just six days later when he wrote a terse note to Knox saying the General Board's work was unsatisfactory.

"Officers of the U.S. Navy are not officers only but are American citizens," he wrote. "They should, therefore, be expected to recognize social and economic problems which are related to national welfare. . . . It is incumbent on all officers to recognize the fact that about one-tenth of the population of the United States is composed of members of the Negro race who are American citizens."

Roosevelt agreed that "to go the whole way at one fell swoop would seriously impair the general average efficiency of the Navy," but he was certain that there were some tasks black men could perform without disrupting cohesion aboard ships.

"I ask you to return the recommendations of the General Board to that Board for further study and report."[24]

Knox thought the president was making a mistake. The fleet was still hobbled from the Japanese attack and about to fight a two-ocean war.

He told his friend Gifford Pinchot, who had served in Teddy Roosevelt's administration, that he was "seriously embarrassed by the effort among a small class of negroes against the Navy."

So many Navy recruits hailed from Southern cities "where the prejudice over the color line is inbred" that mixing crews aboard ship would certainly provoke trouble.

"My serious job right now is to have an efficient Navy to fight this war," Knox said. "To do that, I can't have crews that are impaired in efficiency because of racial prejudice. . . . Somehow, some way, some day, we will have to meet and solve this problem, but I submit to you that during the progress of the most dangerous war in which we have ever engaged is not the time to take up a problem so filled with dynamite as this one."

But Knox had also grown very fond of the president. Less than two weeks after Pearl Harbor, Roosevelt, in front of the entire cabinet, had heartily congratulated Knox for his trip to Hawaii and his "excellent handling" of the situation.

The cabinet all agreed that Knox's trip had been a success and had demonstrated to the nation that the government would not whitewash any mistakes.

Knox, who still felt personally responsible for the failure, was speechless, too overcome with emotion to do more than mutter "Thank you."

That night he went home and wrote the president, the man whose implicit socialism he once considered a threat to the republic, that those two words weren't enough.

"I didn't want to let it go at that," he said. "I want to tell you that it is the finest decoration I could ask for, or have. . . . It is a source of immense satisfaction to me to have a small part in aiding you to bear the fearful load of responsibility which is yours."[25]

So, despite his misgivings over allowing black men to train as more than messmen, Knox, on February 14, dutifully relayed the president's message to the General Board.

"The President is not satisfied with the alternative suggested by the recent decision," he wrote. "He thinks that some special assignments can be worked out for Negro enlisted men which would not inject into the whole personnel of the Navy the race question."[26]

Pinchot thought the president was on the right track and told Knox as much. Knowing of the "very widespread and serious dissatisfaction among Negroes," he suggested "token appointments might be extremely valuable at this stage of the game to neutralize, so far as possible, the very serious discontent in about one-tenth of our population."[27]

Knox thought that a terrible idea. The Navy would never find enough qualified black men to operate a war vessel, he told Pinchot, even "if you had the entire Negro population of the United States to choose from."

Besides, Knox said, black men must be limited to messman duties, because that "enables us to quarter the negroes together on the ship and limit their advancement to ratings within that branch, thus avoiding the promotion of negroes to command white men, a thing which instantly provokes serious trouble."

Pinchot understood better than Knox the grassroots groundswell of discontent that would surely hamper the war effort as much as would integrating ships, if not more so, but his pleas fell on deaf ears and the results were, at least to Pinchot, predictable.

The race question that Knox so hoped to avoid was about to explode.

CHAPTER 6

"A CORDIAL SPIRIT OF EXPERIMENTATION"

On the very same morning that Secretary Knox asked the General Board to redo its report, the *Pittsburgh Courier*, following up on James Thompson's letter, announced a Double V campaign on its front page, and within a month the newspaper was routinely running several Double V stories, photographs, and drawings. A Double V symbol was printed in the upper-left-hand corner of the *Courier's* front page, containing the words "Democracy. Double VV Victory. At Home—Abroad." Between two large V's was an eagle.[1]

The campaign went the mid-twentieth-century equivalent of viral. Soon, all of the other major African American newspapers adopted the slogan, as did Eleanor Roosevelt and two prominent Republicans, Wendell Willkie and Thomas Dewey (the latter of whom would win the nomination for president in 1944 and 1948). House Majority Leader John McCormack, the novelist Sinclair Lewis, and Hollywood's Humphrey Bogart, Ingrid Bergman, and Gary Cooper all lent their support. Prominent black Americans were photographed flashing the Double V sign, including Marian Anderson, Adam Clayton Powell Jr., Roy Wilkins, and Joe Louis's wife, Marva.

The message was simple—a true victory over tyranny would not be won by the surrender of enemies. It would only be achieved by a renunciation of undemocratic principles everywhere: Europe, Asia and, most important, the United States.

The idea was summed up by one African American in North Carolina who said, "No clear-thinking Negro can afford to ignore our Hitlers here in America. I consider a man foolish who kills out mosquitoes in the street, and allows himself to be eaten up in his own bed by bed bugs."[2]

The Negro Baptist Council designated Easter Sunday, 1942, as National Negro Double Victory Day. A week later, the *Courier* printed a drawing of two people standing on a hillside looking upward at Christ, who is emerging from a cloud holding a V in each hand.

The *Courier* recruited two hundred thousand Double V members, making it one of the largest black groups in the United States. There were Double V bumper stickers, buttons, sweaters, and beauty pageants.[3]

The campaign aggravated federal officials who believed that black editors were making too much of segregation, riling up readers when the nation needed unconditional loyalty.

A free press was a privilege, George Barnes, a top aide at the Office of Facts and Figures, told his boss. "The Negro press is flagrantly abusing the privilege every day. Much of the material they print violates every tenet of honest journalism." he said. "As long as the Negro press is permitted to continue its present practices with impunity, we can expect very little improvement in morale of the Negro population."[4]

Jonathan Daniels, Roosevelt's wartime consigliere on racial matters, told the president that the desire among African Americans to use the war effort to further equality was disastrous and called the Double V campaign extortion.[5]

Daniels's father was Josephus Daniels, who had served as secretary of the Navy under President Woodrow Wilson and had been Franklin Roosevelt's boss when the latter served as assistant secretary. Indeed, it was the elder Daniels who, in 1919, had moved to exclude black men from the Navy. Two decades later his son spoke for many in the White House when he said that he was "extremely disturbed" about the state of the "negro-white relationships" because he saw the "rising insistence of negroes on their rights now" conflicting with the "rising tide of white feeling against the negroes."[6]

Any threat to segregation—be it from black troops, Northern white liberals, or the Roosevelt administration—only made Southerners cling to it more desperately.

While many black men wondered whether the war was worth fighting if nothing changed at home, many Southern whites wondered whether the war was worth winning if anything changed back home.

"There's no white man down here going to let his daughter sleep with a nigger, or sit at the same table with a nigger or go walking with a nigger," Lloyd E. Foster, secretary of the Birmingham Chamber of Commerce, told the newspaper *PM*. "The war can go to hell, the world can go to hell but he ain't going to do it."[7]

Alabama governor Frank Dixon refused to sign a contract with the federal government to sell cloth made in prison because the contract contained an antidiscrimination clause. "The war emergency should not be used as a pretext to bring about abolition of the color line in the south," he said.[8]

The White House was regularly reminded by the Southern voters, whom it needed to maintain a governing coalition, that treating black men as equals in the armed forces was not only bad policy but also bad politics.

In an eerily prescient letter, Eugene "Bull" Connor, Birmingham's commissioner of public safety, told Roosevelt that support for equal rights would ruin the Democratic Party in the South. The Fair Employment Practices Committee, he said, was making black men "impudent, unruly, arrogant, law breaking, violent and insolent. There is no doubt that federal agencies have adopted policies to break down and destroy the segregation laws of . . . the entire south," Connor wrote to the president as one loyal Democrat to another. "Unless something is done by you we are going to . . . witness the annihilation of the Democratic Party in this section of the nation, and a revival of organizations which will . . . destroy the progress made by law abiding white people. . . . Don't you think one war in the south is enough. Help us before it is too late."[9]

The pundit Westbrook Pegler called the *Pittsburgh Courier* and the *Chicago Defender* "reminiscent of Hearst at his worst in their sensationalism, and in their obvious, inflammatory bias in the treatment of news they resemble such one-sided publications as the Communist Party's *Daily Worker* and [Father Charles] Coughlin's *Social Justice*."

Pegler, whose syndicated column reached more than six million readers, would later be known for his opposition to the civil rights movement and writing for the John Birch Society. But in the early 1940s he was one of the most influential men in America. In 1941, he finished third in *Time* magazine's Man of the Year poll, behind Roosevelt and the Russian leader Joseph Stalin. Now, he was saying the two leading African American newspapers were "dangerous . . . particularly in their appeal to colored soldiers whose loyalty is constantly bedeviled with doubts and with the race-angling of news."[10]

The *Chicago Defender*'s editors believed Pegler's attack was "inspired by some of his friends in the Navy department who want to smear the Negro Press, and intimidate Negro editors," and dismissed his editorial as the "emotional outburst of a disordered mind or the yapping of a stinking wet mutt."[11]

But Pegler and the Navy were not the only critics of the black press. The editorial slant had become so consistently critical that the War Department asked the Justice Department to consider indicting editors and publishers for sedition, and military intelligence said the black press appeared at times "to achieve the same result as [an] outright subversive publication."[12] FBI agents came to the offices of the *Pittsburgh Courier* "day in and day out" and recommended indicting its editors.[13]

To forestall that possibility, John Sengstacke, the owner of the largest chain of black newspapers in the country, and Charles Browning, who worked in the *Chicago Defender*'s Washington office, went to meet with Attorney General Francis Biddle. They, like the editors who had come to Washington the previous December, expected a welcoming reception. After all, Biddle was one of the most progressive members of Roosevelt's administration on the question of race.

And like the editors who came to Washington in December, Sengstacke and Browning were wrong.

They were brought to a Justice Department conference room and arrived to find Biddle and an assistant sitting at a table upon which several black newspapers were displayed. The papers headlined the racial tensions in Fort Dix, New Jersey, and Tuskegee, Alabama.

These kinds of stories were hurting the war effort, Biddle said, and if the black press didn't take on a more obsequious tone he was "going to shut them all up."

Looking at Browning, Biddle fumed over the *Defender's* report of nine black soldiers who, while traveling through Alabama, had to wait twenty-two hours to eat because white restaurants and railroad stations refused them service. The paper's articles "came very close to sedition," he repeated.

Sengstacke stared back at Biddle, holding his gaze to make sure that the attorney general understood that the next words out of his mouth were well considered and supremely serious.

"You have the power to close us down," Sengstacke said, "so if you want to close us, go ahead and attempt it."[14]

Biddle backed down, and over the next hour the men hammered out a detente. The attorney general promised he would not indict black publishers and Sengstacke said the black press would be "glad" to cooperate if reporters could have regular access to high officials such as Knox.

———

The black press was far from Knox's only critics. African American parents were writing to their congressmen, the Navy, even to the president to protest a policy that deemed their sons unfit to serve. J. E. Branham, a realtor from Cleveland, was dismayed to learn that his seventeen-year-old son, so eager to fight for his country, could do nothing more than wash dishes or scrub pots and floors in the kitchen and dining areas.

"It seems to me that that is a very cold and ugly situation," he said.[15]

Branham sent letters to the president, Senator Robert Taft, and his congressman, Martin Sweeney, who told Knox that "it would be a fine thing for the nation if boys of this type were given special training in Naval schools."

Addison Walker, a special assistant to Assistant Navy Secretary Ralph Bard, told Sweeney, "The Navy recognizes the loyalty and patriotism of the colored people in this country and is not unmindful of its responsibility to encourage the Negroes' desire to contribute their energy, skill and enthusiasm." Walker said the department was considering how best this could be accomplished and promised an announcement would be forthcoming.[16]

Walker was writing several letters like that every day as the General Board deliberated on how to appease the president without condoning conditions it felt would be ruinous to naval efficiency.

The cautious replies and stalling tactics were inadequate and infuriating to the thousands who turned on their radios each night and heard of the sacrifices that must be made in a war to defend democracy.[17]

Wendell Willkie, the 1940 Republican nominee, said the Navy's policies made a "mockery" of democratic principles.[18] Speaking at the Commodore Hotel in New York City during an inaugural dinner for the Freedom House, an organization founded to grow support for America's involvement in the war, Willkie demanded the ideals espoused in the president's own calls for democracy be carried out in the president's own Navy. "Don't you think that as American citizens, we should insist that our government and Navy Department eliminate the bar that prohibits any American citizen from serving his country?"[19]

Willkie called out the hypocrisy embodied by the fact that Joe Louis was allowed to raise money for the Navy but not fight for it. "He was preparing to fight in an Army uniform," Willkie told the two thousand guests. "He couldn't have been preparing to fight in a Navy uniform for his skin was black."[20]

When a reporter asked what could be done about the Navy, Willkie pointed his index finger and said the branch's insistence on limiting black men to the messman branch was "damn foolishness. . . . An order by the President or the Secretary of the Navy would dispose of the Navy's color bar—just like that," he said, and then snapped his fingers.[21]

Knox was furious when he read that in the papers. It wasn't so simple, and he thought it "puny and unpatriotic" to oppose the administration in the midst of a war. Willkie's attacks "were perfectly unjustified and unwarranted and especially his last one on the Negro question," Knox told his friend Paul Scott Mowrer, a Pulitzer Prize–winning foreign correspondent and the editor of the *Chicago Daily News.*

"It is simply impossible in the midst of a war to mix the races on the same ship, and if he had thought on the subject for a half minute, he would have known it," Knox said. "I can only fight one war at a time, and the one on our hands now is big enough without introducing a race war besides." A frustrated Knox wondered whether Willkie had any compunctions when he read about a riot that left five or six men dead at Fort Dix. "That would be a nice thing to initiate right now in the close quarters in which men have to live aboard, wouldn't it," Knox asked sarcastically.[22]

He also felt that Willkie's attacks were disingenuous and politically motivated, which particularly irked Knox, a Republican serving in the Roosevelt cabinet.

"The slightest inquiry on his part would have disclosed that we were working hard on the problem and had practically arrived at a decision when he burst into print," he said.

The solution to which Knox referred was announced April 7, 1942, during an impromptu press conference Knox had called in Washington. The Navy would for the first time in history open the general-service ratings to black men. They would train as quartermasters and engineers, learn how to navigate a ship, and repair a boiler.

The General Board, upon which Knox relied, had devised a plan that offered the "least disadvantages and the least difficulty of accomplishment as a war measure," having finally realized that it would be "unwise and inadvisable" to keep resisting the president.[23]

The board still thought it a terrible idea and, taking another shot at their commander in chief, said this should only be done "if it is determined by higher authority that social economic and other considerations require the enlistment of men of the colored race in other than the messman branch."[24]

It wanted final say as to how many enlistees would be accepted under this new program, but Roosevelt overruled the admirals, telling Knox, "This is a matter to be determined by you and me."[25]

This was a historic moment, but also one soured by needless caveats and dripping with reaffirmed prejudice.

The board recommended that black chief petty officers outrank only other black men—not whites—to avoid having blacks superior in rank to whites.

Admiral Ernest King, the chief of naval operations, said black men should be relegated to construction battalions, known as Seabees, and to shore stations, where they would work on the docks. If absolutely necessary, they were to be put on yard craft.[26] This arrangement could for the most part avoid mixing the races or having black men in charge of white men.

King's biographer charitably referred to the admiral's attitude toward African Americans as one of "benevolent ignorance." He had little personal contact with black men and was influenced by the stereotypes he heard on the radio and read in books, all of which seemed to comport with what Ely and other military minds had said for decades.

King often repeated racist jokes and referred to older black men as "darkies" and younger black men as "boys" and, occasionally, "niggers."

So King was not especially eager to integrate the fleet in any meaningful way and told Knox as much.[27]

Training would of course remain segregated, which the General Board both insisted upon and lamented because "to divert any part of the training effort to the development of Negro crews or Negro battalions would not produce a return in effective fighting units commensurate with the adverse effects on the training program and the efficiency of the fleet."[28]

Segregation required duplication of mess halls, sick bays, instructors, housing, and recreational facilities. It was a luxury and a waste of manpower that the Navy could ill afford, but was kept in place because the top brass still believed that integration would at best "adversely affect morale, and at worst, result in serious racial conflict and bloodshed."[29]

Knox told the reporters gathered at the Navy Department that he'd need three months to ready a segregated camp. Following King's recommendation, Knox ordered the Navy to accept for the general service no more than 277 black men per week and classify them as apprentice seamen. Anyone else who enlisted would serve in the construction battalions, or as messmen, meaning black men would still make up a disproportionate share of laborers and servants. Rated enlistees would serve ashore or on small local-defense craft. No black man who earned a rating would be allowed on a warship—thus African Americans would be denied the chance to test their mettle in battle. Aboard ship, black men would still be relegated to messmen duties. African Americans already serving as messmen were denied the ability to transfer because there was a shortage of servants.[30]

"The whole thing will be carried along in a cordial spirit of experimentation," Knox told reporters. "It is not contemplated they will be commissioned."

The secretary assured Massachusetts senator David Walsh, chair of the Naval Affairs Committee, that any discussion about African American officers remained a long way off.

"As you know, the arrangements for the enlistment of Negroes in the Navy, aside from the messman branch, are just in the making," Knox said. "We will have to develop a considerable body of Negro sailors before we can even approach the problem of the Negro commissioned officer."[31]

He told New Jersey senator William Smathers that "the experience of many years, has demonstrated that [Negro petty officers] cannot maintain discipline among men of the white race over whom they may be placed for the purpose of advancement. It is to be expected, therefore, that members of the Negro race serving as officers in the Navy would face the same difficulties. It is impracticable to so assign officers to particular duties which would make it possible that, in the case of Negro citizens appointed as officers, they would command only members of their own race."[32]

Knox's press conference was a public relations disaster, for he appeared to only begrudgingly accept a black man's role in the Navy, to limit his contributions to menial labor, and to continue the segregation that so insulted African Americans.

The new policy was dismissed as a "mere palliative which doesn't begin to reach the fundamental issues," and a "weak and futile gesture which can in no way claim to pacify the resentment and indignation of the mass of Negroes."[33]

"If Secretary Knox feels that it is necessary to cater to the prejudices of the Navy officials in order to win this war for 'Freedom,' then it would be wiser for him to keep quiet," the *Philadelphia Tribune* told its readers.[34]

The *Pittsburgh Courier* said it was hard not to "feel disgusted at the tricky, evasive hypocritical manner in which the Secretary of the Navy has dealt with this problem."[35]

While some prominent African American organizations such as the National Negro Congress commended Knox for what they saw as a first step, and the Navy did receive many congratulatory letters, most were appalled that the Navy could not bring itself to treat white and black sailors as equals. At best, this was progress of a stuttering sort.

The Washington chapter of the NAACP called the plan a "deliberate insult to all defenders of democracy" and asked the president to fire his Navy secretary. "The demonstration of the Nazi attitude by a cabinet officer strikes at the very roots of our American system," James E. Scott, the president of the local chapter, wired to Roosevelt. "This blow to the morale of the Negro people will be deeply appreciated in Berlin, Rome and Tokio [*sic*]."[36]

The National Urban League's publication, *Opportunity*, said the Navy had passed up a historic chance, and instead had chosen "to affirm the charge that Japan is making against America to the brown people . . . that the so-called Four Freedoms enunciated in the great 'Atlantic Charter' were for white men only."[37]

"Such as it is, this order is a victory for sustained agitation begun and carried on by the *Pittsburgh Courier*," an editorial in the paper said. "But in all frankness it must be stated that fundamentally this order marks a setback in race relations in the United States because it strengthens the vicious institution of segregation, the root and source of all the ills the Negro suffers in this country. It merely extends the borders of segregation and we have too much segregation already. It is a source of sorrow, amazement and shame that in time of war when the United States has suffered defeat after defeat and the fate of civilization hangs in the balance that a high government official should so abjectly surrender to reactionism."[38]

It wasn't only the black press that found Knox's policy lacking. The *New York Times* editorial board lamented the continuing discrimination "for which no warrant can be found in the constitution, the statutes or the Democratic traditions of the United States."[39]

The black press found it notable that "even so conservative a newspaper as *The New York Times* expresses editorial dissatisfaction in stronger words than it has ever used in commenting on racial questions."[40]

A. Philip Randolph thought the new rules were worse than if the government had made no announcement at all because this "accepts and extends and consolidates the policy of Jim-Crowism in the Navy as well as proclaims it an accepted government ideology that the Negro is inferior to the white man. White America must understand that the Negro ... resent[s] the stigma of inferiority and the status of vassals which Secretary Knox has affixed to them," Randolph said.[41]

The dismay from the black community over Knox's timid stance was matched by the horror in the white community, terrified that the secretary had gone too far. Martin Keefe, a retired Marine living in Connecticut, begged his senator to "protest this move to the limit." And a letter signed "just a marine" said that nearly all members of the Navy and Marine Corps "resent this and consider [it] another communistic move by the communistic New Deal."[42]

All Knox could do when responding to howls of protest from civil rights leaders and bigots was to assure all his critics that his decision had not been made in haste.

"I know that many loyal citizens of our country would misunderstand this action," he told Connecticut Senator Francis Maloney, "but I can assure you it was taken with first consideration given to the best interest of our country and the service."[43]

He thought it false and "not in the best interests of the Negro race" for leaders to say that the policies were inconsistent with the nation's democratic ideals. "That all theoretically possible steps are not taken at once cannot reasonably be condemned as undemocratic," he said.[44]

He and Assistant Navy Secretary Ralph Bard tried to make the case that gratitude would go further than griping.

"Rome wasn't built in a day," Bard told the Conference of Negro Churches. "You can't just turn everything upside down in five minutes. The more lack of cooperation there is, the tougher it's going to be for the service as a whole and for your people."[45]

Knox decided that the Navy's experiment with black men would begin at Great Lakes Naval Training Station, on the shore of Lake Michigan just north of Chicago.[46] An isolated section along Morrow Road at the very northwest corner of the station had camps that offered plenty of room for segregated facilities. Rear Admiral Randall Jacobs, chief of the Bureau of Navigation, reckoned that using these existing facilities would make the segregation less conspicuous than if the Navy picked a new site and built segregated camps from scratch.

On June 5, 1942, Doreston Luke Carmen Jr., a nineteen-year-old from Galveston, Texas, who had graduated from high school five days earlier, became the first black man to report to Camp Morrow.[47] The doors were now open—if only a crack—but black men were not rushing to enlist in the Navy. During the first three weeks, only 1,261 black men volunteered, and 58 percent of those men had been rejected for physical and other reasons.

Jacobs thought the recruitment troubles were because the Navy was not doing enough to publicize its new open stance, but the bureau's historians assured him that it was simply black men's "relative unfamiliarity with the sea or the large inland waters and their consequent fear of the water" that kept them from enlisting.[48]

The historians could hang their racist trope on misinterpreted statistics. Of the recruits who reported to Great Lakes, roughly two-thirds of white men could pass the swimming tests, compared to only one-third of black men. Much of this result could be traced to the South's rules that kept black men from swimming at beaches or in public pools, but to many Navy men, it confirmed their fear that recruiting black men was a waste of time and effort.[49]

The real reason black men remained wary of the Navy was because they surmised, not incorrectly, that they'd still be treated as the "vassals" that Randolph described. More than 75 percent of readers polled by the *Pittsburgh Courier* in the fall of 1942 said they did not believe the Navy "offers the American Negro greater opportunity to serve his country than the Army."[50]

As a result, better-educated black men were far more likely to join the Army. Only about 20 percent of young African Americans in the nation had less than four years of schooling. At Great Lakes, it was 30 percent. Consequently, test scores for black men in the Navy consistently ran about ten points behind those of white men. If given more training the black men could equal white men in shop work but remained behind in advanced mathematics and theory subjects, providing fodder to those who thought they were inferior. In reality these differences were an indictment of the "separate but equal" school system that would be challenged a decade later. The eleven states that made up the Confederacy, plus Kentucky, accounted for 91 percent of those requiring, and profiting from, remedial literacy courses, but, as was the case with the swim tests, not everyone in the Navy was inclined to take such a progressive view.[51]

Instead, the poor test scores were among the reasons the Navy gave for insisting on segregated training camps.

In an attempt to address the recruiting challenge, the Navy assigned black men to work at recruiting centers in black communities across the country. Among them was Dennis Denmark Nelson II, who joined the Navy on June 5, the same day as Carmen, though with much less fanfare. Nelson, a thirty-four-year-old with a neatly trimmed mustache and receding hairline, was a prominent Fisk University sociology professor who had already made a name for himself in Tennessee.

A decade earlier, Nelson, then attending Fisk University and working with the Bethlehem Center, a Christian institution for black boys, started Nashville's first black Boy Scouts troop, Troop 65. Nelson was "untiring" in his recruitment and soon there were more than one hundred boys participating from across the city. W. J. Anderson, a Scouts executive, called Nelson "an unusually capable scoutmaster," and asked him to come to Cincinnati to become a Scouts council executive.[52]

It made sense then for the Navy to assign Nelson to the Nashville Navy Recruiting Station, in a community where he already had relationships with many draft-age Boy Scouts. Petty Officer First Class Nelson spent his first eighteen months in the Navy telling potential recruits, uncertain what branch to choose, that the Navy's technical schools offered some of the best training in the world, and in most cases that training was easily adapted to civilian life, offering a chance for employment when the war ended.[53]

Even as black men began to enlist in the Navy in greater numbers and take advantage of the new training offered, African American leaders were pushing to remove the barriers that placed a ceiling on their race's advancement.

In July, the presidents of land grant institutions petitioned Secretary Knox to allow black men into the V-1 program, which combined college courses and officer training. The Navy had blocked all the historically black colleges from the program and was prohibiting black men who were attending integrated colleges from enrolling.

"Obviously, it is a callous, profligate waste of intelligent manpower to take a man who has had (or can get) several years of college mathematics, physics and allied subjects and start him as an apprentice seaman," the college presidents wrote to Knox. "Such a policy of exclusion has caused and will cause more and more colored men to wonder whether the recent action of the Navy in making it possible for colored men to enlist in the Navy other than [as] messmen . . . is to remain a feeble gesture. . . . Such doubts and fears certainly are not conducive to high morale."[54]

A committee appointed by the college presidents told Addison Walker, Bard's special assistant, and Dean Baker, the head of the Navy training program, that ambitious black youths would enter the Army "under the superior opportunities offered . . . to become officers" instead of the Navy, "knowing that the officer program in the Navy is an illusion or practically a closed door."

The V-1 program, they pointed out, would take at least two or three years to graduate a black officer, and if the war actually lasted into 1944 or 1945 the "Navy would need officers so badly that the color of the officer would be immaterial."[55]

Knox didn't care.

The Navy was not ready to train black officers, and he told anyone who protested that black men should first "prove themselves on the present levels and the present opportunities."[56]

The new black sailors were doing just that. According to a report to the Educational Planning Officer at Great Lakes, "The Negro students make up for their poorer background to some extent through their greater earnestness and effort." It seemed obvious to many recruits that the Navy was offering unprecedented opportunities to learn a skill or a trade, the very opportunities that Randolph and White had said were so crucial to the advancement of their people.[57]

The white world was taking notice. The *Chicago Daily Tribune* told its readers that the Navy has "warmed to the Negro because the colored sailor has turned out to be a gentleman."[58]

Black men, despite what the General Board had predicted, could make worthy sailors after all.

CHAPTER 7

"AS GOOD AS ANY FIGHTING MEN THE US NAVY HAS"

Among the very first men to take advantage of the Navy's new open policy was Graham Martin, a reserved twenty-five-year-old from Indianapolis who had just completed a master's degree in education.

A buddy of Martin's, Edward France, had enlisted in the Navy a few weeks before and was already leading a company. Maybe Martin could lead one too, he thought. Besides, anything was preferable to the Army for a germophobe like Martin, whose skin crawled at the thought of cradling a rifle while belly-crawling through muck and mud.[1]

He had been drafted into the Army in April but begged a deferment, telling the draft board that what little money he had was already committed to paying the fees for his final semester at Howard University. He asked that he be allowed to graduate.

"You stay there," the board replied, "and we'll contact you again."

With his master's degree in hand, Martin knew the Army would soon come calling. But before it could, he was on his way to Great Lakes Naval Training Station.

The segregated Camp Morrow at the northwest corner of the station was an all-too-familiar scene to Martin, who throughout his life had been told that he was inferior, incapable of competing with whites, despite all his success in the classroom and on the football field.

His earliest years had been spent in Tobacco Port, a small Tennessee town near the Cumberland River and the Kentucky border.

His parents, Charlie and Carrie Lee Martin, were tobacco farmers who needed every hand they could get. Their fourth and final child, a boy they named Graham Edward, was born January 18, 1917, and not long after he left the womb he found himself in the field pulling large, fat green worms off the tobacco plants.

For his labors, Graham received a penny from his father. Charlie Martin was much older than his wife, already in his sixties when Graham was born. He was a superhero to his young son, a man who possessed almost magical powers.

Graham long remembered the day when he and his dad were coming home from the fields. Up in the tree, two squirrels were chasing each other atop the branches.

Run home and get me my shotgun, his father said.

Graham was just a small boy, and by the time he returned it was dusk. It seemed all you could see were shadows. Charlie Martin raised his shotgun, fired one shot into the tree, and down came two squirrels.

Dinner that night would be fresh.

Graham was only six years old when he saw his father struggling for breath that would not come. The child was led out of the room but peeked back over his shoulder for a final look at his gasping hero.

That was the last Graham saw of Charlie Martin. Soon he'd be saying goodbye to Tobacco Port as well.

His mother, fearing she could not maintain the family farm, moved with her youngest son to Indianapolis, while Graham's three older siblings remained in Tennessee. In Indianapolis his mother would later earn a reasonable living during the Great Depression, thanks to the Roosevelt administration's WPA, which employed her to stitch blankets for the Army.[2]

Carrie Lee Martin and her youngest son were part of a wave of African Americans migrating to Indianapolis, a city that, like Chicago, was seeing a black boom. The black population of Indianapolis increased from 35,000 in 1920 to nearly 44,000 by 1930, amounting to 12 percent of the city's population. The influx strained the infrastructure. The housing stock and the schools could not keep up. The public services pie was the same size, but the slices were getting thinner and the white folks weren't too happy about it.

It is no coincidence that as the Martins and thousands of other black families moved in, the Ku Klux Klan grew exponentially, so that by 1924, more than 40 percent of the native-born white males in Indianapolis claimed membership.

The fifty thousand dues-paying Klan members in Indianapolis provided the organization with a tremendous war chest of tens of millions of dollars, which helped them buy local politicians.[3]

Klan-backed candidates won control of the city council, the Board of School Commissioners, and the Board of County Commissioners. They invented a scandal to remove a recalcitrant and uncooperative governor and replace him with the more malleable Edward L. Jackson, who had served as Indiana's secretary of state. Jackson had the title of governor, but the power belonged to a pudgy, sharp-dressing demagogue named David C. Stephenson, appointed the Klan grand dragon of Indiana.

In 1922, Klansmen in the Indiana General Assembly created Klan Day at the state fair, where events included a nighttime cross burning. Four years later, the city council passed a zoning ordinance meant to prevent blacks from moving into a home without the consent of the block's white residents. The ordinance was declared unconstitutional, but there were other ways to ensure blacks knew they weren't welcome.

It was common for mobs of men, sheets over their heads, to terrorize blacks, Jews, and Catholics. They tarred women accused of prostitution, flogged people in public, and left burning crosses in their wake. Billboards in town read "Nigger, Don't Let the Sun Set on You Here."[4]

This was the Indianapolis that young Graham Martin entered, a Klan-controlled, rigidly segregated town, growing too fast to accommodate the arrival of families fleeing agrarian life.

The Irish stayed in the southeast corner; the Italians and Greeks were to the east; the Jews lived south of downtown. Blacks lived on the northwest side of the city, a neighborhood anchored by Indiana Avenue, where the melodies of jazz musicians perfecting their craft provided a neighborhood soundtrack.[5]

It was a very different upbringing from the one Sam Barnes had in Oberlin and John Reagan experienced in the Englewood section of Chicago, towns and neighborhoods where race remained in the background.

Everywhere Martin looked in Indianapolis, he was reminded that blacks were second-class.

Like Reagan, Martin lacked a positive male role model and soon ran into trouble, joining gangs, breaking windows, sneaking into movie theaters, and stealing from shops. When he was twelve he went into a store, walked behind the counter, grabbed cash from the cigar box, and ran.

A police officer chased him to a dead-end alley.

The officer drew his weapon.

Martin froze.

"I wouldn't shoot you," the cop said, "but maybe somebody else would because you're big for your age. You are going to get yourself killed."

The courts were becoming familiar with Martin's antics. A local judge before whom the preteen had already appeared for breaking windows and shoplifting remanded him to a home for orphans, reasoning that if his mother had to work all day, the young man could benefit from more adult supervision.[6]

The Indianapolis Asylum for Friendless Colored Children had been founded in 1869 by Quakers who saw the need for an institution to care for the children of destitute freed slaves. Most of the children were not orphans. Like Martin, they either came from single-parent homes or had parents who had to work all day to make ends meet and had no time to look after their children.

The orphanage was there to provide the structure that parents could not. The girls helped in the laundry, sewing room, nursery, and kitchen. They were taught to make paper, rag rugs, and baskets.

The boys helped in the kitchen, engine room, shoe shop, carpentry, cement shop, and print shop. They made their own toys, built cabinets for tools, and repaired their own shoes. They had their own magazine, *Orphan's Home*, which they printed themselves. When the weather was nice, the boys gardened.[7]

Martin hated the orphanage at first and even ran away a couple times, but he eventually warmed to the structure and opportunities offered, relishing the positive reinforcement he received for doing well at school.[8]

Children who lived at the Indianapolis Asylum attended PS 37, a segregated elementary school across the street. After school and completing his chores at the orphanage—making his bed, cleaning the floor, washing the dishes—Martin could be found behind a stack of books, his head down and his eyes darting across the page.[9] He proudly told the staff that he was going to be a teacher and spent his time educating himself, in the belief that he would one day educate others.

Martin attended Crispus Attucks High School, which had been built soon after he and his mother arrived in town. Indianapolis high schools had been integrated for fifty years following the Civil War, but the Klan had put an end to that in 1927. The black community protested, arguing that segregating students would require removing black children from schools where they were already enrolled, but their pleas fell on deaf ears. No one in the white world was really interested in their opinion.

Crispus Attucks High School, an unadorned brick building at the corner of West and Twelfth Streets, was built as a segregated school in the worst part of town, where it was surrounded with garbage dumps.[10] When its doors opened on September 12, the Klan organized several parades throughout the city to celebrate. Just a few miles from the school, on Washington Street, "row after row of masked Klansmen, marching slowly to the beat of muffled drums, took an hour to pass."

Black children marched into class, sat down, and opened their books.

That year, Arthur Trester, commissioner of the Indiana High School Athletic Association, denied Crispus Attucks High membership in the IHSAA. The school, he said, did not admit white students, so it wasn't technically a public school. Trester, who was referred to as the czar of the IHSAA and would later be inducted into the National Basketball Association Hall of Fame, told the black students that his hands were tied.[11]

Trester's ridiculous position humiliated parents and teachers, but it also provided an unparalleled opportunity for black students such as Martin, an all-state tackle on the football team.

The players had to travel around the South to find other schools to play against. Young black boys, many of whom were too poor to leave the county, were exposed to a wider world for the first time. Football gave those students a chance to see St. Louis, Tulsa, and Lexington, and as they sat on the bus, towns and farms rolling by, they could for the first time picture a life outside Indianapolis.

By the time Martin reached high school he was a popular student with good grades and president of several clubs, including the boxing club, the student council, and the French club. He was the senior class president. But his life had been the orphanage; what lay beyond, what the world might hold, was something he could only imagine.

Now, hundreds of miles from school, Martin was getting an education. After some of his teammates, pulling a childish prank, poured salt into the mustard in a restaurant in Terre Haute, Martin saw his coach, a talented African American athlete and member of Phi Beta Kappa, pulled out of the restaurant and humiliated by local police.[12]

But he also saw how black men all across the South—across the globe—were achieving every bit as much as, if not more than, white folks, who were supposed to be the superior race. How, he wondered, could Jesse Owens win Olympic Gold in Germany or Joe Louis become a world champion if black men were inferior? Martin even began to suspect that the football teams he played on would beat the white teams if they ever got on the same field.

Segregation also meant that Crispus Attucks High School attracted inspiring teachers, many of whom had PhDs but could not find work in the white world.

The principal, Dr. Russell Adrian Lane, had six degrees, including a PhD from Brown University and another from Dayton University, and was one of the first black men admitted to the Maryland Bar. For thirty years he would tell black students like Martin that they, too, could succeed if they worked hard, and that education was "the way you get out of your cycle of poverty."[13]

The teachers at Crispus Attucks taught the boys and girls never to let race be an excuse. They would have to work harder than white people to succeed. "There were two strikes against you to start with, so you've got to use that last strike," is how Martin remembered it. "You go in there and don't ask for anything and do the job."[14]

Martin enrolled in the University of Indiana, thanks to a merit scholarship for poor but promising youngsters, which offered him $250 per year. He was a walk-on for the football team, where he played tackle for Alvin "Bo" McMillin, the famed college quarterback who went on to coach in the NFL. The teams were not very good, and Martin, at five feet, ten inches and 193 pounds, was one of the smaller tackles in the league. He didn't play as much as he would have liked, especially during home games. He suspected at the time that it may have been because the hometown fans did not want to see a black man take playing time from a white man, although he later came to realize that walk-ons probably always had a hard time getting on the field.

He graduated in June 1941, and one month later married Alma Mae Patterson. He had first met her while living in the orphanage—she lived a few doors down from him. In high school, he'd help her with English and math. Absence made the heart grow fonder—they fell in love while away at college, he at the University of Indiana and she at Indiana State and then Kentucky State.

But they kept their marriage vows a secret. The trouble was, Martin had no job. He still hoped to become a teacher, but he had no means to support his bride and an ailing mother, to whom he was sending what little money he had. Alma moved back home with her parents while Martin enrolled in a master's program at Howard University, studying under Rayford Logan, and teaching history to the freshman class to help pay his way. He lived on campus in Cook Hall and supplemented his income by selling flowers at Sears and cleaning fish at a local market.

Howard was a revelation for Martin. Black history wasn't taught much, if at all, in Indiana, so this was his first chance to study the antebellum South. His thesis was on the Underground Railroad in Indiana, and he spent hours researching abolitionists and slavery, poring over the pages of volumes in the Library of Congress—where, in the nation's capital, signs saying "colored" designated which restrooms and water fountains he could use.[15]

Martin graduated from Howard in May 1942, and eight weeks later he found himself on a train, heading west from Washington, DC, toward a new life in the Navy.

He arrived at Chicago's Union Station with about a dozen other recruits, none of whom had any clue what to do next or how to get to Great Lakes. They had been told to take the train, but these men had never seen an elevated train before so they stood around, uncertain where or how to board it until a passerby explained the platform was up a flight of stairs.

They arrived at Great Lakes Naval Training Station late Friday night, too late for supper. Hungry and tired, Martin looked over his new home.

The barracks in Camp Morrow, like those in the white camps, were laid out in an H shape. They were two stories tall, 100 by 168 feet, with four dormitories, each one housing sixty to eighty men, with four rooms for petty officers.[16] The bare, steam-heated quarters had twelve toilets, six urinals, six shower units, and a laundry room.[17]

Like the white camps, Camp Morrow had eighteen barracks capable of housing a total of about 4,500 recruits: sixteen barracks for recruits in training and two for those in ship's company, the men who worked full-time at Great Lakes. There was one mess hall with cooks' quarters, one physical training building, and one drill hall, where commanding officers lectured and where black enlistees were told they must be "better than good."

There were no guidelines for integrating the general service—nothing like this had ever been attempted in the history of the Navy. These new black recruits could expect to find a hostile, racist environment. They would endure teasing, minstrel shows, racial epithets, and bigoted officers.[18] But the Navy would tolerate no complaints from the new recruits. It was the same lesson Principal Lane had delivered to students back in Indianapolis. Black sailors must keep their cool, keep their heads down, and work twice as hard as whites, they were told. They must "be better than good."[19]

When Martin woke up on Saturday morning and headed to mess for breakfast, he couldn't believe his eyes. They were serving beans and corn-bread, a Navy tradition. He was used to eggs, bacon, and cereal. Beans were for dinner, maybe lunch, but certainly not breakfast. He pushed his plate aside. But if he wanted to eat, he'd have to eat what the Navy offered, and within a week he was asking for seconds.

It was one of the many concessions—some large, some small—that men from across the country were making as they adjusted to life at Great Lakes.

The first few nights could be particularly disorienting.

The men slept in hammocks slung between posts in an open bay. There were five hammocks per bay and six bays on each side of the room. The hammocks were inches apart and barely the width of a human body.

Many men feared falling out, so they'd loosen their hammocks, giving them more sway. But that only made things worse, and throughout the night the sound of fresh recruits falling from their hammocks beat in time, almost as if a drum were signaling another failed attempt.

A number of men also woke up wet, learning the hard way that sleeping in a hammock can activate the bladder.

Those who managed to sleep through the night could find their new alarm clock—an officer charging into the barracks before sunrise, turning on all the lights and screaming, "All right, every living ass, hit the deck!"—a bit disorienting.[20]

Even the military's most elementary tenets could feel foreign.

Marching is integral to the military, but some men did not know their right from their left.[21] The Navy's focus on cleanliness, while attractive to men such as Martin, meant little to the thousands who were coming from homes without running water or soap. Some entered the Navy literally filthy, and special inspections for cleanliness and clothing were established.[22]

But for many black men, particularly those from the South, the Navy was their salvation. Training is supposed to harden recruits, but the conditions at Great Lakes could seem downright luxurious compared to their lives back home. Men who had never owned a decent set of clothing were given three or four uniforms. Malnourished, scrawny teenagers ate three meals a day—a new experience.[23] This was the first time many had ever sat in a dentist's chair or been vaccinated against communicable diseases. Many hadn't seen a doctor of any kind in years.

━━━━━

John Reagan, who enlisted in the Navy on July 1, quickly stood out among his peers. Reagan had dropped out of college, certain that the Air Forces would call, but month after month passed and the call never came. Worried that he'd be drafted into the Army, and still averse to being forced to fight, Reagan enlisted hoping that if he couldn't see action in the sky, he'd find it at sea.

One week into recruit training at Great Lakes, he received orders from the Air Forces to go down to Tuskegee to train with the Ninety-ninth Pursuit Squadron.

Reagan was elated and sought out his executive officer.

"I've only been in the Navy a week, and I've got these orders where I can be a flier. Can't you let me out?" he begged.

"No way," the officer said.

Reagan was crushed, but soon the Navy did not seem so bad. He had a bit of ROTC (Reserve Officers' Training Corps) training and was made an apprentice chief petty officer. Reagan took pride in his company and the work he did, believing that he needed to prove the Navy hadn't made a mistake when it opened the general service to black men.[24] Soon, his chief petty officer came around less and less, trusting Reagan to ensure the company was ready for inspections, on time for meals, orderly.

James Hair was also enjoying his new Navy life. He entered the Navy the same day as Reagan, only he entered as James Hare, a superficial change he wouldn't think much about until forty years later, when the Navy, unable to find him, assumed he was dead and didn't let him know about reunions.

The spelling change had come about in the mid-1930s, when Hair worked at a drugstore owned by the Browns, who were fans of a British tennis sensation, Charles Edgar Hare. They pitied their young employee for having been born the wrong color, but believed his skin was light enough to pass for white if he "whitened" up his name. They told him to spell his name "Hare," the white way. Hair didn't really care as long as he was getting paid, so he went along with the change.

At the time, Hair was saving money for college and needed every dollar he could get. He left Fort Pierce in 1936, the year after his brother-in-law was lynched, and enrolled in a two-year program at Bethune-Cookman College in Daytona Beach.[25] When he graduated in 1938, he had no money, no job, and few prospects. The best work he could find was digging ditches for ten cents an hour while baking in the Florida sun. By the spring of 1939, Hair was wearing out the soles of his shoes looking for work, and he was praying—a lot.

Salvation came, as it so often does, in the form of inspiration.

Hair sent a note to the Peacock family, one of the wealthiest in Fort Pierce, to see if they could provide him with some work. He had two years of college, he told them, and needed to save up for another two in order to complete a degree.

"If you have anything available, I'd appreciate hearing," he wrote.[26]

This was an audacious but not altogether unreasonable idea. The Peacocks were among the most influential couples in the area. They dispatched one of their servants to bring Hair to their mansion. Their butler, also named James, was doubling as the chauffeur and caretaker. James said he'd be glad for the extra help, and so Hair spent the next year as the butler and chauffeur at the Peacocks' mansion.

He saved enough money to enroll in Xavier University, a Catholic school in New Orleans, where he supplemented his savings by working in the registrar's office after class. Then, he'd eat a quick supper and work until 3 a.m. as a porter in the cocktail lounge of the Jung Hotel. He managed a few hours of sleep each night, and then he was back in class the next morning.[27]

Hair had only a semester remaining when war was declared. Like Martin he received an educational deferment that kept him out of the military until he graduated in the spring of 1942. He was expected to report to the Army, but Wright, his murdered brother-in-law, had taught him so much about the water—navigation, swimming, boating, seamanship—that Hair decided to enlist in the Navy. Besides, he later joked, he hated the color of those Army uniforms. "It reminded me of shit."[28]

———

The train that brought Martin, Reagan, Hair, and nearly one million more men to the shores of Lake Michigan stopped just feet from the main entrance to Great Lakes Naval Training Station, on the other side of Morrow Road.

An officer stood at the gate, the first sign that their old civilian life had ended and a new military one was about to begin. As fresh black recruits were driven from the main entrance to the black camp, about one mile away, guards stationed outside other camps would yell, "You're gonna be sorry" or "You had a good home but you left."[29]

Welcome to the Navy.

The thousands of recruits who arrived in the summer of 1942 found a naval station in the final throes of an unprecedented expansion that saw Great Lakes grow tenfold in the months following Pearl Harbor.

Two hours after news of the Japanese attack reached Great Lakes, Captain Ralph D. Spalding, the public works director, walked into the office of the Ninth Naval District's commandant, Rear Admiral John Downes. In Spalding's briefcase were plans that he and his staff had developed during the previous year, a vision that would allow Great Lakes to go from training 6,000 sailors on December 7, to 68,000 by the following summer, to 100,000 by September 1942.

"We are at war, all of us," Navy Secretary Knox had said after Pearl Harbor. "There is no time now for disputes or delay of any kind. We must have ships and more ships, guns and more guns, men and more men— faster and faster. There is no time to lose. The Navy must lead the way. Speed up—it's your Navy and your nation."[30]

And so they did.

More than 13,000 civilians worked around the clock for almost a year to turn Spalding's plans into reality. Blueprints cluttered the admiral's office during those months and decisions that used to take weeks were made in minutes.

Between September 1939, when Germany invaded Poland, and December 7, 1941, when Japan attacked Hawaii, twenty-five new buildings were constructed at a cost of $10 million. During the next ten months, 453 new buildings were constructed at a cost of $75 million.[31]

Spalding requisitioned 375 acres from the Veterans Administration, which had land near the base's hospital just west of the main station, to build 109 new barracks. Another 685 acres of private land were condemned and taken by the Navy to make up the Green Bay area, which held six more camps.

In September 1942, when more space was needed, the hammocks Martin and Hair had gotten used to were replaced by bunk beds, allowing the Navy to cram even more recruits into the barracks.[32]

The building boom transformed Great Lakes from a 172-acre campus to a sprawling 1,600-acre facility that would, by the end of the war, train nearly one million men, close to one-third of the entire Navy, and twice the number trained anywhere else.

It was hell on the men who arrived during those first few months of the war. They trained in mud, flood, and dust the likes of which most had never seen.

"With the rain we've been having around here lately, I might just as well be out at sea," wrote the "Dear Mazie" columnist in the *Great Lakes Bulletin*. "Then, if a couple of hours do happen to get by without any rain appearing it gets so dusty you can't breathe. It is the only place where you can stand up to your knees in the mud and choke to death from dust."[33]

There were times during those first few months when men, both black and white, had to do without heat, hot water, and a full issue of clothing, as the nation's supplies failed to keep up with enlistments. The shortage was so severe that by the fall of 1942 more than thirty thousand men lacked overcoats for the coming winter.

Conditions improved somewhat the following year, once the drill fields were paved, trees and flowers planted, and black dirt hauled into the station, though the air still stank from coal-burning heating plants, nearby industrial plants, and the steam locomotives that spewed cinders and soot.[34]

Recruits began their training with a physical exam and a mental health evaluation, a haircut, and inoculations against tetanus, typhoid, and smallpox. Then they received their first uniforms—woolen "blues" for winter and white twill for summer.

Assignment to company and barracks came next.

During the first week, enlistees learned how to wear their uniforms properly, roll their clothes and stow them in seabags, scrub clean their own laundry, salute correctly, and conduct themselves with proper military decorum. They learned how to secure a gas mask and how to march and were lectured on naval customs and military courtesy. Then came hours of calisthenics and long hikes while carrying a full pack.

The second week, after another typhoid vaccine, was when these "boots," as the recruits were called because of the leggings they wore during training, were given their first aptitude test and swimming tests.[35] There were classes on seamanship where boots learned knot-tying and splicing, about life aboard ship, and lifesaving drills. They learned how to replace missing buttons on their uniforms and repair rips in their clothing. They memorized a new vocabulary. "Port" and "starboard" are left and right. Recruits "come aboard" when they arrive and "go ashore" when they leave.[36] During the third week, there were tests for service schools and lectures on steering and sea watches.[37]

The segregated camp, where thousands of black men spent their first two months in the Navy, was fitted with as many practical training devices as the officers could acquire. There was a five-inch gun moved into the drill hall, and replica ships were built so boots could visualize the location of different parts of a vessel.[38]

The "commando course," built by black recruits themselves, was the pride of the Great Lakes station. It was an obstacle course laid out like a golf course, where different obstacles replaced the holes. Boots raced between sandbags, climbed over high board fences, shimmied up ropes, and swung from handlebars before crawling through knee-scraping tunnels of iron.[39] Meanwhile the Navy trainers attempted to simulate war by broadcasting "battle noises" over loudspeakers attached to the trees.[40]

Among the obstacles was a twenty-foot-wide, six-foot-deep ditch that sailors jumped into and then climbed out of. One anxious recruit, not quite understanding the rules, ran full speed at the edge and leaped across the entire ditch.

"I thought I was supposed to jump across, so I did," he told his dumbstruck superior officer.[41]

Hair didn't mind the rigors of boot camp. The drilling and calisthenics weren't too much of a challenge, as he was in excellent shape when he entered the Navy. Nor did he find the classroom work too difficult. He was a college graduate, more educated than most and more accustomed to academic work. He was selected honor man of his company.[42]

But unlike Martin, Hair never did get used to the beans for breakfast, which wasn't served until the men had been drilled, had cleaned their barracks, and had stood for inspection. The beans were always cold by the time he sat down. The coffee got low marks as well—several chief petty officers said it was the worst they ever tasted—but waste was not permitted. Watchers at each scullery stopped men from leaving the mess until everything edible on their plate was eaten.[43]

Regular drilling didn't much bother Hair, but he hated the drilling done for disciplinary reasons. An officer might enter the barracks at 3 a.m., and if he found a piece of paper on the floor or a Baby Ruth candy wrapper under a hammock, the whole group would be up in the predawn cold doing calisthenics.

"Boy, if we could just find out who that guy is, we'd kill him," Hair remembered thinking.[44]

Punishing the group for one man's actions was standard. If a boot talked out of turn, the whole unit might have to drill with their caps in their mouths.[45]

When one recruit stepped out of line, it fell on his company to mete out justice. One time, a black sailor who thought his undershirt was clean enough to pass inspection did not bother to put on a fresh one. The inspecting officer stopped in front of him, grabbed the T-shirt's collar, turned it inside out, and asked for the sailor's name. He was put on report, the official punishment. The unofficial discipline happened later. When the men in his unit returned to the barracks they undressed and each man grabbed a clothes brush, the type used for scrubbing. The offending sailor was taken into the shower, fully clothed, and each piece of clothing was scrubbed clean while he was still wearing it. When that was finished, he was stripped down and the men took turns scrubbing him. He was red for two days but never again was caught unprepared or unclean.[46]

When boot camp ended, most men would be sent to either a shore establishment or a naval base. Roughly one-third qualified for Class A instruction where they would train for a rating in the general service. Advanced training for above-deck assignments such as gunner's mate, quartermaster, boatswain's mate, and yeoman took place at Great Lakes. Those training for below-deck ratings—electrician's mates, carpenter's mates, shipfitters, machinist's mates, metalsmiths, firemen, and cooks—went to Hampton Institute, a service school in Virginia.

Men received their first leave after they completed boot camp. Those, like Martin, who lived within a couple hundred miles, could travel home to see their girlfriends, wives, or parents.[47]

For men such as Hair, who could not travel home, the opportunities for leisure around Great Lakes were sparse. Most took the bus or train into Chicago, about an hour away.[48] Hair enjoyed the YMCA on the city's South Side and took advantage of the different programs it offered in the black section of the city.

There was also plenty of entertainment inside the black camp.

Movies were shown in the drill hall nearly every night. It was too small to accommodate the whole camp at one time, so select companies would be marched to the movie, and then they were free to return to their barracks on their own, as long as they were back in time for taps.[49]

The Ship's Company Band performed every Wednesday evening and Sunday afternoon for happy hours. During the Wednesday happy hours, the band, thanks to the USO, would be accompanied by an entertainer such as Lena Horne, Dorothy Donegan, or the Jimmie Lunceford Band.[50] The camp also hosted the renowned contralto Marian Anderson and Hazel Scott, the Trinidadian pianist who later married Congressman Adam Clayton Powell Jr. of New York.

On Sundays, when family members could visit, the bands played classical music and jazz. White officers who worked in other camps at Great Lakes considered it a privilege to come over and listen to some of the happy hour shows.[51]

Hair, Reagan, and Martin experienced little prejudice during their first few weeks, but that was not true for every new black recruit. Much depended on the white officers they encountered during training. Some were outstanding leaders, while others were low-class bigots. Hair remembered one graduation ceremony that caused a particular ruckus. Most officers gave a short speech to graduates, something along the lines of "Go get 'em," but one officer, someone who had mistreated the black men under his charge for weeks, refused to be so constructive.

"Look, fellows, we've done a good job here in boot training, and so we're going out," he said. "But before we go, I want all you niggers to know I don't want no shit out of you."[52]

About one month after Hair, Martin, and Reagan arrived, Camp Morrow was renamed in honor of Robert Smalls, a black Civil War hero who
escaped slavery in May 1862 when he commandeered a heavily armed
Confederate ship, navigated it north from Charleston, past Fort Sumter,
and surrendered it to the Union.[53]

Overseeing Camp Robert Smalls was Lieutenant Commander Daniel
Armstrong, an innovative micromanager and workaholic who had impressed Navy Secretary Knox the previous March with a plan for integrating the general service that the secretary deemed "reasonably practical."[54]

"Any plan for the enlistment of negroes . . . requires segregation,"
Armstrong told Knox. "To put untrained negro enlistees alongside white
recruits in Naval Training Stations and on Naval vessels would put the
negro at a distinct disadvantage at the outset because of his background
and the inferior educational facilities which have been available to him."

Armstrong believed there was no need to commission "colored officers
until . . . through meritorious conduct under combat conditions, the service as a whole would endorse commissions"—a sentiment that Knox no
doubt appreciated.[55]

Armstrong's father, Samuel Chapman Armstrong, was a Union general who had helped found Hampton Institute, an all-black college in Virginia where the Navy would soon train some of its recruits. Armstrong
told Knox that he had served as a trustee at the prestigious school since
1929 and was "known to many of the leading negroes in this country."

Hampton's model focused on educating "the head, the heart and the
hands," and those traditions were carried on at Camp Robert Smalls.

Armstrong, a forty-nine-year-old graduate of the US Naval Academy
at Annapolis, who had once taken the future Duchess of Windsor to a
prom, was a bit of a Rorschach test—the men under him saw what they
wanted.

To white men, he was practical, and his willingness, even eagerness,
to work with black men set him apart.[56] Black men's perception of Armstrong depended, in part, on where they came from. Men from the South
typically found him to be fair and open-minded, while many from the

North, as well as better-educated Southerners, generally resented what they saw as his condescending paternalism.

Martin was in the latter group, describing Armstrong as a "great white father," the kind of officer who assumed he understood how black men thought because he had grown up around them.[57]

Dennis Nelson felt that Armstrong was susceptible to some of the most "pathetic stereotypes" of the South and that he could never see black men as anything more than cooks or servants.

"He was definitely the wrong man for the job he was assigned," Nelson said.[58]

Armstrong encouraged black men to be proud of their race and heritage and insisted that everyone at Camp Robert Smalls observe Negro History Week on February 7. As part of those festivities, he had recruits prepare an extensive exhibition of paintings, photographs, and historical documents showing the achievements and contributions that African Americans had made in art, sciences, industry, education, business, athletics, literature, and music.[59]

He asked Owen Dodson, a seaman second class who had graduated from the Yale School of Drama, to produce plays about famous African Americans, naval histories, and wartime allies, in an effort to boost morale. Dodson, already acclaimed for several of his works including a production of *Pygmalion*, would later become one of the most celebrated African American poets and playwrights in the nation, and his contributions at Camp Robert Smalls were generally hailed.[60]

But many black men bristled at Armstrong's efforts to promote black culture.

He commissioned a new marching song composed specifically for black enlistees: "They look like men, they act like men; I think they will be great men of war." Some from the South believed the song represented progress, while many from the North refused to sing along, rejecting the notion that they were "like men." How ridiculous they thought. We aren't "like men." We are men.[61]

Armstrong also required black enlistees to recite a creed on the advancement of their race and had them sing spirituals on Sunday evenings.

Nelson attributed this to a stereotype "that the Negroes are an exceptionally musical people who are proud of singing the 'American folk music' known as spirituals."

Here, too, perception depended in part on geography, for many from the South saw nothing objectionable about singing together. In fact, many enjoyed the break from military discipline and routine and celebrated the camaraderie.

"If you want to hear something, you ought to hear the whole camp singing spirituals," Wayman Elmer Hathcock, who had a doctorate in music and was a professor at Horace Brown College in Atlanta, told a reporter. "When several thousand voices swell the chorus of some sad, sweet spiritual, that is really something."[62]

But those from Northern areas, many of whom had never heard folk music before, resented the implications. For them, the spiritual was a reminder of slavery.[63]

Armstrong believed black men were better suited than whites for vocational training and that black sailors required special treatment and freedom from white competition.[64] He tolerated no overt racism but also felt it was unfair to expect too much from black men. Ely's 1925 report had said that with "unkind treatment" black men "can become stubborn, sullen and unruly." Armstrong refused to let those serving under him punish black enlistees the way they would white sailors.

Some of the officers who worked under Armstrong reported that this leniency led to fights and stabbings inside Camp Robert Smalls, but company commanders who took discipline cases to Armstrong "got the worst of it." That left officers to take matters into their own hands, which usually meant bringing an unruly recruit into a room and, with no witnesses, beating him.

Lieutenant (junior grade) Donald O. Van Ness, one of the four officers who worked under Armstrong, had his own ideas about discipline. There was a black sailor in camp who was a boxer, a sparring partner of the heavyweight champion Joe Louis. Van Ness asked him to set up a boxing academy and teach recruits how to spar. He told members of his companies that they should settle their arguments with words but if they needed to fight they should do it in the ring. Any man reported to pull a knife was sent for boxing instructions with the understanding that he'd be beaten and bloodied so badly in the ring by Louis's sparring partner he'd think twice before pulling a knife again.

"It didn't eliminate knife-pulling, but it made it drop down considerably, because nobody wanted to get in the ring with this fellow," Van Ness later said.[65]

Armstrong did eventually create the "slacker squad," which involved hard labor. Men on that squad slept on the deck and worked twenty hours a day, doing the toughest, dirtiest jobs. When there was no work to be done, they did jump squats.[66]

Among the far less serious infractions that Van Ness and his fellow white officers contended with was the use of marijuana, but it was of such low quality and its effect so mild that the discipline office didn't bother much about it.[67]

Another problem was venereal disease. Van Ness placed boxes of prophylactics in the barracks, which led to complaints that he was encouraging immorality. For Van Ness, the venereal disease, the marijuana, the poor hygiene, the propensity for fights all justified segregation. It was for their own good, he thought. Even decades later, Van Ness rationalized segregated camps by arguing that black men needed to be taught to take a shower, to keep clean and neat.

"I know from actual experience that they were not the type that would do all the things that they were supposed to do, and if they were mixed with the whites, it would only prove that the whites were right, that they were not up to the caliber that the Navy wants," he said.

Of course, many white men came from places where they lacked soap and hot water and had terrible hygiene habits, but Van Ness reasoned that "whites can understand some other white who doesn't come up to par, but it would be very easy for them to grab on and make a stereotype out of all blacks, because, as a matter of fact, there were a higher percentage of blacks who didn't keep clean and didn't do the things that whites generally do in everyday living."[68]

These allowances aside, the training of black men proved less troublesome than feared, and the enlistees proved more capable than the Navy brass had imagined. Instead of realizing that racist assumptions about black ability were misguided, the Navy's senior staff believed that Armstrong, who would soon be promoted, must be a superior leader, an alchemist of some sort who had spun gold from an assumed worthless commodity.

Once the first class graduated basic training, Lieutenant Commander Armstrong shared his successes with the white world.

"It is unfortunate that the Navy has never gotten to know the Negro before, for the Negro has many qualities, which the Navy prizes," he told the *Chicago Daily Tribune*. "They work hard, take their training conscientiously and are very patriotic. There is still an immense reservoir of high caliber Navy material in the Negroes of America."[69]

By the summer of 1942, the recruiting challenges that had so concerned Jacobs were subsiding. Armstrong would soon take over Camp Lawrence and Camp Moffett, two camps near Robert Smalls in the northwest corner of Great Lakes, to accommodate the growing number of black enlistees.[70]

"What we're doing here is bending every effort to make these boys as good as any fighting men the US Navy has," Armstrong told *Time* magazine in August. "The country doesn't yet know what a fine new source of fighting men the Navy has."

The *Time* feature may have been a puff piece, pure military propaganda, but, still, it was running in a national magazine and heralding black enlistees in a Navy that, only months before, had furiously tried to keep them out.

Now the nation was reading that black recruits were so eager to prove themselves that they would race through the commando course three times and ask for more. The officer in charge added a hundred-yard sprint to try to tire them out.

He could not.

"The Negroes take to the training with gusto," the article said. "They carry their shoulders square, their heads up. They have reason to: they have their own racial tradition in the Navy, their own heroes of previous wars. They drill pridefully, rhythmically, marching up & down the parade ground chanting their own songs, composed by a Negro musician, second class."[71]

Jesse Arbor entered the Navy on September 11, about one month after the *Time* feature appeared. He had done so a bit grudgingly, for he had not wanted to give up his life in Chicago. But the draft was calling, and Arbor feared he'd be taken into the Army if he didn't join the Navy first. His uncles had fought in the trenches on the Western Front during World War I and had brought back horrific tales of suffering and death. His three older brothers, already in the Army, also warned him against joining.

"Go anywhere you can go other than this place," they told him.[72]

Arbor went to the Navy recruiting station on Plymouth Court in Chicago to enlist. He entered Great Lakes during one of the station's busiest times, one of 12,241 black and white men to arrive that week, a record.[73]

Like so many others, Arbor struggled to acclimate. He was accustomed to a certain lifestyle, owing to his work at Kuppenheimer and his position as his own boss. The Thom McAn shoes Arbor wore for his flat feet fit so well but were not exactly military grade.[74] His new shoes were too small. They had thick soles that caused blisters and made his feet swell.

Arbor knew what to do. He sat down with his pocketknife and cut the shoes to his liking.

The next morning, during muster, a black chief petty officer confronted Arbor.

"What's the matter with your shoes there, Mac?"

"Sir, they hurt my feet."

"You're in the Navy now, boy," the chief petty officer said. "Didn't anybody send for you; you volunteered. When you're in the Navy, you do what you're told, when you're told and how you're told."

The petty officer walked closer to Arbor and jabbed a finger into his chest.

"Now get out of that line," he screamed.

The petty officer marched Arbor and his ill-fitting shoes one mile, from Camp Robert Smalls to the main side, grabbed a new pair of shoes, and flung them at the stunned sailor.

Arbor walked all the way back to the barracks, climbed into his hammock, and cried, wondering what he had gotten himself into.

His lot improved when he befriended Arthur Collins, an eighteen-year-old from Kansas City whom everyone called Duck. Collins had had

ROTC training, so the Navy routine didn't bother him much, but he was very small—one hundred pounds soaking wet—and some of the older boys in the barracks picked on him.

Collins offered Arbor, the big strong football player, a deal.

"I'm going to make a man out of you," Collins said. "But you're going to have to keep those boys from whipping me tomorrow."

"Good deal," Arbor said.

Arbor had been struggling with the marching drills and Collins offered to help.

The pair snuck into the head after everyone was asleep and practiced. Left, right, left, right.

Arbor was a fast study.[75] After a week of three-hour sessions in the head, he knew how to march and how to call cadence. Soon, he was apprentice company commander.

———

Arbor had been at Great Lakes only one week when President Roosevelt's special train pulled into the station. It arrived at 4 a.m. on a drizzly September morning. Great Lakes was the second stop of what was to be a two-week inspection tour of factories and camps.

The weather had turned cool and wet, and the president and his entourage remained on the train to sleep a few more hours before beginning the official inspection. The president disembarked at 9:35 a.m. and was helped into a convertible, which moved slowly away from the train station and across Morrow Road.

The president paused at 9:50 a.m. to view the USS *Wolverine*, at anchor nearby in Lake Michigan. This was formerly the *Seeandbee*, a very large side paddle-wheel lake steamer that had been taken over by the Navy and converted to an aircraft carrier training ship on which new pilots could practice takeoffs and landings.

Tied up nearby the *Wolverine* was Henry Ford's yacht, which the Navy had also taken. Now, it was the USS *Truant*. Some twenty men at a time would take her out on Lake Michigan to learn the finer points of Navy etiquette, man-overboard procedures, emergency steering, use of the compass, and nautical nomenclature.[76]

The president saw the hospital and the service and training buildings and then passed the detention camp. A company of recruits marched by, heartily singing "Here Comes the Navy" to the tune of "Beer Barrel Polka." Commandant John Downes, who ran the Great Lakes facility, made sure to remind the president that during the previous Sunday, there had been thirty-six church services—"simply to show you that we believe the religious side of the training of a recruit is just as important to the welfare of the recruit and the Navy as is the naval training which he otherwise receives."[77]

At the urging of the First Lady, the president stopped at Camp Robert Smalls.[78] He saw a camp bustling with 4,500 recruits going through basic training. The "gusto" that *Time* had written about one month before was on full display as black men marched before the president in various formations. Roosevelt also watched the black recruits run the famed commando course, and perform a loading drill using the loading machine, dummy shells, and powder charges.

The men who paraded before Roosevelt that day were marching to a song composed by Wayman Elmer Hathcock, the PhD who taught at Horace Brown College.[79] Hathcock composed four songs for the camp, including "Ballad of the Negro Recruit" and "We Are Men of the U.S. Navy," the song that Roosevelt heard.[80] Grace Tully, the president's secretary, called it a "very stirring marching song," though it is unknown whether its lyrics made an impression on the president, who was anxious to return to the train. His entire visit to Camp Robert Smalls lasted just eight minutes.[81]

Of course, not all marching songs were fit for a president's ears, nor were they all composed by men as distinguished as Hathcock. Marching songs were just as often used to keep men in step and their minds off marching. Some included lyrics such as "Eyes right, assholes tight, ankles to the rear / We are men of the U.S. Navy and we all got gonorrhea."[82]

———

Lieutenant (junior grade) Paul Richmond never asked why he was chosen to be one of the four officers assigned to Camp Robert Smalls. He had no desire to stay in Illinois or to work with boots—of any color. Richmond wanted to be at sea. He was an academy man and had been slated for service on the USS *Nevada*, a battleship stationed at Pearl Harbor.

The Japanese attacked two weeks before he graduated from Annapolis, torpedoing both the *Nevada* and his dreams of serving on a ship. Richmond was reassigned to Great Lakes and was told he'd be training new recruits. He reported on January 2, 1942, a fresh-faced naval officer, only weeks out of school, who was suddenly tasked with readying thousands of men for war. His duties also included shore patrol, a common responsibility for junior officers.

Mostly in those first few months he'd patrolled Waukegan, Illinois, and Milwaukee, Wisconsin. Occasionally, he'd get down to Chicago, though the city had its own shore patrol.

When black men began arriving in the summer, Richmond was assigned to Camp Robert Smalls and, as part of his duties, instructed to patrol the South Side of Chicago.

During his first patrol, Richmond rode the train from Great Lakes to Chicago with a black chief petty officer who promised to show the lieutenant, a twenty-one-year-old white kid from Highland Park, Michigan, the ropes in the black section of town.

"When we get there, I'm going to introduce you to 'The Man,'" the chief petty officer said. "'The Man' will take care of you."

It was a little cryptic, but he told Richmond no more.

The Navy needed a white man to patrol black neighborhoods because top officials had given explicit instructions that black men on shore patrols make no effort to discipline white men. If a fight broke out between members of the different races, black shore patrol officers were only allowed to handle black men. The Navy thought it "one of the practical adjustments necessary in accommodating incidents of the Negro program to the existing difficulties in the race situation," though most black men found it yet another example of enforced inferiority.[83]

Richmond and the chief petty officer arrived on the South Side and established their patrol, looking into alleys and bars, just making sure the sailors weren't getting into any trouble.

"Come on, we'll meet 'The Man,'" the chief petty officer told Richmond.

They walked to a busy nightclub called the Cotton Club.

Richmond went inside the dimly lit room, made his way past the crowds, and shuffled toward a back office.

And there was Joe Louis—The Man.

"The lieutenant here is in charge of the shore patrol, and he wants to have things run properly," the chief said.

"I'll tell you what, lieutenant," Louis said. "If you have any trouble, you just come to me. There ain't going to be any trouble."

And there wasn't.[84]

Black men were no more of a disciplinary problem than white men. And the concerns that they lacked innate leadership qualities proved wholly unfounded, Richmond discovered.

He was particularly impressed by a young sailor from Indianapolis named Graham Martin. Renowned for his athletic prowess, Martin had been made athletic petty officer during basic training, leading his company through the drills, calisthenics, and the commando course.

Martin noticed that many of his fellow recruits, especially those from the South, came to Camp Robert Smalls illiterate, and they struggled with the classroom work. *The Bluejacket's Manual* is a sailor's bible and is filled with instruction on policy and procedure, but it all means little to a man who can't read. Martin and a few others took it upon themselves to teach literacy, offering reading instruction to men in the evening, after a full day of training.[85]

After he finished basic training in October 1942, Martin, now a petty officer third class, was made subcompany commander. He worked under a white chief petty officer, helping new recruits through training.[86] He marched the boots, called cadence, and drilled. He'd run through that obstacle course three or four times a day to show them how it was done.

All the while he continued offering literacy instruction and became an unofficial ombudsman, helping a sailor get leave needed to attend a funeral.[87]

One Saturday morning, recruits were lined up for inspection and one of the men had a cigarette in his jumper pocket. The chief petty officer, whom Martin shadowed, was furious. He pulled the cigarette out of the recruit's pocket and pushed it toward Martin.

"Make him eat it," he ordered.

Martin refused the order.

He had a health minor in college and didn't think it was safe to eat a cigarette.[88]

Refusing a direct order is a far more serious breach of protocol than having cigarettes in a jumper pocket. The fact that Martin, black, had refused a white chief petty officer's order in front of a line of black enlistees made the situation potentially explosive.

Martin was put on report and sent to Richmond, the regimental commander, who asked why Martin would disobey a direct order.

Martin explained the situation: Cigarettes were meant to be smoked, not eaten.

Richmond grinned. "I don't blame you," he said. "I wouldn't have made the man eat [it] either. I think it's ridiculous. Let's forget the whole thing."

Richmond also refused to discipline the white petty officer. It wasn't worth it, he thought.

"It was a ridiculous disciplinary tactic that he apparently thought might impress somebody," Richmond later recalled. "I don't know how."

But the white chief petty officer wouldn't let it go. He relayed the story over and over. The white side of the camp was now complaining that black men didn't have to obey orders.

Commander Armstrong was called to answer for the lack of discipline in his camp. Needing to quell the unrest, Armstrong ordered Richmond to write an essay on what he had learned at the Naval Academy about following orders. Richmond turned in a paper on Admiral Horatio Nelson, the British naval hero who disobeyed an order to withdraw that had been communicated by signal flags. Nelson destroyed many enemy ships and later said he hadn't seen the signal flags because he put the telescope to his blind eye, giving rise to a popular phrase, "to turn a blind eye," that seemed particularly relevant to the Martin incident.[89]

Richmond walked away from the episode terribly impressed with Martin, telling anyone who would listen that the young sailor from Indiana "was a better man than I."

His white peers couldn't believe their ears and asked if he could possibly mean what he was saying.

"My God, the record looks that way," Richmond responded. "He's done a hell of a lot more than I have."[90]

CHAPTER 8

"YOU ARE NOW MEN OF HAMPTON."

John Reagan was a member of the first class to arrive at Hampton Institute, a segregated Class A naval training school (the next class after basic training), where black men would spend sixteen weeks training for the below-deck ratings such as machinist's mates, electrician's mates, metalsmiths, carpenter's mates, cooks, and bakers.

He was one of 128 newly graduated boots to make the two-day trip from Great Lakes, stopping first at Chicago before heading southeast to Richmond, and then south to Hampton.

The men exited their Pullman cars at 5 a.m. Saturday September 19, 1942, and marched in formation through the darkened streets of Hampton to the gates of the school that Samuel Chapman Armstrong founded seventy-five years before to educate newly freed slaves.

Lieutenant Commander Edwin Hall Downes, the man in charge of their training, stood just inside the entrance watching the perfect procession. A reporter who was there to chronicle this historic first remarked, "They're a fine-looking body of men."

A smile spread across Downes's clean-cut face.

"You bet your sweet life they are," he said.

The men marched to James Hall, the college dorm, recently leased and renovated by the Navy, which would serve as their new home. Then came sick call, muster, and, finally, breakfast at Virginia-Cleveland Hall, which served as the mess.

College boys from Hampton Institute eagerly greeted the new arrivals and showed the Navy men around their campus. Far more exciting was when the co-eds arrived to extend the tour.

That afternoon, the men filed into Ogden Hall, where Downes made his first formal remarks.

"You are now men of Hampton," he said. "We want this training program to be so good and so successful that all ship's captains will, in a few months, be asking for 'men of Hampton.'"[1]

On Sunday, the men of Hampton attended services at Memorial Church, the college chapel. Physical training began Monday morning with reveille at 5:30 a.m., followed by calisthenics, room inspections, drills, and commando practice. Roscoe Howard Bigby, a twenty-four-year-old cement finisher from Cleveland, worried that the obstacles on the commando course at Hampton didn't seem that tough, certainly not when compared to those at Camp Robert Smalls.

That would "be taken care of," Downes assured him.[2]

Hampton's campus, like Great Lakes, had been expanded to meet wartime demands. The Navy had built a new field house, which held executive offices, a gym, an indoor drill hall, and a swimming pool. There was also a one-story diesel engine and machine shop where men learned welding, electrical science, and motors.[3] A boathouse was built after a coxswain course was added to the curriculum.

Hampton Institute had been chosen to host the Navy's segregated training school the previous June. The announcement, coming just days after the first black boots arrived at Great Lakes, had been made by Dr. Malcolm Shaw MacLean, Hampton's sixth president.

MacLean was a white man, which was not strange for someone running a black college. He was also a firebrand, which was very strange. His appointment to lead Hampton had come just a few days after Frank Knox's Senate confirmation in July 1940 as secretary of the Navy, but whereas Knox deemed it unwise to challenge his admirals' views on segregation, MacLean immediately "locked horns with the . . . status quo who hate his method, fear his pace, and tremble at the boldness of his vision."[4]

Hampton is about seventy-five miles southeast of Richmond, the capital of the Confederacy, and MacLean's striking pronouncements on racial equality stood in stark contrast to the views of his five predecessors, who supported training and educating black men but dared not challenge Southern norms.

That bred resentment from some members of the board of trustees, "who wanted the old pattern of kindly but paternalistic treatment of the Negro continued," and they complained that MacLean had "not conformed with the Virginia pattern of race relations."

MacLean made it plain that his administration would not be content with baby steps toward racial equality or symbolic shows of good faith. For decades, Hampton had run an all-white school for the children of faculty. MacLean abolished it. "Every form of racial distinction on the campus, which had been created in deference to the opinions and prejudices of white Virginia, which contributed little or nothing to the support of Hampton, was thrown into discard," Walter White, executive secretary of the NAACP, later said.[5]

The white ruling class of southern Virginia considered MacLean far too progressive, even dangerous. His calls to increase African American participation in the war effort and for white colleges to employ black professors were bad enough, but it was his habit of inviting both white and black guests to his home and dancing with a Hampton coed that really challenged Southern traditions.[6]

MacLean did not care. He was not of the South. He was born in Denver and went to school in Michigan, Chicago, and Minnesota. He had no patience for the racist preachers he encountered in Virginia, referring to them "bible-pounding bastards."[7]

Only five months into his tenure, MacLean hosted Robert Lee Vann's Committee on Participation of Negroes in the National Defense, which presciently warned that "sound morale among Negroes" could not be maintained if the forces of racism and exclusion continued to dominate the discourse.

When war did come, MacLean was determined that Hampton's hosting the naval training school for black men and its participation in the national defense would be his legacy.

An ardent supporter of the Double V campaign, MacLean was certain that this war would be "the greatest break in history for minority groups," and his school, built on the site of a former plantation in the heart of the Confederacy, would train black naval servicemen in all manner of technical skills and become the launching pad for a generation.

It didn't take long for the first class to see that Hampton was nothing like Camp Robert Smalls. There was no dust, no mud, no lack of clothing. Hampton's grounds were picturesque, especially when the weather was warm and the sun was high in a blue sky, casting shadows along ivy-covered walls, while pretty college girls sought refuge from the heat under the cool shade of the leafy trees that dotted the seventy-acre campus.[8]

The morale and caliber of the men at Hampton were also different from those of the men in boot camp at Great Lakes. Like wheat separated from chaff, the men coming to Hampton had shown an aptitude for these assignments and demonstrated a demeanor necessary for study. A high percentage of these men already had professional degrees. Many were teachers, newspaper reporters and publishers, and doctors and medical school students.[9]

Every day—from 5:30 a.m., when they woke, until 10 p.m., when they got back in bed—was rigidly scheduled.

Reagan and his classmates spent the morning learning math and engineering. They studied Newtonian physics and then put theory to use in the shop, working on diesel engines in the afternoon. They mastered electrical equipment, machinery, ship fitting, and metalsmithing and practiced on sixty-one landing barges and seven motorboats.[10] At night there was study hall, which nearly all took seriously, as it provided the foundation for the material that would be covered the next day.

Outside the classrooms, the men learned boat handling, taught by a chief boatswain's mate who had a penchant for spitting tobacco without regard for where the wind might blow it and gave honor to the expression "cursed like a sailor."[11] There was plenty of recreational activity, including boxing, wrestling, basketball, and swimming, as well as a rifle team. Every Wednesday evening, there was a happy hour featuring guest lecturers and performances by the renowned Hampton glee club, directed by Charles H. Flax, a nationally known baritone.[12]

And though this was no longer boot camp, there was still quite a bit of military drill and focus on discipline.[13] The men were expected to keep their person and their quarters spotless.

1. Recently commissioned black officers: front row (left to right): Ensigns George Cooper, Graham Martin, Jesse Arbor, John Reagan, and Reginald Goodwin; back row (left to right): Dennis Nelson, Phillip Barnes, Sam Barnes, Dalton Baugh, James Hair, Frank Sublett, and Warrant Officer Charles Lear. William Sylvester White was commissioned but is not pictured in this photo. February 1944.

2. Front row (left to right): George Cooper, Graham Martin, Jesse Arbor, and John Reagan; back row (left to right): Reginald Goodwin, Dennis Nelson, Phillip Barnes, Sam Barnes, and Dalton Baugh.

Charles Lear

Phil Barnes

George Cooper

Graham Martin

Dennis Nelson

Jesse Arbor

Frank Sublett

James Hair

John Reagan

Reginald Goodwin

Dalton Baugh

Sam Barnes

Dorothy Donegan, pianist, and Camp Robert Smalls swing band.

Hazel Scott, pianist, performs at Great Lakes.

Marva Louis, wife of heavyweight champion Joe Louis, entertained some two thousand black men in April 1944 at the Naval Training Station, Great Lakes. She is shown here with Ensign Sam Barnes and Willie Smith, musician second class, a nationally known saxophone player.

Lester Granger inspecting facilities in San Diego, California, chats with Rofes Herring, S1c.; Walter Calvert, S2c.; and Nollie H. Million, civilian, as Lt. Roper (far left) stands by.

Chief Specialist R. W. Wallis, in khaki, demonstrates to black recruits the proper way to wear a Navy hat, September 9, 1942.

Lieut. Commander Edwin Hall Downes (second from left), officer in charge of the Navy's training program at Hampton Institute, goes over with his staff the blueprints for new buildings. Left to right: Lieut. (jg) William W. Couzens, Downes, Lieut. Charles M. Dillon, and Ensign Herbert M. Stein.

Recruits balance themselves on the commando course at Camp Robert Smalls, September 9, 1942.

From right: Nathaniel O. Dyson, Richard Hubbard, and John W. Reagan, three electrician's mates, listen as Chief Electrician's Mate John E. Taylor explains the workings of the power system that they would be working with when serving aboard the USS *Mason*. Reagan would be diverted to officer candidate school shortly after this photo was taken.

The highlight of these inspections came the morning Brigadier General Benjamin O. Davis arrived at Hampton. Seeing Davis, the first black general in the Army's history, was like seeing Joe Louis or Marian Anderson, an African American whom no one could deem inferior.

The men of Hampton stayed up until 1 a.m. the night before, determined that no space in the whole United States would be cleaner. Windows were washed; lightbulbs were unscrewed and wiped. The floors were steel-wooled, waxed, and polished. Beds were taken apart so that each bedspring could be cleaned.

When Davis finally arrived, the men lined up in formation, chests extra puffed for the special occasion. Davis inspected the crew, put on white gloves, and went inside the dorm with Downes.

They emerged one hour later. There was dust inside the fuse box, Downes said. The men of Hampton must do better next time.[14]

———

Frank Sublett arrived from Great Lakes in that very first class with Reagan in September 1942. He was, in so many ways, Reagan's twin, and the two men, both born March 5, 1920, began a friendship at Hampton that would last the rest of their lives.

Frank Ellis Sublett Jr. was born in Murfreesboro, Tennessee, a small town about thirty-five miles southeast of Nashville, and was reared in Highland Park and Glencoe, Illinois, the latter a mostly white Chicago suburb on the shore of Lake Michigan. Oftentimes, Sublett was the only black boy in his class, but overt racism was not a part of his day-to-day life.

Like many young boys who grew up during the Great Depression, Sublett worked odd jobs to help the family make ends meet. He cut grass. He was a busboy and janitor in a tearoom where his uncle worked.

His parents, like Reagan's, were divorced, and, like Reagan, Sublett had been a standout high school athlete, excelling in football and track, specializing in the discus throw and shot put. He attended the University of Wisconsin on a football scholarship, followed by a year at Northwestern and a year at George Williams College in Wisconsin. His transcripts show mostly Cs and Ds, and as with Reagan, the war had kept him from completing a diploma.[15]

Also like Reagan, Sublett had wanted to enlist in the Army Air Forces after the attack on Pearl Harbor, even dropping thirty pounds to meet the weight requirement. And like Reagan, he had been rejected.

He loved the water—swimming and fishing—so the Navy seemed a logical second choice, particularly because the general service was now open to black men. Had messman remained the only option, Sublett would have joined the Merchant Marines because he'd be damned before he'd be anyone's servant or cook.

Sublett enlisted at the naval recruiting station in Chicago on July 7 and arrived at Great Lakes three days later, ready to be trained to save the world for democracy, while sitting, for the first time in his life, in a segregated setting.

Boot camp wasn't too hard for Sublett and he received good enough marks to finish in the top third of his class. He was a shade over six feet tall, barrel-chested, and weighed nearly two hundred pounds—a heavy-set athlete who didn't mind the drilling. As a teenager, he had spent two weeks in the Citizens' Military Training Camp at Fort Riley in Kansas. The Subletts didn't have the money to send Frank to a lakeside summer camp in Wisconsin or Minnesota where his friends spent summers, but Fort Riley offered a free program to anyone who passed a physical and mental health test.

At Fort Riley, he learned how to handle a .30–30 Springfield rifle, and at home he used a .22 rifle to hunt rabbits, ducks, and pheasants. So he came to the Navy already versed in drills, marksmanship, and military discipline. That served him well, and he was appointed apprentice chief petty officer, a leader of the company who helped other recruits learn cadence and discipline.

His aptitude test showed that he had a talent for machinery, which wasn't too surprising. He had spent summers working at a Buick dealership installing radios and heaters and making other repairs. He was sent to Hampton, where he would learn to be a machinist's mate.[16]

He adapted rather easily at Hampton too. Some of the other men, most of whom were from the South, teased him over his Midwestern accent, but it was all in good fun.

As soon as there were enough men at Hampton to form a battalion, Sublett and Reagan were assigned leadership roles.

Sublett was named battalion commander. He had a booming voice and would bark out orders. Reagan, his adjutant, would about-face and give the orders to the battalion. The pair kept the barracks in shape, marched the men to chow, and led the exercises and drills. And they were there to greet the second contingent of apprentice seamen when they arrived at Hampton from Camp Robert Smalls.[17]

Leadership had its perks. When Marian Anderson performed at Hampton Institute's Ogden Hall in October, Reagan was tasked with bringing the world-famous contralto a bouquet. Star-struck and entranced by her flowing silver gown and ruby red shoes, Reagan knocked over the vase. Luckily, the shoes were spared being soaked.[18]

Anderson's concert was one of the many efforts Downes made to boost morale, which he defined as "that something that makes people eager to do and to do well those things required of them."[19] Morale was particularly important in 1942, when the war in the Pacific was not going as well as many in the Navy had hoped. It was concerts and comedy shows, movies and jazz that gave men respite from the unending monotony of training and the unrelenting fear of battle and death.

And one particular October concert would long be remembered: Anderson had been scheduled to perform on a Saturday evening, but a terrible storm caused the Rappahannock to flood, stalling her train. She arrived at Hampton after 1 a.m., exhausted from her frustrating journey, but she insisted the show must go on and rescheduled her concert for that same afternoon.

On very little rest, Anderson "held her audience spellbound through her last two spirituals" after singing songs by Purcell, Haydn, and Schubert. Even when a fire broke out on the top floor of Cleveland Hall, the building next door, filling Ogden Hall's auditorium with gongs and sirens, no one stirred, save for the men appointed to the fire service. Though Anderson was so exhausted that her voice gave out during the concert, she performed multiple encores.[20]

Sublett's and Reagan's positions placed them in regular contact with Lieutenant Commander Downes, a Naval Academy graduate who had resigned his commission after serving in World War I and had gone on to earn a master's degree in education from Columbia University. Back in the Navy after being recalled to active duty, Downes set a high bar. He showed up to work an hour early and stayed an hour late. And he had a fantastic memory, which endeared him to subordinates. He asked each man who came to Hampton where he was from and what schools he had attended, and he seemed to remember it all. He could walk the halls and ask Joe how his mother was feeling or Tom if he had beaten back that pesky flu.

Downes called Sublett's mother to personally inform her of her son's progress. It was a call he made for the men he held in high regard, one to make nervous parents proud and bestow upon them some of the glory deriving from the importance of the mission. And Downes held few men in as high regard as he did Sublett.

"If I have one wish in this life," he once told the young sailor, "it is that my own son grows up to be as fine a gentleman as you," which is just about the highest praise Sublett could imagine, a grace he would cherish until the day he died.[21]

With his balding head, Downes looked a bit like the Hollywood actor Pat O'Brien. He didn't bark and rarely raised his voice. He was straight with his men, and they respected him for his candor. He was friendly but firm, never forgetting a courtesy but also never letting anyone forget that they were in the presence of a commanding officer.

Like Armstrong, Downes had the air of a great white father, but he was softer than Armstrong, more human.[22] Much of the Navy considered disrating—demoting—a particularly effective punishment for black men, but Downes thought that too drastic for all but the most extreme disciplinary cases. Disrating, he worried, could be seen as discriminatory and could damage the whole team's morale. Instead, Downes punished badly behaved men by limiting them to bread and water, which the Navy deemed a suitable punishment for black men because of "their heavy eating habits."[23]

"We are not trying to solve the race problem here at our school," Downes told reporters. "We are simply trying to make a constructive contribution to its ultimate solution. . . . We are making men competent so that they can be in demand wherever they are in the post-war world."[24] He hammered home that he was training "good men," Hampton men. That had to mean as much to them as it did to him.[25]

Inside his office hung a sign that reminded him and anyone who visited of the mission that he carried out every day: "Teach the trainees to do better those things they are likely to be required to do afterwards ... [and] be damned sure no boy's ghost will ever say, 'if your training program had only done its job.'"[26]

———

A few weeks after Sublett and Reagan arrived in Virginia, as Hampton started to swell with new recruits arriving from Camp Robert Smalls, Downes interviewed a young African American sheet-metal worker from Ohio who was applying to teach metalsmiths.

George Cooper had completed his undergraduate education at Hampton and so was familiar with the campus. He desperately wanted to avoid the draft, and teaching at a Class A naval training school seemed a better way to do so than teaching aircraft sheet-metal work at Wilberforce University, where he had been the senior foreman since 1941. Cooper and his wife, Margarett "Peg" Gillespie, who had also graduated Hampton, were expecting their first child, and he told his wife that a teaching position at Hampton "might keep me out of the service for two or three years."

Downes immediately recognized Cooper's talent.

"Mr. Cooper, we would like to have you take this job, because we need you, and there aren't many of you around, white or colored," Downes said. "And if you take this job, I'll see what I can do to keep you from being drafted."

Cooper had followed his family's advice and left "little Washington" in the mid-1930s. There was too much racism and violence in North Carolina, they had warned, and they feared for his safety. Hampton, where his brothers and sisters had gone, offered him a fresh start and a chance to earn a college degree, so he enrolled in the fall of 1935.

The school allowed freshmen to take a lighter course load so they could work full-time during their first year and save some money for tuition.

Cooper, who had been a bellhop back home, found a job at the Holly Tree Inn, the guest house on campus, as a bellman, valet, and waiter. About half the guests were Hampton faculty, which made the clientele far less racist and hostile than what he had dealt with in North Carolina.

Cooper added to his income singing spirituals with the Hampton Institute Choir, the Trade School Singers, and the Hampton Student Quartet. The baritone made even more money by chauffeuring the quartet to its gigs.[27]

Singing had taken Cooper all around the South, to churches and to hotels, to Richmond and to Charlotte, but it was back on Hampton's campus that Cooper really found his voice.

Two decades before Rosa Parks and a generation before passage of the Civil Rights Act, Cooper helped lead a student protest over the dismissal of black faculty.

Hampton's president at the time, Arthur Howe Jr., had cut staff to balance the budget, and a majority of those laid off were black.

Howe was married to Margaret Marshall Armstrong—the daughter of Samuel Chapman Armstrong, the school's founder, and the sister of Daniel Armstrong, the commander of Camp Robert Smalls. Howe had been held in high regard since his tenure began in 1930, having been lauded for broadening the curriculum and expanding the campus, but the student protests marred his final year in office.

The layoffs were but one of several grievances that students brought to administrators and alumni. A survey found that whites outnumbered blacks two to one in administrative and supervisory positions, leading to an imbalance in salaries. Students also demanded their own free press and better athletic coaching.

The final straw was the dismissal, on May 13, of James Ivy, a popular African American English teacher, who students felt had been fired without cause, just weeks before commencement. Howe told the students that Ivy's firing was "an administrative problem beyond their comprehension."[28]

The students went on strike, refusing to attend chapel exercises or the junior-senior banquet at which "thousands of gallons of ice cream and punch were wasted."[29] Administrators warned that if their strike continued the students would not be allowed to graduate. The students persisted: if they were not allowed to graduate, so be it. This was more important.

Students involved no faculty, worrying that teachers might face professional consequences. The protest was peaceful and effective.

"Apparently the day of the docile and humble student body which accepted, without criticism or protest, every dictum of a reactionary regime has passed," the *Baltimore Afro-American* opined.[30]

Indeed, a new day had come.

At an assembly on the last Saturday in May 1939, Cooper, a senior just days away from graduating, was reciting the class poem, written by another student, when Howe leaped from his seat, ended the assembly, and announced that he was canceling commencement.

The students were confused. The poem was nothing more than silly couplets poking fun at classes, but Howe, who was partially deaf and may have misheard the words, interpreted it as an attack on his administration and the school.

The students surrounded Howe on the stage, demanding that he recant. He did once he learned that the poem had been written several weeks before the protests had begun, and commencement went forward, though his administration never recovered from the debacle.[31]

Ivy was not reinstated, but he did receive a year's severance. Black newspapers began taking seriously accusations of pay inequity at the school and Jim Crow hiring practices in the campus infirmary.

Howe, the founder's son-in-law, was forced to resign in February 1940, paving the way for the arrival of Malcolm Shaw MacLean and Hampton's role in training black men for the Navy.

"That's something you look back on and say, 'Well, I was a part of that and helped make something happen that needed to happen,'" Cooper said fifty years later. "There are experiences like that in my lifetime that, I suppose make me sleep better at night."

Nearly eighty years after George Cooper graduated, Peggy Cooper Davis said she would not put it past her father to have chosen a poem that could easily have a double meaning to those embroiled in the conflict with students—something just enough to make a point while leaving room for plausible deniability.[32]

Six months after graduation, Cooper married Peg, the homecoming queen. The two had met at Hampton, where she was studying to be a librarian.[33] Returning to Hampton in October, 1942, a place they both knew, seemed like a smart move to Cooper, but his wife had doubts. She loved the campus but hated Virginia and did not want to leave Wilberforce, a racially progressive town.

"Virginia was hell," Peg Cooper, said in 2012, when she was ninety-eight. Even then she could still taste, in an almost visceral way, the bitter discrimination she had faced seven decades earlier.

In Virginia, Peg couldn't try on a pair of shoes or a hat at the store. If merchandise touched her black skin, she had best be prepared to buy.

"I remember walking my toddler across the bridge and she saw ice cream," she recounted. Little Peggy Cooper was screaming in that way babies do when they want something, but black people were not allowed to buy ice cream from a white vendor.

"You just couldn't," she said. "It was—I hated that place. It was demeaning."

Her husband, she said, was less bothered by that sort of thing. Peg had grown up in Ohio. Her husband had grown up in North Carolina, where Jim Crow was the rule, and he had been called a "nigger" countless times. He had been conditioned to have some anxiety about speaking up and had grown accustomed to the racist milieu.

The couple headed south and lived in half of a duplex in the faculty housing section at Hampton. Some of the Navy families who were their neighbors could be pleasant, but Peg found most of them condescending, displaying a paternalistic attitude, as if to say, "I'm here to show you how to be intelligent." Some would be friendly while on Hampton's campus but would not so much as look at the Coopers if they were off campus.[34]

This dichotomy was due in large part to the protective bubble Downes had created at the school. Very little made him angrier than seeing prejudice or racism of any kind, and officers who ran afoul of that precept usually found themselves assigned someplace else.[35]

"Yes, here is one spot in the Navy where democracy is not a rumor," the *Norfolk Journal and Guide* reported. "It is working fine—and below the Mason Dixon line."[36]

But off campus, there existed no such protections or protectors.

Hampton was only a short distance from Norfolk Naval Training Station, the Class A training school for white men. Black men were allowed to visit but were prohibited from boarding any ships.[37]

Black sailors dubbed Norfolk "shit city" and the "asshole of creation" because of the town's overt hostility toward blacks.[38]

Sublett rarely left the campus. Why, he asked himself, should he sit in a separate section of a movie theater when movies were regularly shown at Hampton and he could sit wherever he pleased?

Reagan left the campus more frequently. The answer to Sublett's question, in Reagan's mind, was obvious: girls. Reagan was dating Lillian Thomas, a nursing student, who would become his first wife, and visiting her meant enduring the humiliation that typified life for a black man in Virginia.[39]

State law required that whites enter the front of the bus and sit in front and that African Americans enter through the back and sit behind the color line drawn on the floor. If there were whites standing and seats open behind the color line, then the African Americans on the bus had to move farther back.

But buses were often so crowded that the rules were impractical.

Reagan, an Illinois man who hadn't been conditioned as Cooper might have been to keep his mouth shut, once tried to enter through the front because the bus was too crowded in back.[40]

The driver would not let him on and refused to budge until he got off the bus. Reagan stood his ground.

The police were called and asked him to leave.

Reagan stood firm.

"Well, come on, son, you've got to get off," the officer said. "That's the law."

Reagan, not sure what stand he could make, demanded that his dime be returned.

It was.

He took his coin and, fuming, walked off the bus and returned to Hampton, where men were trained to free the world from tyranny.[41]

=====

Black men from the North, like Reagan and Sublett, were more likely to find the humiliation galling and were less willing to accept it quietly or play the lackey. Many of these men had never before been forced to the back of the bus, or to drink from "colored" water fountains. They had never before walked into the gutter with their heads bowed so as not to make eye contact with a white man walking on the sidewalk.[42]

Only now, in Virginia—where they were picking up arms and putting their lives on the line to defend their country—were they treated so inhumanely.

On bases, black men encountered signs laying out the schedule for religious services that read "Catholics, Jews, Protestants, and Negroes." Off base, black soldiers and sailors were expected to conform to local mores. Those who did not risked being clubbed, jailed, or shot. Many whites let it be known that a black man in his nation's uniform was just "a nigger who doesn't know his place."[43]

An armed bus driver murdered a black soldier in Mobile, Alabama. Local police murdered black soldiers in Columbia, South Carolina, and Little Rock, Arkansas.[44]

Little more than a month after Pearl Harbor, military police in Alexandria, Louisiana, attempting to arrest a black man, triggered a race riot, during which twenty-eight black men were shot. Nearly three thousand black men and women were detained in the city's "Little Harlem" section. The city's entire supply of tear gas was used on black soldiers, almost all of whom were from the North, principally New York, Pennsylvania, and Illinois. One black soldier later wrote, "I would almost rather desert and be placed before a firing squad and shot down before fighting for America."[45]

It was one of fifty-nine known confrontations between black soldiers and military police and civilian authorities in 1942, as black men quickly learned that a military uniform was no protection from a mob.

If an African American soldier or sailor didn't personally experience the bigotry, he could certainly read about it in the black press. A "U.S. Army uniform to a colored man makes him about as free as a man in the Georgia chain gang," one soldier told the *Baltimore Afro-American*. "If this is Uncle Sam's Army then treat us like soldiers not animals or else Uncle Sam might find a new axis to fight."[46]

The bitterness coursing through the black community and the antipathy toward calls for unity were further stoked by the horrific details of lynchings, which belied any notion that the United States was really one nation with a common enemy.

Just a few weeks after Alexandria, the black press screamed the story of Cleo Wright, a thirty-year-old cotton mill worker in Sikeston, Missouri, who allegedly assaulted a white woman and stabbed the arresting police officer. Wright was shot during the scuffle but survived. On Sunday morning, a mob of more than three hundred grabbed Wright from his jail cell, tied him to the back of a maroon-colored Ford, and dragged his near-naked body through the black section of town. They stopped to force his wife to view his bloodied body. Then they doused him with gasoline and set him on fire in front of two black churches, where the pews were filled with men, women, and children who had come for services.[47]

Truman Gibson, William H. Hastie's aide, commented that so many black men were bludgeoned to death in the South that it would only be a "slight exaggeration to say more black Americans were murdered by White Americans during World War II than were killed by Germans."[48]

James Baldwin, the famed novelist and essayist, said that many black families felt a "peculiar kind of relief" when their boys were shipped overseas from the South because "now, even if death should come, it would come with honor and without the complicity of their countrymen."[49]

Almost a year into the war, morale in the black community remained an acute concern. "The men in the barbershop, on the assembly line, sweeping the floors or washing windows know their spirit, concerning the war, isn't right," Enoc Waters wrote in the *Defender*. "It's a thing of which they're not conscious but as they follow the band down the street . . . The cheers of the patriotic crowd as Old Glory flutters by carry their minds back to the angry jeers of the lynch mob, which lynched and burned a Negro at Sikeston, Mo. And the wavering voices of singers of the national anthem are like an echo of the enslaved thousands on peonage farms in the South."[50]

The hypocrisy, so evident across America, stung almost as much as the racism itself. At about the same time that John Reagan was stewing over the color line on the public bus, Lloyd Brown, an African American soldier stationed in Salina, Kansas, went with several compatriots to a lunch counter.

"You boys know we don't serve colored here," the owner politely said.

Of course they knew. They weren't served anywhere in Salina.

But they hadn't come to be served.

The black men just stood there at the door, staring.

Just feet from where they were frozen in place were German prisoners of war who were having lunch at the counter.

The people of Salina would serve the enemy but not American GIs.[51]

———

By the end of 1942, Navy Secretary Knox's policy of refusing to accept black men through the draft and relying on volunteers so as to limit the number of African Americans in the service was becoming untenable. The Selective Service estimated that three hundred thousand black men had been drafted in 1942 and were awaiting induction into the military.[52] The nation could no longer afford to have that many men on the sidelines.

On December 5, 1942, the president issued Executive Order 9279, which ended volunteer enlistments for men between ages eighteen and thirty-eight. By February 1943, all men entering the Navy would come through the draft. Black enrollment was about to explode because Knox would no longer be able to turn black men away.

Knox sought to head off what he saw as a coming crisis, reminding Roosevelt that the Navy could accept no more than 1,200 black men for the general service per month and 1,500 for the messman branch, which was renamed the steward branch in March 1943.[53] Any more than that and crews aboard ships would have to be integrated, an outcome that the Navy secretary reminded the president they had both agreed to avoid.

When Knox did not hear any dissent from the White House, he assumed that Roosevelt agreed that segregation aboard ship must be maintained. Knox told Rear Admiral Randall Jacobs, in charge of recruitment, that the president understood the need to limit the number of black men coming into the Navy (segregation aboard ships must be maintained) and ordered him to resolve the matter with the director of Selective Service.[54]

Two weeks later, Roosevelt, in a snarky note to Knox, made it clear that the secretary had gone too far. Avoiding mixed crews did not mean curtailing the employment of African Americans in the Navy, Roosevelt said. "I guess you were dreaming or maybe I was dreaming if Randall Jacobs is right in regard to what I am supposed to have said about employment of negroes in the Navy," he wrote. "If I did say that such employment should be stopped, I must have been talking in my sleep. Most decidedly we must continue the employment of negroes in the Navy, and I do not think it the least bit necessary to put mixed crews on the ships. I can find a thousand ways of employing them without doing so." The president didn't need to remind Knox that he had served as assistant secretary of the Navy during the First World War.[55] Shore duty and yard craft would be good places to start, the president noted, echoing King's recommendation from the previous spring. Knox, chastened, followed Roosevelt's order: The number of African Americans in the Navy would triple to 78,000 by the end of 1943. It would nearly double, to 147,374, by August 1944.

Knox created twenty-seven new construction battalions: of those, twenty-four were required to have all nonrated men be black and three were made up entirely of black men. Knox increased the number of black crews on harbor craft and the number of black cooks and bakers in the commissary branch for shore establishments. Other black men were sent to shore stations, where they performed guard duty.[56]

Knox's decision to push black men into labor units and shore establishments while refusing to fully integrate ships was, predictably, condemned by the black press. It was a betrayal, it was said, and the only advancement had been in "black sailors trading in their waiters' aprons for the carpenters' hammers and stevedores' hooks."[57]

The Navy defended its position by explaining that segregation did not mean discrimination and that black men were treated on a par with white men. "They undergo the same training given white recruits at the same station and for the same period," Lieutenant Commander P. B. Brannen, director of public relations for Rear Admiral Jacobs, told the *Pittsburgh Courier*. It was, he said, separate but equal.

Why, then, a *Courier* reporter asked, are there no black officers?

The Navy's policy was not to have black men in a position to command white men, Brannen said, and black men couldn't be placed in charge of a ship with an all-black crew because it took years to train a man to boss a ship. Simple as that.[58]

Roosevelt understood how devastating this situation was for morale, and while he wasn't ready to integrate ships, the president leaned on Knox to find more opportunities for black sailors.

"The point of the thing is this," Roosevelt wrote to Knox.

> There is going to be a great deal of feeling if the Government in winning this war does not employ approximately 10 percent of Negroes—their actual percentage to the total population. The Army is nearly up to this percentage but the Navy is so far below it that it will be deeply criticized by anybody who wants to check into the details. . . . You know the headache we have had about this and the reluctance of the Navy to have any Negroes. You and I have had to veto that Navy reluctance and I think we have to do it again.[59]

Four days later, the Bureau of Naval Personnel recommended increasing the monthly quota of black entrants to 5,000 by April, and then to 7,350 per month after that. This increase forced the Navy's highest-ranking officials to consider, for the first time, commissioning African American officers. The men working inside the Bureau of Naval Personnel could read the political tea leaves. The president was responding to pressure from the black community, and there was little chance that the Navy could induct one hundred thousand black men over the next twelve months and not commission a single black officer without setting off a new round of protests.

The bureau circulated a memo in early 1943 outlining a plan to com-mission fifty black men from civilian life and twenty-five more from the enlisted ranks. They would be assigned activities already dominated by black men, such as guarding the ammunition depots, so as to avoid mixing the races as much as possible.

The plan was considered but ultimately rejected, deemed impractical. Black officers remained too great a hurdle to overcome and the General Board's concern about white men refusing to accept a black man in a supe-rior position still held sway, as did Knox's fears that too much integration would dampen morale among whites and damage battle efficiency.[60]

Having black men as officers might not have been the Navy's prefer-ence, but there was an undisputable need for additional officers to handle the thousands of men enlisting or being drafted. So began the V-12 pro-gram, which combined college education and officer training. Dozens of the nation's colleges would teach students to be officers so that they would graduate with a degree and be ready for the Navy.

The admissions test for the program was offered on April 2, 1943. No one had mentioned race when the program was concocted and so no one in the Navy was certain whether the V-12 Navy College Training Pro-gram would be open to African Americans.

True, no V-12 programs were offered at traditionally black colleges, but there were no explicit instructions to turn black men away if they enrolled at one of the fifty-two integrated colleges where the V-12 was offered.

In March, about one month before the exam took place, Lieutenant Commander Alvin Eurich, the director of the Standards and Curriculum Section of the Bureau of Naval Personnel, asked Rear Admiral Jacobs if black men would be allowed to sit for the admissions exam. Jacobs would not rule on his own and forwarded Eurich's memo to Knox, who passed it along to Roosevelt.

"Of course, Negroes will be tested!" Roosevelt scrawled in reply.

Knox would not contradict the president's order, but he made no move to advertise it, either. That left many black men assuming that the V-12 was just another Navy program for which they were not wanted, and Knox was fine letting them believe it.

Mordecai Johnson, president of Howard University, put Knox on the spot just days before the exam, demanding to know "whether the Navy now has a policy, which will admit a Negro student to the real possibility of becoming an officer in the Navy, and whether these examinations in reality do as a matter of fact offer such a Negro student a first step toward this end."

Knox waited until April 3, the day after the entrance exam was to be held, to reply. "The Navy College Training Program admits all students selected for this program, including Negroes, to the possibility of becoming officers in the Navy, and the examinations offer the first step toward this end."[61]

It was the first time the Navy publicly stated it was open to the idea of black officers, though coming as it did the day after the admissions exam, the statement was of little use.

The V-12 program would eventually commission seventy thousand white men and fifty-two African Americans, including Samuel Gravely, who became the Navy's first black admiral, and Carl Rowan, the famed journalist who would later become the first black deputy secretary of state and the first black director of the US Information Agency.[62]

But at the time, no one knew if any black men had bothered to join or were capable of finishing.

Shortly after the first entrance exam, hundreds of teachers in the Virginia Peninsula Teachers Union, which represented employees at Hampton, wrote an open letter to President Roosevelt protesting the Navy's opposition to black officers.

Richard Kidd, president of Local 607, said his members "can no longer afford to continue losing the war at home. What upset the whole Hampton Institute community was the fact that colored members of the faculty who applied for commissions in the Navy were refused, while white members of the Hampton faculty were accepted," he wrote. [63]

"The practice of the Navy in commissioning white men as officers from biracial faculties in a Negro college and refusing to commission equally qualified men of color from the same faculty points up a Navy policy in an ugly way," John W. Davis wrote in the summer of 1943 in the *Journal of Negro Education.* "All of this results in a low ceiling for Negro participation in the Navy. This policy of exclusion has caused many thoughtful Negroes to wonder whether the recent action of the Navy to enlist Negroes in capacities other than 'steward, first, second and third class' is to remain a feeble gesture."[64]

=====

Meanwhile, Hampton's training school was growing exponentially. When Reagan and Sublett arrived in September, Hampton had only 11 officers and 28 enlisted men. Within a year, staff grew to 139 officers and enlisted men in charge of 900 black sailors.[65] Downes kept looking for talented African Americans such as Cooper to teach the mechanical subjects to the thousands of men coming from boot camp. In April 1943, he found just such a talent: Dalton Louis Baugh, a whip-smart sailor from Crossett, Arkansas, who was just shy of his thirtieth birthday.

Baugh had enlisted the previous September, just after his fellow Arkansan, Jesse Arbor. He had spent the previous three years attending Arkansas AM&N, so he was familiar with the discipline needed for classroom work. He excelled at Hampton, finishing second in his sixty-two-man class. He graduated on April 22 as a motor machinist's mate second class, specializing in the maintenance and repair of diesel and gasoline engines. The next day he was an instructor working for Downes.

Baugh had some experience in front of a class, having taught auto mechanics for a year before beginning college. He was a man of few words, but he had a knack for explaining difficult concepts, turning them into basic principles most men could understand. And he had the bearing of an authority figure. He was 6 feet tall and 175-pounds, a solid man with a deep, booming voice that gave an air of importance to whatever he said.[66]

He enjoyed his work and Downes enjoyed him.

Cooper, meanwhile, was teaching sheet-metal work, which he loved, and helping some of the less educated men learn to read. He'd show students a picture of a bolt next to the letters B-O-L-T. It wasn't overly sophisticated, but that's how scores of men learned basic literacy while at Hampton being trained for the nation's defense.

Cooper was very fond of Downes, who invited faculty to lavish parties at his townhouse, where the booze flowed freely.

The pair worked well together, but by mid-1943, with the call for men growing increasingly desperate, Downes knew his original deal with Cooper to protect him from being drafted needed to be altered.

"I can't keep you out any longer," Downes said. "But if you sign up for the Navy, I don't think you'll be sorry. I think I can guarantee you chief petty officer right off the bat. And I think I can bring you back here to do the same job as you're doing now."

"That's a winner," Cooper said. "Let's go."

Cooper enlisted on June 21, 1943, and just by virtue of signing his name he became a chief petty officer. No boot camp, no training, no nothing. The next day he was back at Hampton doing the exact same work, only this time as a member of the United States Armed Forces.[67]

CHAPTER 9

"I FEEL VERY EMPHATICALLY THAT WE SHOULD COMMISSION A FEW NEGROES."

Sam Barnes was on duty in the drill hall at Camp Robert Smalls when Commander Armstrong approached and asked if the young man knew how to play badminton.

"Yes, sir," Barnes said—a lie. He had never played badminton in his life.

"Well," Armstrong replied, "I want you to have the nets up tomorrow . . . because I want to play badminton."

"Yes, sir."

Barnes raced to the library and picked up a book on badminton. He spent the day practicing what he read and let his natural athleticism take over. He held his own in the match, and Armstrong took a liking to the petty officer third class.

Rank had its privileges. If there was a questionable call, Armstrong might say the birdie landed in bounds.

"Commander, you sure that was in? It looked out to me," Barnes would say.

"Yes, it was in," Armstrong would reply.

"It certainly was, now that you call it to my attention."[1]

Armstrong was competitive and had an excellent smash shot, but Barnes, younger and faster, had more stamina and could easily wear down his older opponent. After a while, Barnes had to let his commander win, but not every game: if the men played four games, Barnes won one. If they played six, Barnes won two.

The two played badminton at noon every day for about an hour and grew to genuinely enjoy each other's company.[2]

It seemed everything was going right for the Oberlin native: he had been in the Navy for about a year, had a job he enjoyed, was buddying up to the commander and he was about to get married to Olga Lash, the woman who had stolen his heart five years earlier and would never give it back.

It had all worked out so much better than Barnes had feared when he left his job at the YMCA in Cincinnati and enlisted on September 17, 1942, about two months after his friend Reginald Goodwin.

Like Jesse Arbor and George Cooper, Barnes was a reluctant recruit, but his twin sister, Becky, living back home in Oberlin, was friendly with Hilda, the lady at the draft board, who let it slip that Sam's name would soon be called.

Sam Barnes, like Graham Martin, was a neat freak, and the Navy's emphasis on cleanliness and order appealed to him. He also considered geography. Camp Robert Smalls was in Illinois, the North. Army training was most often in the South. A man who preferred to say his name was S.E. rather than subject himself to the indignity of being called Sam by white men knew he would not fare well in the Jim Crow South. Barnes had a wry sense of humor, but he also had a temper and a history of throwing a punch after being called a "nigger." Best to avoid the South if he could.

His fiancée, Olga, disagreed and begged him not to join the Navy. The branch had not shaken its reputation as a dead-end job for black men. Sure, the general service was now open, but the black press still highlighted a myriad of injustices, and the stories of the Philadelphia Fifteen remained fresh in many minds. Barnes was too smart, too educated, too talented for the Navy, Olga said. His skills would not be appreciated.

The Navy wouldn't even commission black men.

"You'll be a sailor all your life," she warned.[3]

But Barnes's mind was set, and soon he could assure Olga that he had made the right decision. Boot camp and military discipline were easy for the football and track star, a five-foot ten-inch 175-pound rock, who did 100 sit-ups every day (he would wear the same-size clothes his entire adult life).[4]

Barnes had been right regarding the Navy's attention to detail and cleanliness. Uniforms were washed every day, so they were always fresh. Seabags were rolled and ready. Nothing dirty was ever allowed in the barracks. Barnes excelled in that kind of environment.

He was selected company clerk, perhaps, he reasoned, because he was a college graduate and the company commander believed he could handle the work that position entailed. The clerk was charged with keeping all the records for the company, including medical records.

Barnes graduated boot camp in December 1942 as a seaman first class. He was named honor man of the company, which came with the privilege of selecting the service school he preferred to attend. Barnes chose aviation mechanic school but was offered a job at Great Lakes as the assistant in recreation and athletics and intramurals. He was already familiar with athletics and drill, so working on intramural sports seemed like a natural fit, not dissimilar from the work he had done at Livingstone, and staying in ship's company meant he could remain at Camp Robert Smalls, where he had grown comfortable.

It was a great gig for Barnes. Men who worked at Great Lakes were allowed liberty in Chicago with few restrictions. The only real requirement was a "short-arm" inspection for venereal disease upon return. Any sailor who contracted a disease had to give the name of the woman he had been with so that the Navy could warn other sailors.

After about a year working in recreation and athletics, Reginald Goodwin, his friend from Cincinnati, and Lewis "Mummy" Williams asked if Barnes wanted to work in the selection office.

This was a prestigious position, responsible for interviewing new enlistees and assigning them positions once they graduated boot camp. It came with a chance for promotion. Goodwin and Williams were already among the most respected men at Camp Robert Smalls, having both been there longer than almost anyone else, so Barnes took on his next challenge.

It was difficult work. Barnes conducted one-on-one interviews with hundreds of men, trying to discern where their talents might best be utilized. He asked what experiences they had had before the war, what jobs they had held, how much schooling they had. Men who seemed fit for service schools either were sent to Hampton or would stay at Great Lakes. Men not fit for service schools were sent to the outgoing unit and assigned to shore installations, naval ammunition depots, or the operating company at Great Lakes.[5]

Goodwin helped Barnes stand out, offering tips about Navy decorum and interviewing boots who came through the selection office. He explained to Barnes what questions were most likely to elicit the most helpful responses.

Barnes's work ethic and physical prowess impressed Armstrong, who figured an athlete like that must surely be a formidable foe on the badminton court.[6]

———

By the time Armstrong and Barnes became badminton buddies, the training of black men at Camp Robert Smalls, both the basic training and the advanced training for general-service ratings, was proceeding with assembly-line-like efficiency. There were more racist officers at Camp Robert Smalls than at Hampton, but the men who trained were, for the most part, protected from the violence and brutality that was becoming almost routine in the United States throughout 1943 as black men, both in and out of uniform, were targeted, beaten, and lynched.

The escalating violence engendered Northern and liberal sympathies and once again pushed the "race question" to the fore. During the first few months of 1943, several books, pamphlets, and articles were published proclaiming that race relations were the nation's weakest link, and that racism was based on a set of ill-conceived principles and discredited science that were depriving the nation of its full fighting force and wasting precious manpower on pointless bickering.[7]

Wendell Willkie's One World, released in April 1943, excoriated the nation over its treatment of black men in the military. It sold one million copies in the first two months, spent four months atop the New York Times bestseller list, and became one of the greatest nonfiction bestsellers in US history.[8]

"Our very proclamations of what we are fighting for have rendered our own inequities self-evident," Willkie wrote. "When we talk of freedom and opportunity for all nations, the mocking paradoxes in our own society become so clear they can no longer be ignored. If we want to talk about freedom, we must mean freedom for others as well as ourselves, and we must mean freedom for everyone inside our frontiers as well as outside."[9]

The black press, though finished with its Double V campaign, still regularly printed stories about the military's mistreatment of black men, and the Navy provided plenty of material.

Graduates from Hampton Institute's service school, who were sent to a Navy facility in East Boston, Massachusetts, complained they were "assigned to waxing floors in barracks, washing paint, cleaning toilets," and other mindless tasks, while white apprentice seamen were given preference in choosing assignments over the higher-rated black petty officers.[10] The papers explained that the chores assigned black men deprived them of the chance to advance because they weren't doing any work in their ratings.[11]

Dennis Nelson, still recruiting in Tennessee, later said that "many well-educated and experienced Negroes who entered the Navy as enlisted men well knew that their abilities were wasted."[12]

Downes, at Hampton, tried to excuse the assignment of such chores to men who had qualified in general-service ratings, telling reporters that he had done the very same dirty jobs when he came up through the ranks. "Men often are shipped to stations before everything is ready for their eventual jobs," he said. "Hundreds of men loafing would go stale if they had nothing to do, so they clean decks and heads."[13]

But the sheer number of examples of this practical demotion demonstrated that Downes was, at best, willfully ignorant.

At Pearl Harbor, black men who had trained at Class A training schools were working as stevedores, forced to do menial chores and hard labor by the mostly Southern officers in charge of the Hawaii base. At first, the native Hawaiians were welcoming to black sailors, but white officers told locals that they'd boycott any shop that treated white and black as equal. Suddenly a color line appeared in Hawaii.

When the men complained about working as stevedores, they were told that if they didn't like it they were welcome to become messmen, a particularly degrading offer, given how hard black men had fought to leave the messman branch and enter the general service.

Speaking to the *Chicago Defender*, a whistleblowing sailor predicted a racial crisis if something wasn't done.[14]

He was right.

"Longtime warnings to federal authorities that racial tension would bring bloody violence were realistically brought home" in the spring and summer of 1943, the *Chicago Defender* told its readers.[15]

For two years, the drafting and subsequent movement of thousands of black men from segregated towns in the South or racially tolerant cities in the North to boot camps in Southern metropolises or overcrowded cities added fuel to embers that had been smoldering for decades.

Riots erupted in the nation's major urban centers as well as cities critical to defense efforts, including Detroit, New York, and Los Angeles. The Social Science Institute at Fisk University counted 242 such outbreaks during 1943, producing what a later observer labeled "an epidemic of interracial violence."[16]

In May 1943, a riot began at a Mobile, Alabama, shipyard when black welders were assigned to work beside white welders. The chaos came on so suddenly that Alice Gamble, a line worker, did not know what was happening even as her black peers began running past, fearing for their lives. Gamble was frozen in place gawking at the strange scene until someone whacked her in the back and yelled, "Get going, nigger. This is our shipyard."[17]

William H. Hastie, who had resigned his position as Secretary of War Stimson's civilian aide in January 1943 because no one was taking his complaints about the mistreatment of black soldiers seriously, told the National Lawyers Guild at the end of May that "civilian violence against the Negro in uniform is a recurrent phenomenon. It may well be the greatest single factor now operating to make 13 million Negroes bitter and resentful."[18]

The very next day, Private William Walker, a soldier from the 364th Infantry Regiment, stationed at Camp Van Dorn in the southwest corner of Mississippi near the Louisiana border, was shot in the head because a button was missing on his uniform.[19]

Walker had been walking near his post when the military police rolled up in a jeep.

"Say, nigger, what are you doing with your sleeves rolled up?!" a sergeant shouted.

Walker explained that the button had fallen off his shirt sleeve so he'd rolled it up until he could get back to camp and sew on a new one.

"Hit that nigger over the head," the sergeant told the military policeman.

When Walker raised his hands to defend himself, the sergeant yelled to kill "that damn nigger." [20]

Walker was the third African American member of the 364th Infantry Regiment killed at Camp Van Dorn in just that week.

After loading the body into the jeep and transferring it back to camp, the MP bragged, "I just got me another nigger and now I reckon I get my transfer."

"You ought to get a gold medal for that," another MP replied. [21]

The *Chicago Defender* told its readers that Walker's story "leaves one to wonder if the Southern white man isn't hindering the war effort more than helping because of his prejudice." [22]

In mid-June 1943 a riot took place in Beaumont, Texas, a city eighty miles east of Houston, where shipbuilding and petroleum production were booming. Beaumont was typical of Southern towns during the war. In 1940, it had 59,000 citizens, about one-third of whom were black; by 1943, the population stood at over 80,000, with blacks remaining about a third of the city. Surrounding Texas towns underwent similar growth: Orange went from 7,500 to 38,000; Port Arthur from 56,000 to 70,500; and Port Neches and Nederland from 5,500 to 9,100. [23] The situation was as untenable as the violence was predictable.

Trouble began on June 4 when a nineteen-year-old white telephone operator left work and began walking home along Laurel Street. As she approached the intersection of Laurel and Magnolia, Curtis Thomas, a twenty-four-year-old African American ex-convict, allegedly attacked her. He had supposedly been planning an attack for some time: he dragged her to a loading platform at a nearby storage plant where, the victim stated, he had laid out a quilt.

Thomas allegedly stabbed and raped the young woman and told her, "The army is going to get me, and if I do this, I'll get killed for this and I won't be going to the army."

Thomas fell asleep after the alleged attack, and the woman ran home and called the police. Two squad cars raced to the scene, and as they approached, the lights and sirens woke Thomas. He fled into a dead-end alley where policemen shot him four times. Critically wounded, he was taken to the "negro ward" of Hotel Dieu Hospital. Thomas died a few days after, but the seeds for violence were sown. Rumors of crazed black men on the hunt for white women spread in town during the following week and white women were told to stay home because of "nigger mobs on the street."[24]

The following week another woman accused a black man of raping her in her home while her children napped upstairs. Police could not find the suspect. At Beaumont's Pennsylvania Shipyards shift workers decided to take matters into their own hands. More than two thousand dropped their tools and walked off the line. Foremen pleaded with them, appealing to their common patriotic duty, but one worker summed up the feeling of his peers when he said "our duty is for the protection of our homes."

Production at the shipyard halted as the mob began the short walk downtown to the police station. As the men marched, more joined so that by the time they reached the station they numbered three thousand.

The alleged assailant was not at the station, and the mob grew frustrated, uncertain what to do next, until someone shouted, "Let's go to nigger town." They split up, with some heading toward the northern section of the city on Gladys Street while others went downtown, toward Forsythe Street, both areas populated by black families.

For six hours, roving gangs set fires, overturned cars and looted homes, and destroyed cafés, drugstores, and a radio shop. The windows of black families' homes were smashed with rocks. Three funeral homes were torched. Even the pharmacy owned by Sol White, a black man of local repute because he had bought $11,000 of war bonds, was set on fire.

Colonel Sidney C. Mason, in charge of state troops and the enforcement of martial law, told reporters that the black section of town was "literally stomped to the ground."

Just after midnight, about three hundred white men came upon fifty-two black draftees waiting for a Greyhound to take them home to Port Arthur.

"Here they are, a whole bunch of them. Let's get them," someone cried.[25]

Days later the public learned that the second white woman had not been raped. A medical exam by Dr. Barker D. Chunn showed that she had neither been assaulted nor engaged in any sexual activity, but local authorities withheld that information, and by the time it was revealed, the damage was done. The rioting shut down the town and kept five thousand shipyard workers from their posts.[26]

The Beaumont riot was the largest race riot that had yet occurred in the country during the war, and it might have received more national attention than it did if an even larger riot had not broken out only a few days later in Detroit.

The Motor City, like Beaumont, was a powder keg. In early June, more than 25,000 white workers went on strike after the Packard Motor plant promoted three black men to work on the assembly line beside white men. One striker shouted, "I'd rather see Hitler and Hirohito win the war than work beside a nigger on the assembly line."[27]

Detroit's population had ballooned, while its police force had actually shrunk. The police department did everything it could to recruit more officers, offering the highest pay in the United States and recruiting from all over Michigan, but the Army and Navy were taking all the eligible men, and those who weren't drafted were lured into the factories, which paid even higher salaries.

On June 20, a 90-plus degree day, nearly 100,000 men, women, and children went to Belle Isle, a municipal park on an island in the Detroit River, seeking relief from the sweltering heat.

The first interracial fights began around 10 p.m. Soon groups of white men and black men were fighting on the lawn adjacent to the naval armory. White sailors joined the fracas, fueling the hostilities.

Shortly after midnight, at a bustling nightclub in the heart of the black community, a well-dressed black man carrying a briefcase stopped the music, took the microphone, and said he had an important announcement to make. There was fighting between the races on Belle Isle; three black people had already been killed, and a black woman and her baby had been thrown over the Belle Isle Bridge and into the river. He urged everyone in the club—nearly a thousand people—to go home and get their guns. Now was the time to fight. In the white community, someone said a black man had slit a white sailor's throat and raped his girlfriend.[28]

Neither story was true, but both were believed.

Mobs of black men and women smashed windows, stopped streetcars to attack the white occupants, and looted stores, especially liquor stores and pawn shops owned by Jews, who were thought to fleece their black customers.

The mob beat to death a white milkman and a white doctor making a call. By 2 a.m., hospitals were reporting that they were receiving one new patient every minute. A counter-mob formed at around 4 a.m. This time, both sides had rifles. Twenty-five blacks and nine whites were killed, and more than 750 were injured before the riot, the worst of the era, ended.[29]

Japan and Germany, using short-wave radio, beamed exaggerated reports of the riots to countries around the world, especially those with people of color, making the case that the United States didn't really stand for democracy, or if it did, it was democracy for white men only. Anyone who had read Willkie's *One World* would have noted how similar the message sounded.

Congressman Vito Marcantonio, who represented East Harlem, told the White House that it was now inarguable that racial tensions were part of an enemy strategy to weaken resolve at home just as the United States seemed poised for a great victory abroad.

He believed the riots had been spurred, in part, by a fifth column—citizens who sympathize with the enemy—telling the president there "is a peculiar Hitler-like pattern running through all these occurrences, which in my opinion is more than accidental.

"It is significant that anti-negro outbreaks have been stimulated precisely in those areas which are key to successful war production and in and about military training areas," Marcantonio went on. "It is significant that immediate use of these outbreaks is made by enemy short-wave radio broadcasting agencies to spread distrust of American democracy among people of darker races in India, China, Africa, and Latin America who are our allies."[30]

Letters poured into the White House demanding federal action.

"Race rioting on the home front is a dangerous Axis weapon, Jim Crowism in our armed forces is the cause," wrote Sylvia Velkoff, secretary for the United Victory Committee of Park Chester in the Bronx. "You, Mr. President, as Commander in Chief of the Army, must stop it."[31]

Liberal editors in the North wondered how the nation could wipe the Axis from the earth when internal racial strife divided the home front and comforted the enemy. "We cannot fight fascism abroad while turning a blind eye to fascism at home," editors at the *Nation* argued. "We cannot inscribe on our banners: 'For democracy and a caste system.' We cannot liberate oppressed peoples while maintaining the right to oppress our own minorities."[32]

The riots sweeping the nation demanded a national response, and Walter White, head of the NAACP, begged the president to intervene, to marshal the nation as he had done so many times before when a national crisis threatened to overwhelm the republic.

"No lesser voice than yours can arouse public opinion sufficiently against these deliberately provoked attacks, which are designed to hamper war production, destroy or weaken morale, and to deny minorities, negroes in particular, the opportunity to participate in the war effort on the same basis as other Americans," White wrote. "We are certain that unless you act these outbreaks will increase in number and violence."[33]

But the White House made no move, paralyzed by fear of making the situation worse. For every concerned voice that demanded the President intervene to stop Jim Crowism and call for racial equality, there was an equally concerned voice saying it was the very push for racial equality that was causing all these riots, and that Eleanor Roosevelt, in her never-ending quest to promote black men in the factories and the fields, in the Army and the Navy, was responsible for the national discord.

"It is my belief Mrs. Roosevelt and Mayor [Edward] Jeffries of Detroit are somewhat guilty of the race riots here due to their coddling of negro[e]s," John Lang, who owned a bookstore in Detroit, wrote in a letter to FDR. "It is about time you began thinking about the men who built this country. I voted for you three times but next year I am voting for Norman Thomas."[34]

In the South—where rumors of "Eleanor Clubs," which supposedly consisted of black women conspiring to obtain social equality, were so prevalent that the FBI opened an investigation—it was easy to blame the woman who had become the face of a despised movement, an "I told you so" moment for bigots who thought mixing races could only lead to trouble.

The *Jackson Mississippi Daily News* declared the Detroit riots were "blood upon your hands, Mrs. Roosevelt" and said she had "been . . . proclaiming and practicing social equality. In Detroit, a city noted for the growing impudence and insolence of its Negro population, an attempt was made to put your preachments into practice."[35]

Eleanor was despondent. The riots left her doubtful that the nation was ready to live up to the ideals she espoused.

"The domestic scene, as you listen to the radio and read the papers today, is anything but encouraging and one would like not to think about it, because it gives one a feeling that, as a whole, we are not really prepared for democracy," she wrote in her widely read column, My Day. "We might even fall into the same excesses that some other people whom we look down upon have fallen into, for we do not seem to have learned self-control and obedience to law as yet."[36]

The smoke had barely cleared in Detroit when another riot occurred at a Navy ammunition depot in St. Juliens Creek, Virginia, precipitated by segregated seating for a radio broadcast. On June 29, 1943, more than half of the 640 African American men of the battalion who had gathered outside a recreation hall before the dress rehearsal, jeered arriving white people, slashed tires, and cut into car seats.

The disturbance lasted only thirty minutes and no one was seriously hurt. More than 250 black sailors were transferred within twenty-four hours, but that did nothing to solve the larger problem, which was highlighted in a subsequent report from the Navy's Bureau of Investigation. The report concluded that among the causes of the riot was "a prevalent belief that opportunity for advancement was restricted, together with a desire that all battalion petty officers be colored." The report also attributed the riot to the fact that "the leave status of white and colored enlisted men differed [and because of] Virginia segregation laws and local customs."

The following month, more trouble engulfed the Navy. The Eightieth Construction battalion, a unit made up of 744 black men and 258 white officers, went to Trinidad to build an airfield. Tensions had already been simmering when the battalion was in Gulfport, Mississippi, and they boiled over in Trinidad. Black men complained that two separate windows had been set up to sell beer at the ship's store, one for whites and one for everyone else. They complained of discrimination in promotions and of discriminatory limitations on liberty, which the commanding officer justified because of the high venereal disease rate among black men.[37]

Eleanor again took to her My Day column to lament the state of race relations.

> I was sick at heart . . . over race riots which put us on a par with Nazism which we fight, and make one tremble for what human beings may do when they no longer think but let themselves be dominated by their worst emotions. . . . we cannot prepare for a peaceful world unless we give proof of self-restraint, of open mindedness, of courage to do right at home, even if it means changing our traditional thinking and, for some of us, a sacrifice of our material interests.[38]

John Sengstacke, who owned the largest chain of black newspapers in the country and had met with Attorney General Francis Biddle the year before to discuss wartime cooperation between the black press and the administration, implored the president to undertake sweeping action commensurate with the crisis at hand. Calling on the memory of Lincoln, he asked the president for a proclamation declaring that the federal government believed all men to be equal.[39]

But Roosevelt was not Lincoln, and he never used the bully pulpit of the White House to advocate for full racial equality. The president responded impersonally, if cordially, to these pleas, saying that he appreciated hearing the concerns.[40]

Inside the White House, the thought of devoting a Fireside Chat to the subject of race riots was deemed "unwise" by the president's counselors.

At most, Attorney General Biddle argued, the president "might consider discussing it the next time you talk about the overall domestic situation as one of the problems to be considered."[41]

Roosevelt thought even that too much, and when he gave a Fireside Chat on July 28, one month after the Detroit riots, he devoted not one word to race. The twenty-nine-minute speech focused instead on the fall of Mussolini.

Historians Philip A. Klinkner and Rogers M. Smith have argued that Roosevelt's famous political antennae failed to pick up the changes taking place in the spring and summer of 1943. Before the war, it was almost universally accepted by white Americans that they were a superior race. Even among the most progressive class, only a few believed much could or should be done about inequality in the near term. In 1942, when the Double V campaign swept the nation, a National Opinion Research Center Poll found that 62 percent of whites interviewed thought blacks were "pretty well satisfied with things in this country," while 24 percent thought they were dissatisfied. But by 1943 attitudes were shifting, and a year later, 25 percent of white Americans thought black people were satisfied with their status and 54 percent thought they were dissatisfied.[42]

"True, white southerners were becoming more restive, but it seems clear that in the context of the war, nationally public attitudes on race had shifted enough that [Roosevelt] could have been more outspoken for reform," the historians argued.[43]

In August, another large riot began—this time in New York City—when Margie Polite, a thirty-five-year-old black woman, was arrested by Patrolman James Collins for disorderly conduct outside the Braddock Hotel on 126th Street in Harlem. Robert Bandy, a black soldier on leave, intervened. He and Collins scuffled, and at some point Bandy allegedly took hold of Collins's nightstick and struck him with it. Bandy tried to run, and Collins shot him in the left shoulder.

The incident was like a spark to kindling on a hot, sweaty night in the city, the kind where the air is thick and humid, and tempers rise to meet the mercury.

Men and women sitting on their fire escapes seeking relief from the stifling heat climbed down the ladders and formed a mob. They lived in those overstuffed, sweltering tenements because of the color of their skin, because the city wouldn't let them leave the ghetto. They were packed into apartments like animals, and now that they were ready to die so that the best ideals of their country might live, their countrymen beat and slaughtered them like animals.

Their anger wasn't about Bandy or Collins. It was about those shiny plate-glass windows along 125th Street, those white-owned storefronts of shops where black men and women purchased goods but were refused employment. The windows that were smashed that night stood in for those in power who kept in place the redlining and the racism. They stood in for the Army and the Navy.

The Harlem Hellfighters, the black men who made up the 369th Infantry Regiment, had been sending letters home from Camp Stewart in Georgia in which they told friends and relatives, often in graphic detail, of the gratuitous insults and violence they endured. Harlem's black press reported on how soldiers were beaten and sometimes lynched in camps across the South. Residents knew of Cleo Wright, and the riots in Detroit and Beaumont. They knew that airplane factories on Long Island, even though desperate for workmen and -women, would not "degrade" their assembly lines with African Americans.

So it came as no surprise to Harlem residents Walter White and Roy Wilkins, his assistant at the NAACP, that their pleas for calm were ignored, drowned out by the sound of shattering plate-glass windows. Bandy would survive, they told the crowd when they arrived on the scene. "Don't destroy in one night the reputation as good citizens you have taken a lifetime to build," White said. "Go home—now."

As White and Wilkins drove along Seventh Avenue they could see they were having little effect.

It took 8,000 New York State guards and 6,600 city police officers to quell the violence. In all, 500 people were arrested—all black, 100 of them women. One week later, when the *New York Times* examined the causes of the riot, it declared that no one should be surprised: "The principal cause of unrest in Harlem and other Negro communities has been [the] complaint of discrimination and Jim Crow treatment of Negroes in the armed forces."[44]

The military's treatment of African Americans and the racism so much a part of American life was no longer just a political problem. It was a national security issue, impacting war production in the factories and morale in the streets. It was "the worst thing" General George Marshall, the Army's chief of staff, had to deal with, a situation he feared would "explode right in our faces."[45]

———

The Navy responded to the racial tensions by creating the Special Programs Unit, which would be housed within the Bureau of Naval Personnel in Washington. Its mission would be to coordinate policies and protocols for black sailors so that they were used to their full potential and protected—as much as possible—from humiliation and violence.

At its helm was Lieutenant Commander Christopher S. Sargent, a thirty-one-year-old who had clerked for Supreme Court Justice Benjamin Cardozo and worked in the law firm of Dean Acheson, a future secretary of state. Sargent would later be described as "a philosopher who could not tolerate segregation," and he waged "something of a moral crusade to integrate the Navy."[46]

His official job was as an assistant to the head of the Manpower Policies Section of the Planning and Control Division inside the Bureau of Naval Personnel. The formidable title meant that "the Negro problem landed squarely in his lap."[47]

Unlike many more senior officers, Sargent thought the war was the best time to integrate the fleet and told superiors that racial cooperation would create a more efficient fighting force. He brought on two lieutenant commanders: Donald O. Van Ness, who had worked under Armstrong at Great Lakes, and Charles E. Dillon, who was the executive officer under Downes at Hampton. The pair worked for Captain Thomas F. Darden in the Plans and Operations Section of the bureau.[48]

Among the unit's highest priorities was to see to it that black men were no longer bunched together at ammunition depots or other installations with little real work to do, and that graduates of Class A naval training schools were given proper assignments—not the kind of busywork that had so enraged men in Boston and Hawaii earlier in the year.

The Bureau of Naval Personnel knew that when men who had trained as electricians or quartermasters ended up spending their days cleaning toilets, it weakened morale throughout the Navy; in July it ordered that all men must be used for work corresponding to their ratings. But the Special Programs Unit found that some naval districts, especially those in the South, simply ignored that directive, seeing black men as just an extra pair of hands to clean up after and carry cargo for white sailors.

The Special Programs Unit pushed the Navy to go further than it ever had; it ordered that, with the exception of some units in the supply departments at South Boston and Norfolk, no black sailor could be assigned to maintenance work and stevedoring in the continental United States.[49]

But even that wouldn't be enough. If the Special Programs Unit really wanted to reduce the concentration of black men on shore, then there was only one solution. Black men would have to be allowed on warships as more than messmen. Knox's sacred rule could not stand.

It was already obvious to most Navy men that this change was inevitable.

In July, a spokesman for the Navy conceded that Knox's policy made little sense, telling journalists that he "did not know why it is that colored sailors aren't being used" at sea. "I am sure something will have to be done," he said, "but I do not know what."[50]

The answer arrived not long after. The Navy would assign fifty-three black men to the USS *PC 1264*, a 173-foot submarine chaser that cruised three hundred to five hundred miles offshore looking for German U-boats.

Then the Special Programs Unit had its most significant triumph, convincing Admiral Ernest King, chief of naval operations, to place 196 enlisted African Americans along with 44 white officers on the USS *Mason*, a destroyer escort expected to traverse the Atlantic on convoy missions.[51] The ship, still under construction at the Boston Navy Yard, was named for Ensign Newton Henry Mason, a fighter pilot shot down during the Battle of the Coral Sea. Many in the Navy gave it a different name: "Eleanor's folly" they called it, another slight aimed at the First Lady for her advocacy of integration.

Manning the ships did not, of course, represent total integration or full equality. The two ships would have all-black crews serving under white officers. White and black men would still sleep in different quarters and eat at different tables.

"We are trying to avoid mixing crews on ships," Knox told reporters. "That puts a limitation on where we can employ Negro seamen."[52]

Still, the black press heralded the announcement. For years, civil rights leaders had said that the right to fight and die for one's country was a crucial step toward making the United States a more perfect union. Having black sailors outside the messman branch serve at sea marked "a distinct departure from present Navy policy and is the culmination of a five-year fight," the *Pittsburgh Courier* told its readers.[53]

But one problem remained beyond the unit's reach, one symbol of inequality so glaring that it outshone all other successes: at the end of 1943, there were no black officers.

———

Among the more galling aspects of the Navy's policy was that, in this case, African American ambition was not being stymied by the usual suspects: Southerners who masked their hatred with talk of tradition. Secretary Knox was from Boston and Michigan. Rear Admiral Jacobs was from Pennsylvania. Admiral King was from Ohio. "Every last one of these men responsible for the Navy's Jim Crow policy, from stooge to the President himself, is a northerner," the *Baltimore Afro-American* said. "The men who are responsible for this un-American policy are not race-baiting hillbillies from the south but northerners whose family trees go back in some instances to the Civil War abolitionists. . . . If Wendell Willkie or Thomas Dewey were president we would not have lily-white fighting ships."[54]

The job of convincing Knox that it was finally time to commission black officers fell to Adlai Stevenson, the secretary's speechwriter and confidant. Stevenson had been brought into the Navy Department in August 1941. Knox, certain that war was imminent and needing a legal advisor and an assistant, had turned to a personable forty-one-year-old lawyer from Chicago whom he had met years before. Stevenson and Knox hit it off right away.

"I've a grand job, and I confess I don't know yet precisely about my duties," Stevenson told his sister. "Apparently most anything the Secretary wants to unload."

The two men saw "eye-to-eye on foreign policy," and though they had strong disagreements on domestic politics, they came to respect one another's abilities and patriotism.

Knox, always a fan of nicknames, began referring to his more liberal friend as "my New Dealer." He would tease Stevenson, the future two-time Democratic nominee for president, and tell other government officials that he needed a New Dealer like Stevenson around "to protect me from the New Dealers around here."

Then, Knox would turn to his speechwriter. "Adlai," he'd say, "you're not letting any of 'em creep in here, are you?"

The two men golfed together in the late afternoons and on weekends, and lunched together in the Navy Department's private dining room.[55] Stevenson became Knox's alter ego and consummate traveling companion. Stevenson accompanied Knox on his tour of the Pacific in January 1943, writing his speeches, hearing his thoughts, and inspecting naval stations and ships.

"It was 18 nights and a lifetime of adventure," Stevenson wrote in his diary. Knox spent the long hours traveling from island to island by seaplane, reading dozens of books, and amazing those around him with his concentration, boundless energy, and the rapidity with which he devoured another tome.

It was during that trip that Stevenson first broached the idea of black officers. He suggested it, rather casually, to Admiral Chester Nimitz, who replied that he did not think "Negro units" could make effective "service units."[56]

Eight months later, Stevenson understood as well as anyone that the Navy could not postpone meaningful action any longer. The policy was not feasible, the politics no longer tenable.

And no man in the world knew better than Stevenson the precise words that would move Knox.

On the question of integrating the officer corps, Stevenson explained to the efficiency expert that refusing to commission black men was now unquestionably inefficient. The Army, he said, was still recruiting better-educated, better-disciplined black men in large part because that branch offered a path for advancement. If the Navy wanted to keep up, it would have to consider commissioning African American officers.[57]

There were 60,000 black men in the Navy, and 12,000 more were entering every month, Stevenson wrote to Knox on September 29, 1943. "Obviously, this cannot go on indefinitely without accepting some officers or trying to explain why we don't. I feel very emphatically that we should commission a few negroes."

The V-12 Navy College Training Program, Stevenson conceded, might one day produce an African American officer, but no one knew when, though it was certain to take at least another year. That was too long, Stevenson said, and besides, "The pressure will mount both among the negroes and in the Government as well."

Indeed, one day earlier, Roosevelt had told Lester Granger, president of the National Urban League, "We cannot stand before the world as a champion of oppressed peoples of the world unless we practice as well as preach the principles of democracy ourselves for all men. Racial conflict destroys national unity at home and renders us suspect abroad."[58]

Stevenson suggested "10 or 12 negroes selected from top notch civilians just as we procure white officers." He ended his memo by telling Knox, "If and when it is done, it should not be accompanied by any special publicity but rather treated as a matter of course. The news will get out soon enough."[59]

Knox understood Stevenson's point, but he would not give the order without his admirals' consent. Knox punted the matter over to the Bureau of Naval Personnel and waited for a response.

———

While Knox waited for his admirals to decide whether black men deserved a chance at being commissioned as officers, William Sylvester White, a twenty-nine-year-old lawyer who had sought to avoid the military, was finally forced to enlist.

White had hoped that his work as an assistant US attorney for the Northern District of Illinois would keep him out of the war. After all, he reasoned, he was serving the government in another capacity.

He owed his job, an uncommonly estimable position for an African American, to an old friend, some old-school politicking, and good luck.

Back in 1939, White, two years out of the University of Chicago's law school, had been a small-time lawyer working at a prominent African American law firm. Charles Browning, a friend from Hyde Park High School, dropped by one day to ask White if he might like to be an assistant US attorney.

White laughed. "I'd like it very much," he said. "I'd like to be a United States Senator. I'd like to be President of the United States. What else is new?"

But his friend wasn't joking. Roosevelt was ready to appoint William J. Campbell as the new US attorney for the Northern District of Illinois, and Campbell wanted a token African American lawyer in his office.

Roosevelt owed Campbell, who had formed the Young Democrats for Roosevelt in 1932, when Chicago's powerful Democratic machine was squarely behind Al Smith's campaign for the nomination. For his loyalty, Campbell was first named Illinois administrator for the president's National Youth Administration in 1935. When the US attorney spot opened, it was his as well.

White's career to that point had been rocky. After graduating from law school in 1937, he had clerked for Joseph Clayton on the South Side of Chicago. Clayton, a talented and well-respected lawyer, paid White five dollars per week.

"I wasn't worth any more than that either," White later recalled.

Like much of the nation during the 1930s, White was a little desperate and greatly depressed. He even considered abandoning law and gave social work a try, working alongside Lewis "Mummy" Williams, whom he had first met when they were both at the University of Chicago.

But that life wasn't for him. White's first big break came when he was hired by Earl Dickerson, one of the few African American attorneys with an office in the Loop, the central business district in the heart of Chicago. Working for Dickerson, the dean of Chicago's black lawyers and one of the first African American graduates of the University of Chicago Law School, was an entry point for any promising young attorney. But a job as a federal prosecutor came with prestige of a far higher order.

White was now a mini-celebrity, with his photo appearing in magazines that listed him among the "outstanding Negroes in Chicago."[60]

It seemed all at once to validate White's decision to stay in law and his preternatural self-confidence. He had grown up at 6342 Eberhart Avenue on the South Side, two miles south of Arbor and two miles east of Reagan. White's father, a chemist and pharmacist, was a precinct captain in the city's sixth ward. His mother was a public school teacher. Together, they instilled in their only son the value of a good education, reminding him that material assets can be stolen, lost, forfeited, and repossessed, but knowledge is a person's for life. "My father used to tell me," White said, "that his mother told him that almost anything you get, the white folks can take away from you—except learning."

White enjoyed trying almost anything someone said was too tough for him to accomplish or was reserved for older boys. He did well in school and excelled at ROTC.

In the US attorney's office, White handled civil matters, mostly contracts and torts. His superiors kept most criminal cases off his plate, fearful that a jury might not believe an African American prosecutor.

His position as the "token black" was exploited in early 1943 when the government brought sedition charges against Charles Newby, a forty-six-year-old African American who publicly called on black men to avoid the Navy and the Army. Newby, speaking in Chicago's Washington Park, said that the war "was a white man's war" and that the Japanese were the black man's best friend.

It was a sentiment rippling through black communities across the country because of how blacks were treated in the South, in the military, and in the halls of Congress. It was the same expression of resentment and defiance that had concerned Hastie during the war's first days so much that he asked for a vote on whether black men truly supported the war effort. Newby's crime was saying in public what many black men had been saying quietly for years. White was selected to prosecute so that no one could say Newby received unfair treatment on account of his race.

White secured the conviction, which he had mixed feelings about for the remainder of his life, and Newby was sentenced to three years in prison.[61]

As prominent a position as federal prosecutor was, White was restless and wanted to try something new, so he applied to join the FBI but was told the bureau had no need for black agents. "It used to disgust me that whenever they had some undercover work to do, they would take on a smart black detective and have him work with them, thereby eliminating the necessity of having black agents," White later said.[62]

When it became clear that his work for the federal government would not keep him from being drafted, White, in October 1943, went to the same recruiting station as all his white peers from the US attorney's office and applied to be an officer. An Ensign Drips went through the formality of taking White's information before, red-faced and tense, he explained that black men were not qualified for commissions.[63]

But White wouldn't give up on the Navy. His buddy Mummy Williams was working in the selection office at Great Lakes, not too far from where White lived. White thought Williams could get him into a good service school once he made it through boot camp, so he enlisted later that October.[64]

Because of his work with the US attorney's office, White knew plenty of reporters who would print announcements of indictments and convictions, as well as when members of the office went off to war. "Be sure you don't miss when I'm leaving for the service," White told them. "Get it into the paper and say I'm going into the Navy."[65]

A small item announcing that "W. Sylvester White Jr., Lone Negro Assistant U.S. Attorney," was reporting to the Navy appeared in several of the nation's most widely read black newspapers.[66]

White was only two weeks into boot camp when he needed to have nine teeth pulled, a procedure that kept him on bed rest for three days with little more than a bag of ice on his cheeks to numb his swollen gums. That unpleasantness aside, White performed admirably during boot camp and was selected recruit company commander, thanks, in part, to his ROTC training.

After basic training, White intended to go to quartermaster's school, intrigued by the intellectual challenge. Mummy Williams was supposed to make it happen, but the opportunity never came.

Instead, White was called to the main side and asked if he thought he could carry out orders—even orders that are unpopular. The black press was attacking how the Navy was—and wasn't—using black sailors, he was told, and the Navy was considering making him a public relations officer.

"Now," White was asked, "if the Navy makes decisions regarding the utilization of Negroes and that decision comes under attack by Negro leaders and Negro writers in the press, would you be able still, to carry out the Navy policy?"

White was smart enough to know there was really only one answer to a question like that.

"Well, we are at war and men are dying in following orders," he said. "And if men can die to follow orders, I guess I can follow orders."[67]

The Navy informed White he would not be training as a quartermaster. They had something special in mind for him.

———

As White was going through boot camp, Graham Martin was growing ever more frustrated with his lack of advancement. Less-educated and, frankly, less-intelligent white enlistees were rising through the petty officer ratings, but Martin, who had already earned a master's degree from Howard University, was held back because of the color of his skin.[68]

It was a common refrain throughout 1943. Black men in segregated camps, particularly university graduates, felt that the Navy had little stomach for them, that their talents were wasted, and that the white officers over them "resented their superior education or manliness and that their chances for promotion were far less than those of smiling, knee-bending, 'cotton-mouth, cotton-tops' as they termed more subservient trainees."[69] Those suspicions were routinely validated by condescending white officers, many of whom were Annapolis graduates.

"Recruits who felt they had been treated as sub-citizens found it likely they would be classified as sub-sailors as well," Dennis Nelson remembered. "They were carrying a psychological burden that killed the morale and destroyed the initiative."[70]

In the fall of 1943, Martin found an outlet for his frustration when he was finally offered the chance to prove his mettle on the gridiron. When Martin, a football stud, first arrived at Great Lakes in 1942, he'd asked about playing on the station's team, but he was told that it was for whites only.

Segregation was still the rule at the beginning of the 1943 season, but after an ugly 23–13 loss to Purdue, resulting from some particularly poor tackling, Lieutenant Paul "Tony" Hinkle—a famed coach at Butler University and a future member of the basketball Hall of Fame—came to Camp Robert Smalls and asked whether any of the "boys" wanted to play football.

Hinkle gave the black men tennis shoes and drilled them on asphalt. He had them demonstrate pulling out, blocking left and right, and pass blocking. Martin could do it all and made the team that day. Five days later, he was first string.[71]

Integrating the football team wasn't easy. Martin was one of only a handful of black men selected, and he found Hinkle, and his constant warnings to stay out of trouble, condescending.

"Yes, sir," was really all Martin could say, no matter what he felt. He was addressing a lieutenant.

Hinkle explained to Martin—who had never had any trouble getting along with anyone—how he needed to behave if he was to get along with other players.

"Yes, sir," Martin said.

Keep your head down and do your job, Principal Lane had instructed him all those years ago.

The one game Martin looked forward to above all others was against Indiana and Bo McMillin, the coach who had underplayed him during his college career. The Great Lakes team stayed at the athletic club, but Martin, who had already played in seven games, was not assigned a room. Instead, they put him in an alcove in the locker room.

"If this is my room, I'll go home," he told Hinkle. He'd stay with his mother.

"Okay, Martin, go on home."

Yes, sir.

Before his biggest game of the year, the one for which he swore he would finally show his old coach what he was capable of, Martin, not welcome at the athletic club with his white teammates, stayed in his mother's house.[72] The next day, Great Lakes beat Indiana 21–7.

Martin helped lead the Great Lakes team to a string of victories and the 1943 award for the nation's top military team. They played so well that there was an investigation into whether sailor-players were being kept at Great Lakes longer than necessary simply to help the team. Great Lakes was cleared of suspicion. Martin and his teammates were just that good.

Great Lakes played undefeated Notre Dame the last game of the season on Saturday, November 27, 1943. The Fighting Irish were favored by forty points, but Great Lakes beat them 19–14, and Martin was one of the reasons why, protecting the quarterback with near-flawless play.[73]

Captain Robert R. M. Emmet, the new commandant of the Great Lakes Naval Training Station, "bubbling over with pleasure," gave the whole team a three-day pass.[74] Martin was congratulated for not causing any trouble with whites, no doubt a condescending gesture but one that proved propitious when his superiors decided they needed to find a group of black men who could succeed in a white world and break a color barrier without ruffling feathers.

The following Thursday, December 2, Rear Admiral Jacobs told Navy Secretary Knox that he approved of Adlai Stevenson's proposal to commission black officers. He explained that the Navy now had 82,000 black sailors and it wouldn't be too difficult to find a handful who were officer material.[75]

Even Commander Armstrong got on board, telling Knox that black men should be commissioned, that they'd be capable of commanding white enlisted men. Armstrong insisted that the move could not have been made sooner because black men had only just recently begun training for the general service, and he had done African Americans a great favor by opposing commissioning them as officers until now.

"My own opinion is that there would have been no surer way for this program to have ended in disaster than by the commissioning of officers before either the prospective officers or men whom they were to command were trained to discharge the duties and responsibility incumbent upon them in a satisfactory manner," Armstrong said.[76]

Admiral Ernest King, chief of naval operations, consented on December 15, and that was enough for Knox. If his admirals were on board, so was he. Knox approved the plan on December 18, as well as the additional recommendation that the Navy promote to warrant rank no more than four men nominated to the officer candidate group who performed well but did not meet the education requirements.

This was not a blank check, Knox said. He told Admiral Jacobs that the issue of black officers "should again be reviewed" after the first wave completed its training and "before any additional colored officers are commissioned."[77]

Martin, just back from a three-day pass and still a hero at Great Lakes, was told something good was about to happen to him, but no one would say exactly what it was.[78]

━━━

In December, Sam Barnes finally had saved up enough to get married.

He and Olga had been engaged since 1940, but nuptials had been postponed because he had been saving for their wedding and she had taken a job teaching in Trenton, New Jersey, where women could not marry until they had been on the faculty for at least three years. Barnes, in order to earn a little extra, took a part-time job at the Johns Manville asbestos plant near Great Lakes. Every weeknight, Barnes ate a quick dinner and then worked at the plant until midnight.

On the weekends, when the plant was closed, he'd work at the Campbell Soup factory in Chicago. He would leave Camp Robert Smalls at noon on Saturday, work through the night, and then catch a few hours of sleep at the USO club. He'd work all through Sunday as well. On Monday morning, he'd wake early and take the 7 a.m. Skokie Valley line back to the base and report at 8 a.m. He kept up this pace for three months so he'd have enough money to travel to North Carolina, where Olga's family lived, get married, and then enjoy a brief honeymoon in his hometown of Oberlin.

While Barnes was in Ohio introducing his new bride, friends kept asking why strange white men from out of town had been inquiring about him—his past, his associations. These men had interrogated the town's clergy, Barnes's high school teachers, people at Oberlin College.

Barnes had no idea what his friends were talking about, and he certainly did not know who these strange white men were or why they were interested in him.

The white men were FBI, and they were running a background check. The Navy was taking no chances.[79]

———

In the fall of 1943, Reagan received orders to head east and report to duty on the USS *Mason*, a coveted assignment. He had spent much of the year stationed at Point Loma, near San Diego, where he worked aboard the USS *Firefly*, an auxiliary minesweeper.

He sent a note to Downes saying he wasn't aware of the discrimination that his peers were complaining about, a letter Downes showed off to reporters who asked whether Hampton graduates were really getting a fair shake in the Navy.

"There are close to 60 colored boys here now from Hampton and the Lakes," Reagan wrote. "The officers seem to be a fine bunch of men—fair and with the Navy's and the men's best interest at heart. And they do have the men (every one of them) doing the work they were trained for."[80]

But Point Loma had been no easy assignment.

The base commander, a white captain, had named his black dog "Nigger" and walked around yelling, "Here, Nigger, here, Nigger."[81]

Off base wasn't much better. Black men stationed at Point Loma called San Diego "little Georgia," owing to the signs in windows stating "No sailors, dogs, or colored allowed."

Reagan's time aboard the *Firefly* was uneventful. Occasionally, a generator would break, and Reagan would fix it. The young man who had two years earlier dreamed of being a fighter pilot was spending the war repairing equipment on a small converted fishing boat. It was pleasant enough duty, providing the seas were calm, but it was far from the action he had imagined for himself the day he exited that movie theater in Montana.

At night, he'd enjoy a few beers at the famous Douglas Hotel, the "only quality place of lodging and entertainment for black visitors to San Diego," and swap sea stories with the other sailors.[82] On weekends, he would take three or four guys to Los Angeles, to his mother's house, for a home-cooked meal.

But the *Mason* would be a chance to see real action. Reagan, now a petty officer second class, was elated. He arrived in Virginia, feeling spry and ready for his new assignment, when he ran into an old friend, Downes.

The commander would not let him board the *Mason*. He had something else in mind but would not say what.

"Reagan, you're to report to Great Lakes on the double," Downes said, smiling and tossing a sealed brown envelope across his desk. "Your orders are sealed. Don't open them. But I got a hunch you'll like what's inside."[83]

Downes also sought out Dalton Baugh and George Cooper.

"You've got orders to go to Great Lakes, and I think you will not be sorry," he said.

He would provide no further explanation.

Just before leaving for Great Lakes, Reagan was waiting for the ferry to take him from Hampton to Norfolk. There was supposed to be a line for whites and a line for blacks, but it was crowded that day and several whites were in the "black" line, looking to board. Reagan, just trying to beat the crowds, got into the "white" line.

Almost immediately, he was given a hard time.

"The hell with it," Reagan said. "You know, it's crowded over there and there are whites over there."

He had given in to this racism the year before, when he was pulled off the bus by police, but this time Reagan would not budge.[84]

This was a perfect metaphor for what was about to take place: Sixteen black men would meet at Great Lakes to break a color barrier. They, too, would immediately be given a hard time, and they, too, would refuse to back down.

CHAPTER 10

"YOU CAN MAKE ME AN OFFICER, BUT MY PARENTS MADE ME A GENTLEMAN."

The very first night when they convened in January 1944, the sixteen officer candidates sat together at the long table inside Barracks 202 with textbooks and syllabi before them. They shared with one another their life experiences, their academic strengths, and their previous assignments, determining who was most proficient at the subjects they'd be expected to master. Those already familiar with a topic volunteered to help the rest.[1]

"We decided that same day that this was an experiment which could not fail because it meant too much to too many people," George Cooper said. "We would either excel as a group or fail as a group."

Each man around that table represented thousands more. They were certain that if they failed as officers, "the evil of segregation in the Navy, as related to black officers, would be set back for only God knows how long."[2]

"We were the hopes and aspirations of the blacks in the Navy," William Sylvester White recalled. "We were the forerunners. What we did or did not do determined whether the program expanded or failed."[3]

"We knew we were putting ourselves—and all blacks—on the line," Jesse Arbor said. "It was a literal test of our abilities. If we didn't score high, we would be held accountable. People would point to us as proof that blacks couldn't be leaders in the Navy."[4]

For these sixteen men, the coming trials would be like fighting in the dark, for they could not know what obstacles the Navy would put in their path, only that there were sure to be many. Nor could they know during those first days whether the Navy was making a good-faith effort to train them as officers or whether they were pawns in some larger game, there only to appease some liberal minds in Washington.[5]

All they were certain of was that many in the Navy hoped and assumed they would fail, simply so that someone high up could say "Well, we gave them a chance and they couldn't hack it."

"But we were going to fool all of them," Barnes remembered thinking, "because we were the foot in the door for the other blacks, and we were determined not to be the ones responsible for having the foot removed."[6]

———

Training began on Monday, two days after they were first told of their new assignments, and for the next two months, the men lived like lab mice caged for experimentation. They were prodded to see how they'd perform, with little regard for how they might feel or for what message segregated training conveyed to them or to the hundred thousand other black men in the Navy.[7]

They were a diverse group. Frank Sublett and John Reagan were only twenty-three years old, fresh out of college. Dennis Nelson and Reginald Goodwin were thirty-six, men who had wives and professions prior to the war.

Sam Barnes had grown up in a town relatively free of prejudice. James Hair had seen his brother-in-law lynched, wiped the blood from his head, and listened to him take his last breaths.

Graham Martin had his master's degree and White his law degree. Charles Lear had not made it past the tenth grade.[8]

There were friends among the group. Barnes, Goodwin, and Mummy Williams had worked together in the selection office at Great Lakes. Cooper, Reagan, Sublett, and Dalton Baugh knew each other from their time at Hampton.

And there were new faces. Hair had come from New York and Arbor, from Boston.

But no cliques formed, and all the superficial differences faded quickly. They would not survive as sixteen individual men; they could only succeed as one unit.

Sam Barnes kept thinking of the Three Musketeers: all for one, and one for all.[9]

And if any one man tried to assert himself over the group, perhaps because he was older or had served longer, the others would remind him— sometimes gently, sometimes not—that no player was more important than the team.

When Cooper suggested that he should march in front of other men because he was a chief petty officer and an instructor, Barnes shut him down. "Hell, don't let them stripes go to your head," he snapped. "I ain't walking behind you. You're one of us. Take that coat off, you look just like us."[10]

Barnes needed to say nothing more. Whatever differences they saw in one another—their backgrounds, their age, their education, their rating— the Navy didn't see it. All the Navy saw was their black skin.

They had to remember that.

They were brothers, and they'd need to fight for every mile in this marathon, which would test them, physically, mentally, and emotionally.

Suggestions were welcome. If consensus was reached, they'd move along, but no one gave orders and it would be futile to try.[11]

Dennis Denmark Nelson II, the undisputed peacock of the group, was the man hardest to keep in line. It was said of Nelson that he could strut while sitting down. He took every paycheck straight to the bank and asked the teller for crisp, new dollar bills. A man of his stature would carry nothing but new money.

Nelson would, as soon as he could, purchase every kind of uniform the Navy sold, complete with all the accoutrements. He even bought the cape, which might have looked ridiculous or ostentatious on anyone else, but it suited Nelson perfectly, for reasons no one could ever explain. His tie was always straight and his uniform always pressed.[12] He loved the way his .45 looked at his side, and he'd tilt his hat jauntily, instead of wearing it straight as Navy regulations demanded, because he wanted a more dapper look.[13]

Nelson was a sailor with Navy blue running in his veins. His father had worked for the Navy Department and his father-in-law, Charles Stewart, had been a seaman aboard the USS *Maine* when it was blown up in Havana Harbor.[14]

Nelson's brashness and alpha-male attitude had to be tamed in the winter of 1944, and when he failed to do it on his own, one of his compatriots was there to provide a little extra encouragement, warning that they'd lock him in the head if he didn't pipe down and act like a teammate.

Even as they rolled their eyes at Nelson's antics, the other men grew to love him because they all knew that behind the pretty-boy facade— the perfectly pressed uniforms and the crisp new dollar bills—was a fiery intellect. Nelson, the "untiring" Boy Scout leader who had started Nashville's first black troop, knew what he wanted and how he was going to get there. He was a human spark plug, a man who could activate things.[15] Everyone knew, just knew, that Nelson was going to succeed.

The other two senior citizens of the group were Goodwin and Williams, both of whom worked with Armstrong, and both of whom were among the first black yeomen in the Navy.

Goodwin was reserved but had such bearing and presence that he made an instantly positive impression when he entered a room.[16] Good looks, intelligence, and a sturdy build had endowed him with the kind of confidence associated with command.

Some Navy men might look disheveled, especially when on liberty, but Goodwin, the social worker from Cincinnati, was always immaculate. His Clark Gable mustache was neatly trimmed every morning.[17] And because he and Armstrong had worked together and developed a rapport, he felt at ease among those in the white power structure at Great Lakes in a way few black men did, acting at times as a liaison for the officer candidates.

It was a valuable if not always appreciated quality. Barnes looked up to Goodwin, grateful for his help, whereas White thought of him as an Uncle Tom.[18]

Goodwin was the member of the group most likely to remind his peers of the Navy's rules, especially on decorum—whether they wanted him to or not. There was no frivolity in the Navy, and there would be no display of such from Goodwin, nor would he tolerate it from others. On duty meant on duty, no distractions. Clothes were to be kept straight and the ditty bag always ready.

Hair one night suggested shooting dice, just something to break the monotony and blow off a little steam. They were sitting on the floor of Barracks 202, playing penny stakes, when Goodwin walked out of the head, saw what was going on, and started screaming.

"Fellows, fellows, what's going on here?" he demanded. "Look here. You are officers! Down there on your knees, shooting dice. Up, men! We will not have that as officers in the United States Navy. No! I cannot take this. Stop it, or I will report you."[19]

They knew he meant it, and that was the last time dice ever appeared in Barracks 202.

Arbor was the antithesis of Goodwin, a loosey-goosey sailor with a penchant for running his mouth. He had a story for every situation, a quip for every occasion, and a joke for every tense moment. He seemed to possess a sixth sense, always knowing exactly when the men around him needed a pick-me-up or when they were starting to get on each other's nerves. Just before the breaking point, Arbor would fire off a one-liner that invariably cleared the air and loosened the mood. Whatever they were so hot about a moment ago seemed a distant memory, especially if Phil Barnes started laughing. Barnes, no relation to Sam Barnes, had a big belly laugh as infectious as any virus, and soon everyone in the room was laughing. Arbor was the antidote to every poison, unforgettable to everyone he met no matter how many decades passed. He was self-aware enough to know that his mouth was both a strength and a weakness, endearing and enraging all at once. When he invariably stepped over the line, he was met with the same threats as Nelson: "Jesse, if you don't shut up, we're going to put you in the head and lock the door."

And like Nelson, he was embraced for his eccentricities. He didn't take himself too seriously and downplayed a lot of his own skill, but he was a deep thinker. And because he was a quartermaster, he offered a lot more than laughs. He was invaluable in helping the group learn navigation and identifying aircraft.[20]

Phil Barnes had a roly-poly physique and was self-conscious about his weight, which led to a bit of shyness in this group of physically imposing athletes.[21] He packed 216 pounds onto his five-foot, eight-inch frame and carried a lot of weight in his face, giving him the appearance of an overgrown baby, though he had no trouble with the physical drills.

Barnes possessed a contemplative soul. He trained racehorses, loved the sea, and spoke of becoming an angler, a path for which his temperament was ideally suited—although, ironically, he struggled with seamanship.

He had enlisted in the US Army Reserve Corps in 1931 and served for three years before taking a job as a bookbinder in the Government Printing Office in Washington, DC, where he worked until he enlisted in the Navy on Christmas Eve, 1942. He had spent most of 1943 at Hampton, first at the diesel school learning to be a shipfitter and then as an instructor.[22]

Barnes was not the easiest man to know, but those who took the time to pierce his shell were rewarded with a sincere, loyal, hard-working friend. He had a finely honed, almost biblical, sense of justice. Break a rule or cut a corner in front of Phil Barnes, and he'd calmly explain, almost like a preacher, that "it's just wrong for us to do this. It's wrong for us to go this way, morally wrong. We just can't afford to do it."

When tempers were at their hottest and Arbor's one-liners failed to break the tension, it was Barnes who would say, "Gentlemen, let's cool it. Remember what we are here for and what we decided to do and how we decided to do it."[23]

Sam Barnes, like Arbor, brought a sense of humor to the bunch, though his was far more dry. Unlike Arbor, he wasn't constantly talking, but he would long be remembered for the moments of good-natured cheer he brought when men needed it most. Perhaps because of his teaching background, he was an exceptional listener. Have a problem? Talk to Sam Barnes. His stature was elevated when the other men learned he had graduated from Oberlin. Anyone with Oberlin on his diploma was no dummy.

Cooper also relied on his teaching background to help his peers. He had an organized mind and a gift for conveying difficult material.

Graham Martin saw officer candidate school much the same he way he saw his chance to play on the Great Lakes football team. He could certainly do as well as any white man, and so, he believed, could the men around him. If anybody was going to be the first black officer in the US Navy, it might as well be him. Why not, he thought. He was smart and well educated, tough and talented. He was fluent in German and French, and had a knack for solving equations. The football player from Indianapolis viewed this new challenge just like a contest on the gridiron: if you are going to be on this team, you've got to make the grade, he'd say. "You've got to make the grade on classroom work; you've got to make the grade out here in the field; you've got to make the grade, period, if you're going to be on this team."

When morale was low, Martin was the no-nonsense coach, telling the men, "Let's get our crap together here," and accepting no excuse for lackluster performance.[24]

Hair was one of the few who had spent considerable time at sea, having served for the better part of a year as a quartermaster aboard the USS *Penobscot*, a 122-foot-long, 415-ton harbor tugboat. Hair did most of the steering on that ship and had become quite adept at handling craft, as well as updating charts by noting the location of shipwrecks and new buoys. He was proud of his work at sea and often bragged that he had "more salt in my socks from washing them in seawater than all the rest of you guys put together." He was chummy and talkative, but in a different way than the garrulous Arbor. He wasn't trying to be the center of attention. He was an easy mixer, with a boyish and sometimes raunchy sense of humor. He liked to joke that his last assignment was to give short-arm inspections to a contingent of WAVES (the women's naval reserve). Hair, like Phil Barnes, had an infectious laugh. When he found something amusing, he'd bend over at the waist and clap his hands, his whole body getting into the act.[25]

Augustus Alves was the only other member who had spent extensive time at sea, owing to a stint in the merchant marine before the war began. Though not nearly as collegial as Hair, he was second to none when it came to seamanship, and the group would gather around the long table to learn the proper way to tie knots and fold equipment, a useful skill for men who would be penalized for even the slightest infractions.[26]

Sublett, perhaps because he was the baby of the bunch, rarely volunteered an opinion, though he was eager to help when asked. A philatelist who loved animals, Sublett was himself a bit of an overgrown puppy: very friendly, open, and eager to please. His Hampton training had given him expertise in lathes, drill presses, milling machines, and shapers. He was a machinist's mate, who could fix just about anything and relate to just about anyone.[27]

At 5 feet, 7 inches and 130 pounds, William Sylvester White, whom everyone called Syl, was not nearly as physically imposing as the men around him, but his self-confidence and piercing intellect made him seem like a giant. Because he had entered the Navy only three months before, much of boot camp was fresh in his mind. He could remind his comrades of the basics they may have forgotten, and his time as an assistant US attorney made him a natural choice to explain Navy regulations and court-martial proceedings, which as officers they would be expected to master. He was quiet and analytical, almost withdrawn. He chose his words carefully, and when he spoke it was because he had something important to say.[28]

Charles Lear, a hard-nosed chief petty officer, was born in Keokuk, Iowa, but had spent much of his adult life working in the fields and factories of Illinois and Missouri. He was the only one of the sixteen who had spent no time in college. Husky and square jawed, Lear was the kind of man for whom the Navy was love at first sight, the kind of sailor who at reveille was always first on deck.[29]

Dalton Baugh was one of the more brainy of the bunch, beloved for his salt-of-the-earth, commonsense touch and plainspoken Midwestern vibe. He had an engineer's temperament: Problems have solutions. They just need to be found. When the coursework seemed impossible to master and frustration built, Baugh's logical approach guided the group to an answer. He'd stand up from his chair at the long table, his arms akimbo, processing the information, working it all over in his head. "What's the situation here?" he'd calmly state. "Let's look at it." If the answer eluded him, he'd say, "We'll see, we'll see," a sure sign that he was turning the problem over.[30]

And if anyone was slacking, it was Baugh, with a baritone voice that never needed to be raised to be heard, who would say, "Oh, man, just stop this crap. We just can't do this."

During those early months of 1944, when the burden appeared too great to bear, the pressure too intense to tolerate, and someone said, "Screw the whole thing, let's just forget it," or "The hell with it, this is just too damn much," Baugh would stand and say, "You can't do that, you can't let that happen."[31]

———

Their days began at 6 a.m. Six mornings a week, they rose from their cots and donned an enlisted man's uniform: undress blues—plain without white piping on the jumpers. Their pants were bell-bottoms, and they wore the standard Navy white hat.[32]

Once dressed, the men marched to chow and were seated and eating by 6:30 a.m. After breakfast they lined up for muster and sick call, ready for the rigors of another day.

On Monday and Wednesday mornings, the officer candidates drilled for four hours, until lunch. On Tuesday, Thursday, and Friday mornings, they took classes in seamanship, gunnery, navigation, naval law, and Navy regulations. On Saturdays there was a course in navigation, followed by an inspection of the barracks before lunch, and then a class in gunnery.

There were quizzes most afternoons, followed by an hour of exercise. Thursday afternoons were devoted to drilling.

Dinner was from 5 to 6 p.m. On Wednesdays, they were free for the rest of the evening, but every other night of the week was set aside for study.

Lieutenant Paul Richmond, the Great Lakes officer who had been so impressed with Martin's demeanor and abilities, designed the curriculum, which he based on the so-called "90-day wonder" program that was used for V-7 officer candidates. Richmond was a natural choice to head up the training program, having become the senior regimental officer at Camp Robert Smalls the previous summer when Donald Van Ness went to Washington to work with the Special Programs Unit.

Richmond, himself only two years out of the Naval Academy at Annapolis, gave the candidates an abbreviated version of what he had studied there. He taught navigation and assigned Benjamin Dutton's classic textbook, *Navigation and Nautical Astronomy*, and George W. Mixter's *Primer of Navigation*, which had been published to help yachtsmen, not train professional sailors. Richmond figured it'd be easier to learn from a basic primer, given the time constraints.

The men were assigned about thirty pages to read before every lesson, which covered rules of the road and right of way at sea, piloting, the use of the sextants, the points of a compass, dead reckoning, and other basic topics. Some of the men had never seen a sextant before, so Richmond brought some from the main side to demonstrate how to take star sights.[33]

Lieutenant Paul Perkins taught Fundamentals of Naval Service, using A. A. Ageton's *The Naval Officer's Guide* and Leland P. Lovette's *Naval Customs, Tradition and Usage* as well as *The Bluejacket's Manual*. Lieutenant W. I. Quattlebaum was the gunnery instructor, while Ensigns Joe Redwine Jr. and F. G. Headley taught aircraft and ship recognition, and seamanship, respectively.

Martin felt that many of these teachers acted as if they thought they were gods trying to pass on wisdom to a hopelessly inferior group, who, with much patience, might learn a fraction of what was being taught. They didn't seem all that interested in whether the men passed, failed, or learned anything at all. Sublett was certain that some of the teachers felt their efforts were a waste of time because no one expected black men to succeed.[34]

There was a six-part lecture series on the current war in Europe, intended to "establish a pattern of the war for the indoctrinee."[35] The course was taught by officers from the War Orientation Office, who explained the causes of the war and analyzed current events. It was, essentially, a European history class. The men studied the nineteenth-century empires and conflicts that explained the rise of fascism and Adolf Hitler.

The men also studied the history of the US Navy, beginning in 1775 with the Continental Congress's establishment of a three-member Naval Committee.

They learned the history of signal flags, how they were used on ships during the twelfth century, how the colonies used them during the Revolutionary War, and how their meaning had evolved down to the present day.

Time was spent on the firing range practicing with 20-millimeter guns, and on an anti-aircraft simulator that gave them training in the use of 40-millimeter guns.[36]

They trained in distance swimming, and swimming fully clothed. They had abandon-ship and lifeguard drills. They learned how to fashion life preservers from trousers, mattress covers, hats, and ditty bags.

They studied the sweet science of boxing—pages 72–82 in the Navy's *Physical Fitness Manual* described how to land an effective blow and use self-defense techniques. Pages 88 and 89 explained how to wrestle and prepared men for hand-to-hand combat.

They instructed basic training companies and performed duty watches in regimental offices and the service schools.[37]

They memorized nautical terminology such as "cockbill" (to position a yard at an angle to the deck or place an anchor ready to be dropped) and "Irish pennants" (the untidy ends of a line or loose end of a poorly tied knot).

"Officers are friendly, honorable, just," Cooper wrote neatly on lined loose-leaf paper, which he kept in a three-ring binder.

"Duty is that which should be performed with as much accuracy as possible," his notes say. "The smallest order should be executed with as much interest and zest [as that] of a larger one."

Cooper would commit these rules to memory at night, as he did the courtesies he was being taught to recite, such as "Call enlisted men by [last] name only. . . . Pass senior officer to left only after his permission has been given. Ask—'by your leave, sir,'" and "Avoid conceit." Cooper had those words underlined in his notebook.

The men learned how to keep a ship's log and how to write a formal letter, where on the page to sign one's name and how to respond to a request from a higher-ranking officer. They attended lectures on leadership and expected conduct.

There was a class on naval courts and procedures, and the men were quizzed on summary courts-martial and general courts-martial. They were quizzed on traditions, customs, and military insignia, as well as on Navy history and the different types of warships.[38]

The pace was brutal.

Most of these men had only a passing familiarity with these subjects. This is where Cooper and his knack for breaking down complex concepts into digestible nuggets came in handy. "Yeah, it went pretty fast, but here is what it meant," he'd say at the end of another long day. "Here is what you *really* have to understand."

The men were supposed to be in bed with the lights out at 10:30 p.m., but well past that hour, the sixteen candidates sat together in the bathroom, flashlights in hand, studying the lessons of the past day and preparing for the day ahead. They draped sheets over the windows so no one outside would notice the light.

They were intent on proving that their "selection was justified," Sam Barnes said, "and that we weren't a party to tokenism."[39]

Arbor, the quartermaster, taught semaphore and Morse code, tapping out sentences on the wall of the restroom. He'd give a clue—say, "a ship approaching on such-and-such side." The men would tap it out. If they got it wrong, they'd go back and start again. Even their toughest instructors weren't as demanding of them as they were of themselves, so when the men went to class the next day there was little a teacher could do to catch them off-guard.

They'd average five or six hours of shut-eye a night, but sleep was never scheduled.

They studied until they felt prepared for the next day, or until the fatigue and stress overwhelmed them. That's when Arbor's sixth sense kicked in: "All of this is a lot of bullshit," he'd say. "I'm hitting the sack."[40]

"It was a long day," Hair remembered. "Day in and day out, right on through."[41]

Sublett described the training as "pure hell."[42]

Cooper leaned on his wife, Peg, to help during the darkest hours. She had not wanted to remain in Virginia—a place she'd never liked—without her husband, so she took their baby girl to Hamilton, Ohio, where her family lived, while he trained at Great Lakes.

When Cooper wrote or called, he often spoke of the camaraderie he had found and how it was solace amid the enormous pressure he felt. He was studying all the time, he said, and the people in charge weren't making it easy.[43] His voice betrayed the doubt he felt, and he often appeared on the verge of tears.

Peg, on the other end of the line, promised her husband everything was going to work out. "You can do this," she'd repeat to him. "You are smart enough to do it and you have to do it."

It could not have been easy for Peg to say. Even decades later she never felt all that patriotic for a country that had treated her race so poorly. She related to the African Americans who wrote letters to the *Pittsburgh Courier* wondering why they should lay down their lives to live half-American; to Charles Newby, whom White had prosecuted for stating that black men had no business fighting for a nation that treated them as a subspecies. She didn't want to participate in the war effort, and certainly didn't want her husband to travel the world for it. She felt that way about all of the nation's wars, up to and including America's second war in Iraq. Why should black boys die for this country in some faraway place when they were treated as second-class citizens at home?

"It's like Cassius Clay said," Peg later told an interviewer, referring to the boxer who changed his name to Muhammad Ali. "No Vietnamese ever called him a 'nigger.'"[44]

Whatever ambivalence she harbored about the nation and the war she kept to herself during those first ten weeks of 1944. The war had nothing to do with her husband's struggle, and she told him he'd have to fight through, past and beyond whatever the Navy threw at him.

"That's the way I feel about things," she later said. "You go out and you fight, you fight like hell."[45]

Her husband was going to become one of the first black naval officers. She was certain of it.

"Any accomplishment, if I can claim any, has to do with my wife and the support that I've gotten from her," Cooper later said. "You call on the telephone and just cry your heart out, and there's somebody on the other end of the line who's going to listen to you and she's going to say, 'Keep your chin up.'"[46]

One Saturday morning, not long after their training began, Phil Barnes received a letter from his sister, who was living in Washington, DC. She instructed him to call her as soon as he could. When he did, she sounded very strange. She needed a phone number where he could be reached. She wouldn't say why, but she told her brother to be by that phone at 4 p.m. the following Saturday. She'd explain then.

When they connected, she said she was working as a janitor at Navy headquarters, cleaning offices, including the office of Undersecretary of the Navy James Forrestal.

Something funny is going on, she told her brother.

"I see a list of men here—that they're going to be some kind of offi-cers," she said.

"What do you mean?" Barnes asked.

"Don't tell anybody now, because it's top secret, and it's not supposed to be on this desk. I can't pick it up, but I can read. It doesn't say what date it's going to be, but they're going to make the first colored officers."[47]

Barnes's name was on the list, which is why she had thought to call.

The training program was still a secret, but that fortuitous connection confirmed for the men that they weren't engaging in a pointless exercise. The Navy, all the way to the top, was taking this seriously.

If the men passed their tests the Navy was prepared to commis-sion them.

White men knew it, too, and many were aghast at the prospect. And the surest way to prevent it from happening was to prove that the Navy's worst fears—that black men were incapable of discipline—were correct.

If the sixteen officer candidates ever lost their cool, ever broke ranks, ever screamed at an injustice, it could be enough for someone to say that African Americans lacked the temperament to be officers—enough to end this experiment.

Naysayers goaded the men in the hopes that one would lose his tem-per and blow it for the whole group.

On one occasion, the officer candidates were lined up for a medical exam.

"All right, you boys, strip down," someone yelled. "Everything off. Strip down."

So they did.

"Stand over there," came another order. "Stand at attention."

Jesse Arbor, a well-endowed man, had white splotches on the skin near the top of his penis. A white pharmacist's mate grabbed a thirty-six-inch ruler and yelled out, "Look at this, look at this. Here's this Negro here. Look at this man, half white and half black."

As he spoke, he rapped Arbor's penis with the ruler, causing him to wince with each whack.

Hair was certain a riot was about to start. This was it. This was the moment they would surely be kicked out.

"Hey, boy, where did you get this thing from?" the pharmacist's mate asked, still whacking Arbor's penis.

Arbor looked him directly in the eye, just the way the Navy had taught. "Well, you see, sir, I was raised in a white neighborhood."

Nothing more than a snicker escaped his comrades' lips, and the white men, furious that they could not get a rise out of the sixteen officer candidates, stormed off.[48]

Arbor was determined to respond to provocation with tranquility and creativity. He felt he owed it to the group.

Their restraint was neither an accident nor a character flaw. These men had been winnowed from hundreds of candidates, chosen because the Navy deemed them not too "extreme" in their attitudes.

"They are all good leaders and they are not radical in any sense of the word," Richmond wrote a friend shortly after the men received their commissions. "They were picked because we knew that we could count on them to benefit the Navy and they will not raise racial issues, I am sure, such as coming to the Officers' Club or anything of that nature. They are loyal to the Navy."[49]

In short, Armstrong and Downes had chosen these men because they expected them to suffer these indignities quietly and gracefully.[50]

═══

The instructors during officer candidate school were all white, except for Chief Petty Officer Noble Payton, who had earned a master's degree from Howard University in 1934. He was a renowned chemistry professor and physicist who had worked with Sam Barnes at Livingstone, had taught at Howard University, and had worked with Cooper, Baugh, and Phil Barnes at Hampton. He was brought to Barracks 202 to teach mathematics, which was necessary to calculate the speed and direction of a ship as it passes through water, and he provided a familiar face and a sympathetic ear.[51]

The one other person they could lean on, the only white man who seemed to empathize, was Lieutenant John Flint Dille Jr., who had been a classmate of White's at the University of Chicago, though the two did not know one another until they met in the Navy.[52]

Before the war, Dille had worked for the National Newspaper Service, a syndicate that his father, John Dille Sr., had started and made famous with a comic he helped create called *Buck Rogers in the 25th Century A.D.*

Dille Jr. created his own syndicated puzzle called "Brain Twizzlers by Professor J. D. Flint," a play on his own name. It proved quite successful and ran in several newspapers.

But when Japan attacked, he left it all behind. Dille, a handsome six-foot, three-inch man with brown hair and blue eyes, had a new baby boy at home and might have received a deferment, but like so many men he felt a duty to serve. He enlisted on April 13, 1942, six days after Knox announced that black men would be trained for the general-service ratings.

Dille chose the Navy because, like Martin and Barnes, he was a germophobe. That meant the Army was out. And at twenty-eight, he thought he was too old to learn to be a fighter pilot. Besides, he figured, he was a big guy, and those cockpits looked a tad too small to accommodate a man who wore size 13 shoes.

Dille passed the physical exams, but the Navy discovered he was partially defective in color perception—an irony not lost on the men of Robert Smalls, who would become his protégés—and, worried he would not be able to read signal flags correctly, denied him sea assignments.

Instead, Dille was put in charge of training a battalion of new recruits at Great Lakes Naval Training Station, only ten miles from his home in Highland Park. He formed new recruits into marching units and taught them correct pace and rhythm, and good military bearing. Dille himself actually had very little natural rhythm, but he knew how to teach.[53] Eyes straight ahead, Dille would order. There is a proper length of stride and a correct distance for how far out the arms should swing.

Knowing that his "fellow officers wouldn't have been happy to see black faces in their dining hall," Dille asked his superior officer, Lieutenant Commander William Turek, if he could be assigned to work with the black recruits at Camp Robert Smalls.[54] It was a chance to distinguish himself, Dille thought, and perhaps earn a promotion. And he figured black men would need all the help and understanding they could get from the officers in charge.[55]

Dille came from a home well ahead of its time on matters of race relations. His mother, Phoebe Minerva Crabtree, was a Chicago chapter president of the Daughters of the American Revolution. She had reared Dille on the ideals of the Declaration of Independence and to appreciate a person regardless of skin color. Her father, Dille's grandfather, John Dawson Crabtree, had fought with Illinois's Thirteenth Infantry Regiment during the Civil War, helping the Union lay siege to Vicksburg.[56]

Dille grew up in Evanston, Illinois, which had a sizable black community, and he had African American friends in high school. This set him apart from many white officers at Great Lakes, most of whom had grown up in the South, had graduated from the Naval Academy at Annapolis, and wanted little to do with the latest Navy experiment.

Turek told Dille that Robert Smalls was an assignment reserved for Naval Academy graduates and sent him on his way. But when Ensign Robert E. Blackwell, one of the four men assigned to work with black boots, was ordered to sea, Turek, remembering the eager young man, brought Dille back to Camp Robert Smalls.

Eighteen months later, when Dille learned that black men were to be trained as officers, he volunteered for that assignment as well. He figured he could help indoctrinate these candidates in protocol and military courtesy; once again, he correctly assumed that they'd see few friendly faces during their training.

Almost immediately Dille found these officer candidates to be some of the finest sailors he'd ever met.

"But they were going to face problems, and they knew it and I knew it," he said. "To the extent that I could be helpful, I tried to articulate these circumstances and set the warning signals up."

Dille talked to them about how to comport themselves around other officers and enlisted men. He spoke of the importance of keeping their cool when they were invariably shunned at—or excluded from—an officers' club, and of proudly wearing the uniform no matter what invective is hurled their way.

Dille never had anything written down in advance; there were no formal lectures on racism in the Navy. There didn't need to be. "More often than not, being the intelligent, educated, and, for the most part, sensitive men that they had to be to be qualified, they would anticipate those things and very well bring it up themselves, whether with me or among themselves," Dille later recalled.[57]

Mostly, though, Dille listened. He was a morale booster at a time when the men needed it most and provided a link to the world beyond their barracks. In early February, Dille dropped by to inform the men of the invasion of the Marshall Islands. It was a key battle in the war and Dille explained why. The mood brightened. This was all part of a larger mission, and the United States was winning. Everyone's spirits lifted.

Dille offered practical help as well. The officer candidates took turns as officers of the day, training companies in boot camp. They were graded on how well they inspected and drilled the enlisted men.

Dille was among the officers assigned to grade their work. If someone made a mistake or did not know what to do, he could ask Dille for advice.

The admiration the men felt for Dille and the sympathy he felt toward them remained a closely guarded secret. Outwardly, Dille was businesslike, an officer training candidates. He maintained a military posture. There was no fraternizing. But on occasion, he might flash a smile or give a knowing nod that conveyed his understanding.

That was enough.[58]

Richmond, on the other hand, appeared in view of the men to be Dille's opposite. It seemed he was purposefully harder on them than he needed to be. Richmond had always wanted to be at sea and made plain that he resented being stuck at Great Lakes. The men felt his brusqueness was an attempt to provoke them in the hopes that their resentment of him would get the better of their judgment. Then Richmond could fail them all. Only after the men were commissioned did he congratulate them on completing a semester's worth of training in half that time. Even then that seemed to the men to be a halfhearted gesture.[59]

Decades later Richmond would say he had no malicious intent but wanted to make the course as tough as he could because he knew the men would be scrutinized once they graduated, and because he had so much to teach in such a short period of time. At the Naval Academy, Richmond had studied navigation for a year. Now, he'd be teaching it in a month.

Richmond, a Michigan native, was a by-the-book sailor who sought to carry out every order to the letter. It was his duty to see that these men became officers. But he felt awkward about his role, his cousin later explained. He was very much aware that these men were older and better educated than he was. He was supposed to train leaders, but these men, he thought, were already leaders. He was teaching people whom he felt really had a lot to teach him, a sentiment that he could never outwardly express. He was an officer, and decorum must be maintained. So this twenty-three-year-old, charged with training the first black officers, fell back on what he knew from his Annapolis days.[60] Making it difficult—being gruff, callous, even indifferent—was how you molded men into officers. And if he scared them a little by telling them that they weren't up to snuff or that they weren't going to make it, it was only to motivate them.

It's impossible to know whether Richmond's intent was as pure as he later said, and it is irrelevant because the men did not know and could not have known his motives. All they knew was that Richmond, who was younger than every one of them, seemed far more interested in explaining why they'd fail than in helping them succeed.

Whether Richmond's attitude was for their benefit or his, it had the effect of making the group more determined. They took everything he threw at them and came back for more.[61]

They were going to show him and every other Richmond-like figure they'd ever met.

And so they did.

As their training drew to a close in March, the group was posting grades like no other officer class in history. Their marks were so good, in fact, that some in Washington did not believe they could be real. The men were forced to take some exams a second time. They scored even higher, a collective 3.89 out of 4.0, the highest average of any class in Navy history.[62]

———

The Navy had been working on the assumption that one-fourth of the class would fail, in line with the attrition rate for white officer candidates.[63] No one expected all the men to pass, certainly not with top marks. Toward the end of their ten-week course, when it became obvious that all of them would not only pass but pass with flying colors, the Navy decided it would commission only twelve of the sixteen men and a thirteenth would be made a warrant officer.

No explanation was given for this decision.

Perhaps some felt uncomfortable having black men succeed at a better clip than white men, or perhaps they took Stevenson's memo literally and decided to commission no more than twelve officers. Whatever the reason, the decision meant that the first black class, a group that posted the highest marks ever, would have the same pass rate as a class of average of white officer candidates.

The sixteen men were told that three would be dropped, but not which three. Instead, men were excused from Barracks 202 to be processed into officer ranks one by one, while the others sat, nervous and dejected, waiting to see who would be cast off. Nelson recalled that "morale was at an all-time low" during this "sweating out" period.[64]

When Arbor walked into Armstrong's office, the commander looked him over and asked, "Now that you're an officer, how do you feel?"

"Sir, having never been an officer before . . . I will first have to be an officer a day or two before I know how I feel."

"I understand all of you made good grades over there, and that's commendable," Armstrong said. "Now you know you will have to make choices as an officer instead of an enlisted man."

"Yes, sir."

"Now, in the event that you would be in a position where there was a colored sailor and a white sailor in a fight, whose side would you take?" Armstrong asked.

"Sir, I have to wait until that occasion arises."

Armstrong stared at Arbor. It was not the answer he wanted and he waited a beat to give Arbor a second chance.

"The first thing I would think of to do is as an officer, as has been taught to me," Arbor said. "It's the only thing I could rely on. My personal judgment would not enter into the case."

"Well, that sounds pretty good," Armstrong said. "Now you know there are no quarters for you."

Arbor did not know that.

It was the first of many times these newly commissioned black officers would learn that they may wear the same stripes as white men, but they would not be given the same privileges. In fact, their commissions came with far more warnings and admonishments than respect and plaudits.

And one more thing, Armstrong added, as Arbor was about to leave. "I don't want any of you fellows going to the officers' club."[65]

For Reagan, this was a particularly dispiriting order and darkened what he otherwise considered the "outstanding event" of his life. Becoming an officer was like a dream, a minor miracle. He had been denied the chance to fly for his country because of the color of his skin. Now, he was an ensign.[66]

Sam Barnes entered Armstrong's office uncertain what to expect.

The conversation was brief, perfunctory almost to the point of absurdity. The man he played badminton with, the man he had worked under at the selection office, could conjure no kind thoughts.

"Now you are an officer and a gentleman," Armstrong said.

Barnes could not let that suffice.

"Well, I wish, sir, to say one thing," he replied. "I was a gentleman before I came. You can make me an officer, but my parents made me a gentleman. So I respect what the Navy's saying, but I just wanted you to realize that these values were taught to me prior to coming into the service. I want to give my parents credit for that."[67]

When it was Cooper's turn, it was Armstrong who seemed uncertain what to expect.

"I don't know what kind of an officer you'd make for the Navy," he told a stunned Cooper. "In the first place, you're what we call a hell-raiser."

"Sir, I don't recall having raised any hell since I've been here, and certainly not at Hampton when I was down there as a chief petty officer," Cooper responded.

"This goes back to when you were eight-years old and the fight you had with a white boy in Washington, North Carolina."[68]

It had been decades since that day when Cooper was delivering milk for his father and a little boy, standing on Market Street, called him a nigger. A fight broke out. The white boy went home and told his father, who spoke to Cooper's father, but nothing came of it, a fortunate circumstance at a time and place where that was enough of a transgression for a black family to be run out of town. The incident was literally childish, and Cooper couldn't believe Armstrong was bringing it up now—or that he even knew about it at all.

It had turned up during the FBI background check, and Armstrong's message to Cooper was clear: stay in line, know your place.

It was another example of Armstrong functioning like a Rorschach test. White saw a commanding officer simply trying to protect this new crew, telling them to keep their heads down and stay out of trouble.[69]

Cooper saw something else.

"Prejudice is exerted in so many subtle and unobvious ways that a black person senses it and smells it and feels it," he later said. "There are so many subtle ways of demonstrating prejudice, but as a black person, you just have antennas out, and you sense it and you feel it instinctively."

It can be a glance or in the tone of voice, or a demeanor.

"And it's so frequently done by people who, if you're on the bitter end of it, are so much your inferior in so many ways until it takes a hell of a lot of guts to even stomach it," Cooper said. "And you know this. And you sense this. And you feel this. And it takes me back to what Mama used to say: 'Son, it ain't no sin being colored, but it's darned inconvenient.'"[70]

Lear, the candidate with no college experience, was made a warrant officer. The Navy also announced that Willie Powell, a pay clerk who first enlisted as a messman in 1918, would be appointed a warrant officer when he returned from the South Pacific.[71]

Armstrong offered no explanation as to why Augustus Alves, Lewis "Mummy" Williams, and J. B. Pinkney were not commissioned. They simply disappeared from the group and returned to enlisted duty.

Alves, the rumor was, had once passed for Portuguese. He was light skinned with straight hair, so he could have passed for European and that might have been enough for the Navy to deny him his commission.[72] Or maybe, Hair guessed, Alves was rejected because he had once told men to boycott the Red Cross on account of its policy of segregating blood donations.

"He was quite militant at the time," Hair said.[73]

Whatever the reason, Alves was let go, though he would later make history as the first African American chief specialist in the Naval Reserve, and as adjutant of the Twenty-Ninth Battalion at Camp Robert Smalls.[74]

Williams always felt that it was his participation in the labor movement that rubbed some in the Navy the wrong way.[75]

Pinkney, too, was considered radical, an agitator, because he had worked for the labor movement in Atlanta.[76]

The Navy kept the commissioning a quiet affair. There were no graduation exercises, no ceremonies, no celebrations.[77]

But just as Stevenson had predicted, "the news got out soon enough."

The *Pittsburgh Courier* and the *Chicago Defender* ran the new officers' names and photos on their front pages, cheering the twelve new ensigns. The *Defender* reported that the "United States Navy is moving closer to the principles of Democracy by gradually erasing its color line."[78]

There was only one problem: the story wasn't entirely accurate. There were not twelve ensigns. White had not yet received his commission. Just days before the end of officer training he started complaining of headaches, chills, and chest pain. He likely had a respiratory infection, which was diagnosed as "catarrhal fever," a catchall term used at the time for lung diseases. He was placed on bed rest for three days and was absent when the Navy took the first official photograph of its black officers.

The fever wasn't White's only problem. He hadn't passed his physical. He'd had teeth pulled in November, shortly after enlisting, and the replacements were still missing, which was enough to deny him a commission. The week after their training began, White requested a medical waiver. By March 20, it still had not arrived and the Navy refused to grant his commission until the paperwork cleared, which left White in limbo for about a week. The waiver was finally granted on March 29, and White, a man the FBI said it had no use for because of his color, became an ensign in the United States Naval Reserve.[79]

White's respiratory infection cleared up that week, too, so he was ready to be photographed for *Life* magazine's April 24 issue under the caption "First Negro Ensigns." The photo was "historic," the magazine said, but the editors did not bother to print the officers' names.[80]

Three weeks later, J. L. Jones, a *Life* reader from Great Neck, New York, wrote in a letter to the editor that he was "shocked" by the photo. "Every real American will bitterly resent the breaking down of our great naval traditions. There is no place for the black man in our white Navy, and there is moral and political dynamite in trying to mix the white with the black."

No doubt Jones spoke for many, but his is the only objection that *Life* printed. Ronald Spiers, a naval reservist in New Hampshire, wrote that he "would be proud to salute any of them."

"Shame on Mr. Jones for this thoughtlessness," wrote W. W. Ritter Jr., a reservist from Chapel Hill, North Carolina, in a subsequent issue. "His ideas are of the kind which start race riots and prevent closer collaboration between the races. I am a Southerner, but more than that, I am an American—and white."

Eight reservists from Princeton, New Jersey, expressed "great distaste" for Jones's letter. "Our nation is engaged in a life-and-death struggle to insure equal opportunity for all men," they wrote. "If any man, regardless of his race, color or creed, can hasten our victory by his efforts he should be given that opportunity."[81]

———

Cooper, by virtue of his size, was the only one who could buy a uniform off the rack from the ship's stores. He needed no alterations and walked out with it that day, becoming the very first black man to wear a naval officer's uniform: a dress blue, double-breasted coat with a half-inch gold stripe and gold star on each sleeve above the wrist.

They had gone through hell, Cooper thought as he put on that uniform for the first time. But having been through that hell, they had laid the groundwork for others to follow.[82]

Arbor took Baugh, Hair, and Reagan to Finchley's, a clothing store in Chicago where there was an expert tailor who would have their new uniforms fitting perfectly. The tailor gave them a deal on the suits, so proud was he to be sewing on gold braids for the first African American officers.[83] James Hair, the son of a slave, a man born to a man owned, fastened the gilt brass buttons on his coat and walked out into the Chicago streets wearing the uniform of a United States naval officer.

The men received a ten-day pass after they were commissioned. Cooper took advantage of his first free weekend in a couple of months to visit his wife and daughter in Hamilton, Ohio. When he walked into Union Station in Chicago, wearing his uniform, everyone stared. Same on the train. No one quite knew how to react to what they were seeing.[84]

White also went home to visit his wife, George Vivian Bridgeforth, whom he had not seen in three months. Twin girls, Carolyn and Marilyn, were born nine months later.

"The Navy chow really does something for you," he used to joke.[85]

Sublett, the day after he received his commission, married Henrietta Beck, a young woman who grew up in Evanston not far from his own home.

Baugh suggested that he and Arbor visit their alma mater, Arkansas AM&N, and the two were greeted like conquering heroes. Everyone wanted to know the story of how two of the first black officers came from a small, little-known school.[86]

Arbor also used his free time to visit Duck Collins, the sailor responsible for acclimating him to the Navy two years earlier. Collins hadn't heard anything about black officers, and when he saw Arbor standing before him in his perfectly tailored uniform, wearing a cap with an officer's insignia, he broke down and wept.

"I'm proud of you," he said, tears rolling down his cheeks. "You wouldn't have been a damn thing if it hadn't been for me."

And Arbor thought then, and for the rest of his life, "No, I probably would not have."[87]

CHAPTER 11

"HIS INTELLIGENCE AND JUDGMENT ARE EXCEPTIONAL."

James Forrestal, the undersecretary of the Navy, flicked a switch in his boss's office. The microphone came alive and carried his taut voice through the cavernous halls of the Navy's sprawling headquarters and the corridors of the annex across the Potomac.

His voice choked and cracked as he told thirty thousand Washington-based Navy employees, "The Navy has suffered a great loss."[1]

Frank Knox was dead.

The secretary suffered a massive heart attack on April 25, 1944, and died three days later, surrounded in his final moments by his wife and closest friends, including Assistant Secretary Ralph Bard.[2]

Funeral services were held at Mount Pleasant Congregational Church. His flag-draped casket was taken to Arlington National Cemetery, where a Navy chaplain read the committal service, a bluejacket detachment fired three volleys, a Navy bugler sounded taps, and Frank Knox was lowered into the ground.[3]

He had been appointed secretary of the Navy nearly four years before. He was an efficiency expert to whom the president entrusted the task of transforming a meager fleet into an armada that could defend the world from fascism. When Knox took over, in July 1940, the Navy had just 385 combat ships. At the time of his death, it had nearly 1,000. The Navy had

2,112 aircraft when Knox took office. When he died, it had 42,600 aircraft, of which more than 2,000 were tactical combat aircraft.[4]

President Roosevelt, a man who so treasured matching the right words to the right moment, could find few to express his grief to Frank's widow, Annie Reid Knox.

"It seems so futile for me to say anything at this moment except that I am sure you know that I am thinking of you and that you realize that in these four years I have come to have not only a deep respect for Frank's ability but also a great affection for him personally with a high appreciation of his outspoken honesty and underlying devotion to duty," wrote the president. "He has very literally given his life in the cause of his country."[5]

The flags of the ships of the United States, Great Britain, and Canada flew at half-mast. The Allies mourned.

Inside Camp Robert Smalls, the newly commissioned officers wondered whether the reality of black men wearing gold stripes had been just too much for Knox to bear. The news, they joked, must have literally killed him or at the very least hastened his demise.

"We had a little laugh about that," Sam Barnes admitted.[6]

Secretary Knox may have been gone, but the Navy's fear of black officers commanding white men in battle remained.

Sea duty was out of the question for the men of Barracks 202. For the time being, they had to remain in the United States, performing clerical duties and other menial jobs. If they were assigned to shore installations, they were to be sent in pairs, because the Navy reasoned that no white officer would speak to, or be seen with, them. Keeping the men in pairs would ensure they had a modicum of companionship; the policy lasted through the fall of 1944.[7]

But no one it seems had given serious thought to what assignments these black ensigns should be given.

Commander Armstrong offered one idea. He suggested that one of the new black officers be assigned public relations duties. It was a nod to John Sengstacke, who had visited Camp Robert Smalls just before the men received their commission. Sengstacke owned the largest chain of black newspapers in the country and had founded the National Newspaper

Publishers Association, which had been asking for some time for a black officer to be assigned to the Navy's bureau of public relations.[8]

Captain Leland Lovette embraced the proposal and told Knox, weeks before the secretary's death, that it would satisfy the demands of "the Negro press" for a "Negro public relations officer."[9]

Knox gave the green light, and Syl White was assigned the position on April 6, 1944, one week after he was commissioned. He worked at Great Lakes, where he functioned as a liaison to the black press, feeding reporters and editors story tips and ideas that put the Navy in the best possible light.

He traveled to New York City; New Orleans; Davenport, Iowa; Corpus Christi, Texas; and Norfolk, Virginia, promoting the contributions of black men, the segregated service schools, and the Great Lakes athletic teams.[10]

When he began, White's superiors complained that the black press seemed to cover only stories that made the Navy look bad.

"Do you ever offer them good stories?" White asked.

No, he was told, but no one was offered good stories, not the Jewish press, not the German press.

White called a few reporters working for large black newspapers and asked why the coverage appeared so negative.

We're busy, they said, and we assume if the Navy has a good story, it would be shared with the press. They weren't about to waste precious hours investigating stories that the Navy should by all rights be bragging about.

White solved the problem by providing a steady supply of copy that made the Navy look good, helped by a staff "that would make good reading out of stories that really weren't all that great."[11]

Captain M. Collins recognized that White, the only black officer assigned to the Ninth Naval District, "has been in an unusually difficult position," and Collins was impressed with how well White performed. "He has conducted himself very well and has been instrumental in improving the attitude of the negro press toward the Navy," Collins told his superiors.[12]

Those comments were typical of the performance reports the newly commissioned officers received wherever they went.

Ensign Sublett's "personal and military character is excellent."[13]

Ensign Arbor "exhibited good judgment, [with] a pleasing personality and ability to direct enlisted personnel."[14]

Ensign Cooper was "capable, conscientious and cooperative."[15]

The Navy's brain trust in Washington took notice. Black officers, it seemed, were no different than white officers, and their exemplary performance gave the Navy confidence to do more.

On May 15, 1944, Edward Swain Hope, a member of the Civil Engineer Corps, became the Navy's first black lieutenant. Nine other staff officers—chaplains, dentists, doctors—soon followed.[16]

Adlai Stevenson's vision was realized eight months after he first suggested to Knox that the Navy commission black men. The second round of black officers proved just as capable as the first batch, which meant the Navy was ready to take another baby step.

At the end of June, Dalton Baugh became the Navy's first black chief engineer when he was ordered to Boston and assigned to the USS *Migrant*, a schooner conducting antisubmarine patrols along the northern New England coast.

Phil Barnes, who was first assigned to work in the outgoing unit at Great Lakes, joined Baugh two weeks later.

Barnes had never been to sea, and this hampered his performance at first, but he made himself useful wherever he could. He helped in the commissary, which everyone was grateful for as the ship's experienced cook had just been reassigned, leaving in his stead a much younger cook whose organization, ability, and cuisine left much to be desired. Barnes proved a quick study and after only a few months was deemed a competent watch officer.

Jesse Arbor and Charles Lear were the first of the group to be sent outside the continental United States, arriving at the Manana Naval Barracks adjacent to the Pearl Harbor Navy Yard on July 29.

The officers who remained at Great Lakes—Sam Barnes, Reginald Goodwin, and Dennis Nelson—proved more than capable of handling the white petty officers and enlisted men who served under them.[17]

Goodwin returned to the selection office and performed so well that he was eventually placed in charge of it.[18] "His intelligence and judgment are exceptional, his personality and leadership outstanding," Commander William Turek wrote in Goodwin's performance report. "His military bearing, neatness and poise are evident to a high degree."[19]

Goodwin shared an apartment in Lake Forest with Sam Barnes, who was placed in charge of the recreation and athletic program for the three black camps: Camp Robert Smalls, Camp Moffett, and Camp Lawrence. The pair drove to base each day in Goodwin's 1941 Pontiac Coupe, not a bad way to get to work.

Barnes arranged the company competitions for softball and basketball, setting the schedule for the drill hall so that it was available for special events when needed. He created and administered a two-week course on venereal disease control. The Navy figured black sailors might heed warnings from an officer who looked like they did, an example of what would later be called cultural competency.[20] These were some of the most fun times Barnes had in the Navy, and for decades he kept a photo of himself drilling a field full of cadets.

Nelson was placed in charge of the remedial reading program at Camp Robert Smalls, where he helped formalize the curriculum. The program in 1942 had 200 students. By the summer of 1944, when Nelson was in charge, there were 1,400 enrollees at any given time.[21]

Nelson referred to himself as the "Dean of KU," for Knucklehead University.[22] Though he made light of his role, he took it extremely seriously and was a driving force behind the education of thousands of men who spent two hours a night, five nights a week, and two hours on Saturday afternoon learning to read and write.

Attending literacy classes was in addition to their regular drilling. The instructors were all volunteers. At the end of the six-week course, 72 percent of the men had attained a fourth-grade reading level.

More than just providing basic literacy, the coursework gave these sailors a heretofore unknown civic pride. Many registered and voted for the first time in their lives, using absentee ballots.[23]

Nelson, ever the peacock, drove to and from work each day in a blue Mercury convertible. He washed that car every morning and almost always had the top down, even in the winter. Shore patrol routinely chased Nelson around the base, reminding him that the speed limit was fifteen miles per hour.

"My car won't go that slow," Nelson replied.[24]

Unlike Sam Barnes, who enjoyed his new role, Nelson chafed under Armstrong, who he felt took every opportunity to "embarrass and belittle them before other officers and enlisted men."[25]

Barnes, who held Armstrong in higher regard, thought it ironic that Nelson felt that way because the two were so alike. Both were cocksure and so supremely confident in their own abilities that they were often unaware of how condescending they could seem to others.[26]

Nelson's gripes with the commander weren't all superficial or driven only by personality. Armstrong insisted on keeping the new ensigns out of the officers' club. He worried that a fight could break out and racial strife would diminish the likelihood that the Navy would commission other black officers.

Lieutenant Paul Richmond thought much the same. "For Pete's sake, you want to be successful," he said. "Now don't be bringing up a lot of things that would quash the program." His orders weren't explicit like Armstrong's, but he made it clear it "wouldn't be wise for them [to push for entry into officers' clubs] . . . foolish actually, because they would be jeopardizing the program."[27]

Nelson didn't buy that logic. Armstrong's order was a "disastrous blow to the group," because it further marginalized black officers, he said. "And the only opportunity for friendly contacts and to meet [white officers] on common ground was forbidden."[28]

Nelson's opinion of Armstrong wasn't unique among the first black officers, but it wasn't held unanimously either.

Syl White, Sam Barnes, and Goodwin all thought highly of Armstrong, whereas Arbor, Nelson, and Martin detested his attitude toward African Americans.

Armstrong's actions provided enough evidence for both sides to believe they had the correct view. He could glorify the contributions of African Americans and tout them as inspiring role models, while simultaneously justifying segregation and exclusion.

The very same month that he insisted the officers' club remain for whites only, he commissioned twelve large paintings depicting the history of African Americans in the Navy, and ordered them displayed in the lounge of the Camp Robert Smalls recreation building. One showed Scipio and Cato, two black men who fought in the Revolutionary War battle between the *Bonhomme Richard* and a British frigate, the *Serapis*. Other paintings portrayed the Battle of Lake Erie, Robert Smalls, and Dorie Miller.[29]

But all those men were dead. The living heroes, right there in Camp Robert Smalls, were shown little respect. The new ensigns were designated "Deck Officers Limited—Only," which was typically for officers who were physically unfit or lacked requisite education. Of course, none of these men met that definition. They were standout athletes, and many had advanced degrees. There was only one reason to give that label, and it was painfully obvious to them—and to everyone else—what that was.[30]

It would take several months before these ensigns were allowed to be officer of the day, which meant they were temporarily in charge of the camp—a standard task for commissioned men. Instead, the black officers were first assigned junior officer status and trailed behind a white officer. It was demeaning to the black ensigns and deflating to black enlisted men, who saw that the first officers who looked like them still had to play the lackey.

Nelson remained bitter for years over that treatment, which "left Negro officers in inferior positions which produced in the minds of Negro enlisted personnel a lack of confidence to follow such leadership." He and his peers knew their abilities were being wasted "or dissipated under a continued plan where color and race determined assignments, rank and responsibility."[31]

Many white sailors at Great Lakes—either because of their own prejudice or because they felt Armstrong did not have the new officers' backs—were publicly dismissive and openly insubordinate toward the new black officers.

White sailors would cross the street to avoid having to salute black officers. Baugh at first ignored the insult even as it ate him up inside. After a while, he made a little game out of it. He'd cross the street, too, just to catch them.[32]

Off base, the treatment was often even more hostile.

Shortly after receiving his commission, Graham Martin and his wife, Alma, dined at a fancy Chicago restaurant, excited to share a romantic dinner. When Martin walked through the door in his dress blue officer's uniform, patrons and staff stopped what they were doing and stared.

No one said anything, though, and the couple took their seats. They both ordered the stuffed bell peppers and enjoyed their evening—until they got home. For the next twelve hours, the two took turns in the bathroom. Someone in the restaurant's kitchen had put a laxative in their meal. Martin suspected croton oil. Years later, he joked that he would have sued but he flushed the evidence.[33]

Nelson told a tale of a meal he ate at the Palmer House, a posh Chicago hotel, shortly after he was commissioned. After his plate had been cleared, he pulled out a cigar and asked a wealthy-looking white woman at the next table whether she minded if he smoked.

"I don't give a damn if you burn," she said.[34]

It was a very different story in the black communities of Chicago and Milwaukee. In those sections of town, these officers were heroes, celebrities who could do no wrong and would pay for no drinks.

When Lena Horne, the famed singer and actress, performed for the troops in the spring of 1944, Ensign Sam Barnes had the privilege of planning the logistics of her visit and catering to her needs.[35]

A young enlisted sailor, a white man named Ted Sherman, who was only a few months out of boot camp, remembered escorting Horne and a quartet of musicians to the auditorium at Great Lakes so they could rehearse. He asked if she had any requests.

Just one, she said. The first three rows, normally reserved for top officials, were to be assigned to black sailors.

Sherman didn't know what to do. Black sailors had to sit in the balcony. He went to find his superior officer. Horne insisted, telling the commandant that "if discrimination enters the picture, then we don't appear." The Navy gave in. Black men would sit up front.[36]

Horne sang a host of hits that night, including "Stormy Weather," "The Lady Is a Tramp," "Honeysuckle Rose," and "Someone to Watch over Me," all to loud applause. But the loudest applause all evening, the loudest applause Horne said she had ever heard, came when she walked to the stage on the arm of Ensign Reginald Ernest Goodwin, a black officer in the United States Navy.[37]

———

George Cooper, John Reagan, and Frank Sublett were sent back to Hampton, where they resumed their friendship with Commander Edwin Hall Downes. Downes refused to tolerate any act of racism or condone any condescension; anyone who violated those tenets could expect a transfer order. The commander could enforce his rules, even with higher-ranking officers, because Washington felt so indebted to Downes for running a topnotch segregated training school. Navy bureaucrats in Washington assumed—as they had with Armstrong—that this was all due to Downes's talents instead of to the simple truth that black men were every bit as a capable as white men.

It also helped that Downes was a savvy politician who knew which wheels needed greasing and how best to grease them. He had Joe Gilliard, who worked in Hampton Institute's art department, make beautiful pieces of copper and brass so the commander always had a small gift for whichever high-ranking official he visited. The pieces weren't much more than trinkets such as candlesticks, lamps, or small coal scuttles, but they were useful for winning friends in high places.

So when Downes needed to take a stand, he could be reasonably certain he would not be overruled. And that stand, more often than not, was in the service of protecting the black officers and enlisted men under his watch.

Shortly after arriving back at Hampton, Cooper was ordered to pick up a captain at the airport.

The captain gazed warily at Cooper, a black man wearing an officer's uniform, and asked where he'd be sleeping that night.

Bachelor officer quarters, Cooper said.

"Where do you stay?" the captain wanted to know.

"I live in an apartment, sir."

"Good. But before I go to bed, I want to see the skipper."

"Sir, you can't see the skipper tonight," Cooper said. "You can see the skipper at quarters tomorrow, because I'm not going to call him tonight."

"Well, I've got a problem," the captain said.

"Can I help you with the problem?"

"You are the problem."

"There's nothing I can do about it then," Cooper said. "I'm not going to call the skipper tonight, and you'll have to, sir, see him at quarters the next morning."

By the time Cooper arrived at Downes's office the next morning, the captain had come and gone.

Downes called all his staff—white and black—together and addressed the men.

"We had a new officer come in last night," Downes said. "George met him, and he came in this morning early to see me. He told me that if he had known there was a colored officer on this base, he would have asked not to be sent here, because he never wanted to see another nigger as long as he lived."

Downes took a breath.

"I've been in touch with [the Bureau of Naval Personnel], and he won't stay here," he continued. "We're going to ship him out. He's going to Alaska."

Three weeks later, Downes came to see Cooper.

"You remember that captain who came in here and said he never wanted to see another nigger?" Downes asked

Yes, Cooper remembered.

"We sent him up to Alaska and he never saw one, because he died yesterday."[38]

Downes, though, could only do so much to protect his men. Many members of ship's company at Hampton refused to salute Reagan, Sublett, and Cooper, or they'd cross the street to avoid them.

Sublett had a live-and-let-live attitude about the whole affair.

"If he saluted, okay. If he didn't, okay," Sublett explained. "I was wearing a United States uniform. That was due the respect. . . . If they chose to respect that, fine. And if they didn't, they didn't."[39]

It wasn't easy for everyone to be so magnanimous, though they knew it was part of their duty—to the Navy and to each other. Officer training was only their first test. The black officers were under the microscope now, and they understood that whatever progress the Navy made in 1944 was tenuous. All could be stalled or reversed if anyone gave the Navy even the slightest reason to suspect that black officers were less than perfect. This group carried a responsibility to ensure they were the first, not the last.

They were expected to be little wooden soldiers, Hair said.[40]

There were close calls, times when the disrespect and dehumanization pushed them to the brink, but no one ever saw these thirteen men crack.

Once, when Cooper and his wife, Peg, were walking with their baby girl in Newport News, just outside of Hampton, a white sailor got right up in Cooper's face and yelled, "You black son of a bitch, I read about you guys, but I never thought I'd meet one."

Cooper, the hell-raiser Armstrong worried about, was ready to fight and cocked his fist.

Peg, the woman who had told her husband he'd absolutely become an officer, grabbed his arm. It's not worth it, she whispered.

"Peg, you're right," he said. "Thank you."[41]

It may have seemed to the first black officers, so often the subject of scorn and epithets, that racial progress in the latter half of 1944 was proceeding at a snail's pace—if at all. But what they couldn't see and could have no way of knowing was that a revolution was taking place in Washington, emanating from the very office that had done so much to inhibit black ambition.

James Forrestal, the new Navy secretary, felt the branch had for too long been too slow to take advantage of all the talent and effort African Americans could offer. A wealthy Wall Street executive and longtime member of the National Urban League, Forrestal had a far more progressive take on racial issues than Knox. "Bigotry damages the spirit of the bigot more than it injures the object," he once said at a National Urban League dinner.[42]

Forrestal thought democratizing the Navy amounted to a great "challenge to the white people and to the colored people" and told President

Roosevelt that segregation was inefficient and bad for morale, that "Negroes resent the fact that they are not assigned to general service billets at sea, and white personnel resent the fact that Negroes have been given less hazardous assignments."[43]

He proposed using black men on large auxiliaries, the vessels that bring fuel, food, and other supplies to ships at sea. He told the president that black sailors would make up no more than 10 percent of the ship's crew. If this worked without too much trouble, black men could be sent to other types of ships "as necessity indicates."

Forrestal received a two-word response: "OK, FDR."[44]

Like Knox, Forrestal wanted support from the admirals. Unlike Knox, he took the initiative.

The new secretary met with Admiral Ernest King and said he remained unsatisfied with how the Navy was using black men.

"I don't think that our Navy Negro personnel are getting a square break," Forrestal said. "I want to do something about it, but I can't do anything about it unless the officers are with me. I want your help. What do you say?"

King sat for a moment, looking out the office window.

"You know, we say that we are a democracy and a democracy ought to have a democratic armed services," he said. "It certainly ought to have a democratic Navy. I don't think you can do it, but if you want to try, I'm behind you all the way."[45]

Admiral Jacobs told the commanding officers of twenty-five large fleet auxiliaries that black men would soon make up as much as 10 percent of the ship's general-service ratings. Of that cohort, about 15 percent would be petty officers third class taken from shore installations around the country. The remaining men would come from Class A schools and boot camp.

"Inasmuch as the assignment of Negroes to duty aboard ship has been limited to the steward and commissary branches, the present plan is somewhat experimental in nature in that no recent past experience is available from which to draw conclusions and to establish policies," Jacobs wrote the commanders of the chosen ships. "Commanding officers are cautioned to check closely to assure that Negroes are given the same consideration in duty assignment, and are accorded the same opportunities for training and advancement in rating as are others. . . . It may be helpful to point out . . . that past experience has proven the desirability of thoroughly indoctrinating white personnel prior to the arrival of the Negroes. It has been the experience that when this is done and the whites thoroughly understand the commanding officer's policy, and what is expected of them, the chance of racial friction is materially lessened."[46]

A few months later, the Bureau of Naval Personnel asked the skippers how this experiment was going.

Captain Robert Barber Twining, of the USS *Antaeus*, said that black men were berthed indiscriminately, same as whites, and that "the assimilation of the general service Negro personnel aboard this ship has been remarkably successful."[47]

Forrestal had predicted as much, but word from the fleet convinced King that the experiment could proceed, and he approved a plan to integrate all auxiliary ships.

King sent a missive to the entire Navy in which he stated that mistreatment of African Americans would not be tolerated. "It is expected of each officer assigned to the command of Negro personnel that personal attitudes inimical to the best interests of the naval service be completely suppressed."[48]

He pushed officers to have Class A graduates assigned appropriate duties. "It will be readily understood the value of training programs set up by the Bureau will be lost if individual commands are not careful to see that graduates of the training schools are placed in jobs which will enable them to use the training they have received," King wrote.[49]

Forrestal also wanted to integrate the WAVES. Knox had told Captain Mildred McAfee, director of the WAVES program, that blacks would be in the WAVES over his dead body, which turned out to be morbidly prescient.

Forrestal had no objections to integrating the WAVES, but on this point the president demurred—at least at first. Election-year politics once again forced Roosevelt to pay attention to African American demands. The 1944 Republican nominee, Thomas Dewey, had been courting the black vote since his run for governor of New York in 1942. He had been an early supporter of the *Courier's* Double V campaign. Now he was accusing the president of discriminating against black women.

Roosevelt, one month before the election, told Forrestal to go ahead and integrate the WAVES.[50]

⸺⸺⸺

Shortly after Roosevelt secured a fourth term, Walter White, executive secretary of the NAACP, visited the Pacific theater on a mission to boost morale and address grievances. Armstrong was detached from Great Lakes and assigned to act as White's guide.

At Pearl Harbor, White met with the commander of the Pacific Fleet, Admiral Chester Nimitz, who had been one of the more vocal proponents of segregation, and discovered that the Texan now held a more enlightened point of view.

An attack cargo ship manned by a mixed-race crew arrived shortly after White. Nimitz called the captain and White to his office. White arrived to find the captain and his first officer waiting nervously in the anteroom, uncertain of what to expect. Nimitz beckoned them inside and asked how integration was going.

The captain, perhaps thinking of Nimitz's Southern upbringing, said that even though the sleeping quarters were integrated the black sailors were at one end of the room.

"That's bad, Captain," Nimitz said. "If you put all the Negroes together they'll have a chance to share grievances and to plot among themselves, and this will damage discipline and morale. If they are distributed among other members of the crew, there will be less chance of trouble. And when we say we want integration, we *mean integration!*"[51]

The next day the segregated sections were gone.

With Armstrong no longer at Great Lakes, Nelson and Goodwin asked his successor and former aide, Lieutenant Commander Vance Kauffold, if they could revisit the rule prohibiting them from the officers' club. Armstrong had said the orders had come from above, so they were hoping Kauffold would intercede on their behalf. Kauffold took the request to Commodore Robert R. M. Emmet, who said he had never been aware of Armstrong's policy and had certainly given no order of that kind.

Emmet, who twelve years earlier railed against the idea of opening up the messman branch to black men saying then that Filipinos were "cleaner" and "more efficient," now said black officers should avail themselves of any and all club facilities and if anyone had a problem with it, he would deal with it personally.[52]

Goodwin got his privilege and then never used it. He didn't want the club. He wanted the equality. Like Nelson, Goodwin understood that his officer status came with a responsibility to make life just a little easier for the men coming up behind him. He argued for the Navy to change its tone when recruiting black men. Recruiters, he said, were painting too rosy a picture. They focused on the glory of fighting on the high seas and the $50 monthly paycheck and glossed over all the hard work, drilling, and dangerous labor. When the rhetoric didn't match the reality, black men were disillusioned, leading to a drop in morale. Goodwin said potential enlistees should be told they would be seamen second class in eight or nine months, that their jobs would be hard, and that many of them would handle ammunition. The Navy also had to be better at "internal public relations," Goodwin said, so that African American sailors knew their opportunities.[53]

The Navy was thinking along the same lines. Black sailors in the Pacific would soon benefit from seeing black officers.

CHAPTER 12

"YOU FORGET THE COLOR AND YOU REMEMBER THE RANK."

Jesse Arbor and Charles Lear arrived in Guam in February 1945, the first African American naval officers to reach the central Pacific.

The marines stationed in Guam had a reputation for violence toward black sailors. Only three months before, a race riot nearly broke out on the island when, according to an Army orderly, "some Navy niggers got uppity."

Walter White visited Guam two days after Christmas, 1944, as a war correspondent and was struck by the casual racism he encountered. On account of his light skin, most soldiers and marines assumed he was white and certainly would not have guessed they were telling the executive secretary of the NAACP that "niggers [were] raising hell."

Guam, at the time, was a key supply base and home to Marines training for the invasion of Iwo Jima. The jungles had been cleared and in their place came roads, bridges, and airfields that could accommodate the heavy B-29 bombers that would lay waste to Japanese cities. Most of this construction was handled by black sailors, who worked twelve hours a day, seven days a week under a sun so hot "it made the earth seem like a hamburger grill."

As the black soldiers toiled, Marines routinely threw stones and empty beer bottles at them while screaming "niggers," and "black sons of bitches." Two hand grenades were hurled into the black camp.

When black men complained to their superior officers, they were ignored. On Christmas Day, a white Marine shot and killed a black sailor, and a second black sailor was shot and critically wounded by a white sailor.[1]

This was Guam in early 1945.

On the night Arbor arrived, he and Ensign Joe Hise, a Jewish sailor from Rome, Georgia, decided to avail themselves of the officers' club.

Hise was tickled by the prospect. "Man, this is going to be a party in itself," he said.

"What's that, Joe?" Arbor asked.

"A black and a Jew going to the officers' club," Hise said. "Neither one of us is wanted."

"To hell with what they want now," Arbor said. "The war is on now. I didn't ask to come over here. You give me a damn ticket, and I'll leave here tomorrow. I didn't come over here to stay. I came over here to do a job."

Arbor was enjoying the officers' club when a Marine called him over.

"What the hell has this world come to now?" the Marine asked. "After a while, they'll have [black] marine officers."

The Marine took a shot of whiskey. Arbor poured himself a shot, too, and said he was every bit a man as anyone else.

"I don't mean no harm," the Marine replied.

"That's all right," Arbor said.

He poured another shot, threw it back, and walked off.

The next morning the Marine apologized.

Arbor was congenial, saying he hoped to see him after the war. What he thought but dared not say was that he hoped to see the Marine after the war to find out if he had learned any sense.[2]

What Arbor learned later was that his arrival had been preceded by a letter from Lieutenant Commander S. B. McCune in which McCune had warned other officers against showing any kind of discrimination toward black officers.

Walter White had taken his complaints to Forrestal, and the Navy responded by trying to protect the black officers it was sending to Guam.

"There are now attached to this depot two Negro officers," McCune said, referring to Arbor and Lear. "Their services are sorely needed by the naval supply depot, and they were therefore requested by the supply officer in command. These officers are to be given the same respect as any other officer in the U.S. Navy. They will be quartered and messed in regular quarters and mess halls in this depot. No discrimination of any kind will be shown these officers, and they will be treated equally with all other officers. Any officer violating this order will be sternly dealt with."[3]

So Arbor and Lear were for the most part left alone, mere curiosities to most officers, many of whom had never seen a well-educated black man.

Others weren't as fortunate.

Sam Barnes landed in Okinawa in June 1945, commanding a 120-man logistics company preparing for the invasion of Japan. By then, there were nearly 60 black officers in the Navy—staff officers in various bureaus and V-12 graduates.

Most, like Barnes, were sent overseas attached to logistical support and advanced base companies, supervising stevedore work at Pearl Harbor, Eniwetok, Saipan, the Philippines, Kwajalein, and Okinawa.

Barnes had the night shift, overseeing men as they unloaded cargo from ships from 10 p.m. until 7 a.m. the next morning. His crew, which later received a citation for effectiveness, would take the cargo from ships and place it onto trucks, then drive the cargo to another supply base on the island, where another company would unpack the crates and boxes.

It was hard labor, made no easier by the fact that by the time Barnes finished his shift and got a bite to eat, the morning heat was so oppressive that he could hardly sleep.

The subtropical climate contrasted with the ice-cold reception Barnes, the only black officer on the island, received from his fellow officers.

His only friend was Lieutenant (junior grade) Steve Belichick. Barnes and Belichick had met years earlier when Barnes played football for Oberlin and Belichick, who later coached at the Naval Academy and whose son Bill would become one of the most revered and reviled coaches in the NFL, played for Western Reserve.

The first time Barnes entered the officers' club in Okinawa, every officer except Belichick walked out.

Two men—one black, one white—and a bartender stood amid the awkward silence.

"Well, Steve," Barnes said, almost apologetically.

"Hell, Sam, don't even worry about it," Belichick said. "Let's enjoy having the club to ourselves."[4]

That scene played out again and again until the white officers grew tired of abandoning the club and decided to stay, despite the presence of a black man.

There were no incidents. Barnes had little more interest in knowing them than they had in knowing him, and that's how the Okinawa officers' club was integrated.

Barnes, like his peers, knew he must keep his cool in the face of discrimination, but he also demanded respect, not just for his own sake but for the Navy's.

Barnes and a Marine he knew from Cincinnati were once in a jeep, stopped at an exit post in front of a petty officer third class who refused to salute.

"Sailor, did you forget something?" Barnes asked

"No."

"No, what?"

"No, sir."

"Let me remind you of something you already know," Barnes said. "You see this eagle on my cap? You see this bar on my jacket?"

"Yes, sir."

"You're not saluting me," Barnes said. "You're saluting that emblem of rank. Hereafter, you forget the color and you remember the rank. You forget everything except that in the future. And whenever you see one, you salute this. You don't have to salute me as a person, but you salute that insignia as long as I have it on. I'm going to put you on report."

"Oh, don't do that," the sailor said.

"I certainly am," Barnes said. "This is not Navy regulations, and you know it, and I know it. You're not saluting me because I'm colored, but that has nothing to do with Navy regulations. Maybe you ought to go back and read your *Bluejacket's Manual*."[5]

―――――――

Graham Martin, after he was commissioned, was a battalion commander at Great Lakes. He wanted to be aboard a ship but instead found himself running men through drills. He knew in his bones he had this assign-ment because the Navy could not stomach the thought of black officers commanding white men at sea. Reagan and Sublett were given similar make-work jobs at Hampton. Reagan was first made an officer in charge of the electrical school. He'd give a lecture and check in on how men were performing. Sublett instructed a company in small boat handling, sea-manship, and military bearing before being sent back to Great Lakes to lecture on venereal disease.

Fortunately for the three officers, these assignments lasted only about a month. In July, Martin and Sublett were sent to San Francisco and given command of the *YP-131*, a converted yacht assigned to patrol the waters off the California coast. Sublett was the skipper. Martin was second in command.

It still felt like busywork, the kind of job that probably did not require one officer, let alone two. "What the heck am I doing?" Martin thought.[6] But remembering those Hoosier lessons Principal Lane had taught him all those years ago, Martin thought he had best complete these orders as well as he knew how. He was part of a team, and his job was to execute the play to the best of his ability—"because if I don't," he thought, "that will give them something to talk about."

Coast patrol may not have been the flashiest assignment, but it wasn't all bad. San Francisco was a hospitable town, and Navy nurses were always clamoring for tours of San Francisco Bay or an up-close look at Alcatraz.[7]

Dealing with bigotry was just part of a day's work, and Martin, like his shipmate Sublett, mostly ignored the white men who crossed the street to the other side or pretended they did not see him in order to avoid saluting. But like George Cooper and Sam Barnes, Martin had a breaking point.

On base at Treasure Island, which is connected to San Francisco by a bridge that spans the bay, a white sailor walked right by Martin as if he did not exist.

"Hey, sailor. Would you come back here, please?"

The sailor turned around, stared at Martin, and walked toward him.

"Are you supposed to salute officers?" Martin asked.

"Yes, sir."

"Well, you didn't salute me."

"No, sir."

"What's the matter? Why didn't you?"

The sailor didn't say a word.

"Oh, I see what it is," Martin said, removing his cap and holding it in front of the sailor's face.

"Now salute the insignia of the United States Navy."

The sailor snapped his hand to his cap and said, "But you understand that I'm not saluting you."

"I understand, but you understand that you're supposed to salute this insignia."[8]

Martin worked yard patrol for nine months. In the spring of 1945 he was placed in charge of the *YO-106*, a yard oiler. It was his first assignment with a mixed-race crew and was a far more challenging detail than any of his previous tasks. His job was to take oil from a refinery off the coast of San Francisco, pull up alongside battleships, aircraft carriers, cruisers, and destroyers and refuel them, day and night.[9] Oilers required skilled officers to help handle the ship in the currents and waves as the ship pulled alongside much larger vessels.

Martin received a commendation for his quick thinking after one incident when a cruiser lurched as it was being filled with oil. The hose snapped and oil shot up in the air like a geyser in the Pacific. Martin was on the bridge at the time and cut off the oil flow in seconds.[10]

Commendations from ashore were nice, but what Martin cherished was the respect he earned at sea. The plan for the oiler when Martin came aboard was to gradually replace the white crew with black sailors, but a white engineer said he had no desire to leave. He liked the crew and he liked the skipper. Could he stay?[11]

On June 7, after only a couple months on the oiler, Martin went ashore for the evening and left a warrant officer in charge of the ship.

"If a fueling order comes in after dark, give me a call," Martin told him. An order came in, and the warrant officer thought he'd try to make the run himself but hit the *YO-106* against the dock. To the Navy, the accident was Martin's fault. If he hadn't thought the warrant officer could handle the assignment, he never should have left him in charge. A letter of admonition was attached to his file, citing his "lack of proper appreciation of his duties and responsibilities."[12]

The next week, Captain Roscoe H. Hillenkoetter ordered Martin to Hollywood for a five-day assignment to participate in a propaganda film. Hillenkoetter, who would later become the first director of the CIA, was in charge of the Committee on Negro Personnel, which Forrestal had created "to assure uniform policies" across the Navy with regard to its treatment of black sailors.

Among the efforts that emerged from his committee was a propaganda film entitled *The Negro Sailor*, which tells the story of Bill Johnson, a black man in the Navy. Production was supervised by Frank Capra, who directed *Mr. Smith Goes to Washington*, among other classics.

The theme of the film is cooperation regardless of race, and Martin appears for a few moments as the skipper of an oiler. Ironically, one of the Navy's first black officers appears in a film that stresses the value of the messman branch, now called the steward's branch. Johnson is informed that stewards are every bit as important as any other member of "the team" and no black man should see that branch as mere cooks or waiters, because they may be called on to fight if the ship comes under attack. "They may pour soup between battles but in battle they pour lead with the best of them."[13]

———

Off the Atlantic coast, John Reagan and James Hair were assigned to operate a large harbor tugboat, the *YTB-215*, responsible for the waters near Connecticut, down almost to Cape May, and all around New York Harbor.[14] They were stationed in Tompkinsville, Staten Island, and their tug worked around the Ambrose Channel, the only shipping channel in and out of the Port of New York and New Jersey. Reagan and Hair helped with docking and undocking larger ships, breaking up ice floes on the Hudson River, and putting out fires on ammunition piers in New Jersey.[15]

It wasn't long before Hair had a chance to prove his worth. In September, a powerful hurricane moved up the East Coast, and the tugboat was ordered to help a distressed ship. Visibility was less than five feet and the waves were crashing over the sides. For the first time since he had enlisted, Hair feared for his life. One of the crew, a fellow everyone called Shorty, came up to the pilothouse wearing just about every life jacket he could fit on his body.

"What in the hell are you doing," Hair screamed. "What kind of damn sailor are you? Get those damn jackets off! Get 'em off!"

Shorty ripped off those jackets as fast as he could.

Hair suspected that everyone in the crew was just about as frightened as Shorty, and with good reason. He needed to demonstrate that there was nothing to fear. If the skipper wasn't scared, then they had no reason to be. He put on a brave face for his crew, but as Shorty scampered off, Hair thought to himself he sure would like to grab a bunch of those life-jackets, before steeling himself and skillfully steering the ship to safety.[16]

Captain John M. Gill, the gruff but fair base commander on Staten Island, said that Hair was the kind of sailor who'd succeed no matter what color he was: "He seems to have that little extra something that makes him click in whatever he does."[17]

The assignment allowed Reagan and Hair to spend their spare time in New York City, a sailor's dream, for that was the "best liberty town in the world."[18] The two hung around the Hotel Theresa, known as the Waldorf of Harlem, where sailors and soldiers mingled with celebrities such as Sugar Ray Robinson and Joe Louis, the heavyweight champion. It was the perfect place to get a drink or meet a girl. One evening Hair asked a beautiful young woman to join him for dinner that night. She accepted his invitation, but when he returned to the hotel to pick her up, he ran into Joe Louis, who was there to pick up the exact same woman.

Hair figured he'd win the young lady's favor by showing he was as tough as any boxer.

"You're not taking her out. She's my date. I'm taking her out," Hair told Louis.

"No, you're not." Louis said.

Hair pulled off his jacket and challenged Louis to a fight, right there in the hotel lounge. He guessed there was no way Louis would actually hit him, and he thought the gesture would impress the girl.

It was brave. It was valiant. It was stupid.

She was not impressed. She left Hair standing in the lobby holding his jacket and the prizefighter walked out with his prize.[19]

The Hotel Theresa was also where Reagan came to realize that one of the greatest disappointments in his young life was really one of his luckiest breaks. Among the regular guests at the hotel were members of the Ninety-ninth Pursuit Squadron, the famed Tuskegee Airmen, the unit that Reagan had so longed to join when he dropped out of college in Montana after the attack on Pearl Harbor.

Many were broken men now, missing legs or arms. Many more had been lost forever.

"Maybe it was for the best," Reagan thought.[20]

It was during these months that Reagan earned the dubious distinction of being the only member of the first group of black officers to lose men under his command. Hair wasn't aboard, and Reagan was in command as the crew helped a loaded tank landing ship pull away from the dock at an ammunition pier in Bayonne, New Jersey. The tug was on the LST's starboard side, and Reagan wanted to speed around to the port side. The current was stronger than anyone realized, and as they were swinging around at full speed, the tugboat tipped just enough for three sailors to fall overboard. Only one survived.

"That was the worst thing that personally has ever happened with me in the Navy," Reagan later said.[21]

It was on this tug, in May 1945, that Hair caught the attention of Lieutenant Commander Norman Meyer, the skipper aboard the USS *Mason*, the ship that Arbor and Reagan had been so excited to join before being diverted to officer candidate school. The destroyer escort was making its way toward the Earle ammunition depot at Sandy Hook, New Jersey, not too far from New York City, and Hair's tug was helping the *Mason* dock. Meyer couldn't believe how good that tug looked. The brass on its rails sparkled, the maneuvering was flawless. "Who is in charge of that ship?" Meyer wanted to know.

Meyer invited Hair to lunch aboard the *Mason*, quite an honor. Senior officers rarely requested the presence of junior officers, certainly not black junior officers.

When Hair boarded the ship Meyer greeted him while holding a copy of Gunnar Myrdal's *An American Dilemma*, which had been published the year before and was already considered a seminal work on race relations in the United States. Myrdal's central argument was that white Americans were free to choose whether black men and women would be their liability or their opportunity, a theme Meyer was mulling over when he first met Hair.

The two officers spent the next forty-five minutes discussing race relations, Myrdal's book, and the war's effect on black men.

Meyer was impressed and the next day called Commander Eddie Fahy, a detailer in the Bureau of Naval Personnel. He asked for Hair to come aboard the USS *Mason* as the first lieutenant.

Meyer, a Naval Academy graduate from Minnesota, had recently replaced the *Mason*'s first skipper, Lieutenant Commander William "Big Bill" Blackford.

Before taking over command of the ship he had been warned that the *Mason*, on account of its black crew, was a disgrace, one of Eleanor Roosevelt's flights of fancy. If he took this assignment, his friends said, his reputation would be ruined.

"My reputation is back at a factory in New Jersey," he told them. "I'm just trying to get this war over with, and that's my aim in life—to get back to my wife and a baby I hardly know."[22]

Meyer was Christian, but because of his last name was occasionally the target of anti-Semitic attacks. He had Jewish classmates he knew to be as bright and talented as anyone else, and his sympathies for minority groups were stirred.

He didn't think he was prejudiced against African Americans, and he had attended an integrated high school, but he knew he had lived a segregated life. Perhaps because of the Navy's presumptions about black men or perhaps because Meyer harbored more bigotry than he cared to admit, he came aboard and almost immediately decided that the ship and crew were in bad shape. Meyer let it be known that he thought little of Blackford, who was beloved by the crew. Morale on the vessel tanked.

Perhaps, he thought, Hair could help.

"If the enlisted men had some doubts about this honky Meyer, he [Hair] could tell them I was sincere," Meyer later recalled.[23]

Hair, the only black officer aboard, was placed in charge of all deck operations and the topside appearance of the ship. He made sure that everything on deck was spotless—the boats, the hatches, portholes, rigging, and anchors.[24]

By the time Hair arrived, the war in Europe was over and the crew figured they'd soon head to the Pacific to help with the invasion of Japan. Those orders never came. Instead, they tested depth charges that would be set off at the sound of a submarine's propellers. It was dangerous work. One misstep and the crew could blow up the ship.[25]

The crew dropped nearly 200 of these depth charges off the coast of Atlantic City, killing thousands of fish but bringing no harm to ship or crew. The next day they dropped 225 mark-14 depth charges. These caused some superficial damage to the ship but nothing too serious. The USS *Mason*, "Eleanor's folly," earned a commendation.

———

The stories of the *Mason* were told in the pages of the black press, which was now filled with positive news about the Navy, thanks in no small part to Syl White's work in the press shop.

White, who had been promoted to lieutenant (junior grade) in July, did his job so well that by the end of August 1945, Rear Admiral Harold B. Miller, the Navy's director of public information, requested that White be transferred to Washington to work in the Navy Department. White needed to be in the nation's capital by September 20 because the Navy already had a special assignment in mind for him: he was to travel alongside Lester Granger, executive secretary of the National Urban League, who was leaving for an inspection tour of overseas naval bases on September 25.

It was Granger's second tour. Secretary Forrestal, who had been a classmate of Granger's older brother at Dartmouth, had asked Granger to help improve morale among black sailors and try to ease some of the racial tensions.

"I want you to report everything you find that is not right," Forrestal told him. "I ask only one thing of you—if you find anything that's wrong you report it to us and give us a chance to handle it, before you go to the public. But if in the end you're not satisfied with the way in which the Navy has handled it, you can relieve yourself of your Navy connections and say anything you want."[26]

Granger had become Forrestal's personal representative and during the summer of 1945 had toured shore installations to assess how integration was progressing.[27]

The "Navy is so far out in front of the Army it isn't funny," Granger said during a press conference on July 21, 1945, following his first tour. "The Navy is now doing things which the Army insists would be bad for morale."

At the time of Granger's press conference black men were still not allowed to be aviation pilots or to serve in combat posts in submarines. Some barracks remained segregated but at mess halls and on recreation fields the color line was gone.

"I don't think any of us is prepared to give the Navy a blank check of confidence," Granger said. "But any reasonable person who has been around the country must give it credit for not being the same Navy so far as the Negro is concerned."[28]

The second trip would be overseas, and White's role was press officer. They visited nine naval bases during their thirty-one-day trip. They began in San Francisco, meeting with the commandant of the Twelfth Naval District. Then they traveled to Manus Island, Espiritu Santo, Guam, Saipan, Okinawa, Nansei, Iwo Jima, and the Philippines.

It was a bit of reunion tour for White. In Saipan he saw Reginald Goodwin and Phil Barnes. And at Eniwetok, "a little godforsaken stretch of sand less than a mile and a half long and a quarter-mile wide," he saw Martin, Sublett, and Nelson, all members of Logistics Support Company 515.[29]

The base at Eniwetok hosted five thousand men who had been preparing for the invasion of Japan. The officer in charge was Lieutenant (junior grade) George Reed, a Pennsylvanian. Sublett was his executive officer, Nelson was the personnel officer, and Martin was the athletic officer.[30]

There wasn't much to do on the base. Martin, when he wasn't supervising men loading and unloading cargo ships, spent most of his time in the surf gathering seashells.[31]

Nelson, who couldn't stand to be idle and needed to be the best at something, boasted to anyone who cared to listen that he had the best seashell collection of any man on the island.

The peacock had arrived a few months before, after having finally worn out his welcome at Great Lakes. The final straw occurred on a very cold morning with the wind whipping off Lake Michigan. Nelson, driving his blue Mercury convertible and looking as dapper as ever, spotted an attractive young white woman walking alone on the main road and stopped to offer her a ride.

It was Mrs. Gumz, the wife of Commander Donald G. Gumz, who was a bomber pilot serving in the Pacific.

Per usual, the top was down, so everyone saw a handsome black officer giving the commander's wife a ride. Shortly after, Nelson was shipped out to Kwajalein. He turned right around and wrote the staff at Great Lakes a nice letter, thanking them for sending him to such a lovely part of the Marshall Islands.

Sublett found his time on the island depressing. He wanted to be aboard a ship. What was the point of being commissioned if he couldn't see some action? But the opportunity never came, and Sublett resented his token status for the rest of his life, feeling he had been denied the opportunity to prove his worth in battle.[32]

Granger's second report was less positive. He found that the farther you got from Washington, DC, the less impact Secretary Forrestal's words had, and the farther down the ranks of command the policy descended the less likely it was to be enforced.[33] He told Forrestal that while progress had been made, the Navy was not where it needed to be.

"The final answer to a Democratic and completely efficient Navy," Granger said, "is going to be found in the abolition of all types of segregation."[34]

White performed admirably during the trip, and Rear Admiral Miller, in charge of assigning photographers and correspondents to battlefronts, said White "has at all times been a credit to his race and the Navy. He has handled his assignments with tact, foresight and sound judgement. It can be said he contributed in large portion to a better understanding between the Navy and the Negro public."[35]

Miller recommended to White that he meet with William Hastie, who was in line to be the next governor of the US Virgin Islands. Hastie's appointment would entitle him to a naval aide, and if White was selected, he'd earn a promotion to lieutenant commander.

White liked the idea, but Hastie did not.

"If I do have a naval aide the one thing I don't need is another lawyer," Hastie told White. "So I wouldn't be interested in appointing you to the task."

That conversation effectively ended White's service, as he decided to return to his job at the US attorney's office.[36]

———

With the war now over, the hustle and bustle that defined Camp Robert Smalls slowed. Fewer than 2,000 black men remained at Great Lakes, down from the 13,550 who had been training there fifteen months earlier.

Black men had performed ably as quartermasters, gunner's mates, shipfitters, radiomen—even as officers in the US Navy. The discrimination justified so steadfastly in 1942 was by 1945 considered a terrible mistake, and Armstrong was singled out for blame.

"Armstrong was an evil influence," said Captain K. E. Bond, who led the technical training schools at Great Lakes. "Segregation was an egregious error. It was un-American and inefficient."[37]

Bond asked Commodore Emmet to integrate the aviation metalsmiths school with a similar school in Norman, Oklahoma. Emmet agreed and further recommended integrating the literacy training program.

"We are making every effort to give more than lip service to the principles of democracy in the treatment of the Negro and we are trying to do it with the minimum of commotion," Forrestal told Marshall Field III, the publisher of *PM*, founder of the *Chicago Sun*, and owner of the publishing house Simon & Schuster. "There is still a long road to travel but I am confident we have made a start."[38]

Commander William Turek, the officer in charge of recruit training, had always been uneasy with integration, but in June 1945 he was relieved of his position and replaced by Captain Richard Penny, who was eager to carry out the new directives. Goodwin thought that Turek was "too much aware of imaginary problems." He assumed black men would make poor sailors so he took every opportunity to try to prove himself right. Penny had no such predispositions. When asked what allowances he was going to make for the supposed inferiority of black men, he said, "None."

Penny integrated recruits first by companies in July 1945, placing two black companies with four white companies in a battalion. Finally on the same playing field, the black men showed they were every bit as talented as their white peers and earned six consecutive battalion "Rooster" flags for military proficiency.[39] In August, just before the war ended, Penny moved for full integration, placing eight or ten black men in each company. Once again, the black men proved more than up to the task, and a black man was voted honor man of his company.

Even Armstrong appeared to have a change of heart, acknowledging in December 1945 that integration should have occurred from the outset of the war.[40] White remembered running into Armstrong, then a captain, in Washington, DC, and congratulating him on earning his fourth stripe.

"Too bad I couldn't have gotten it earlier, during the war," Armstrong told White, "because there's so much more I could have done if I'd had the power of the fourth stripe."[41]

=====

After the war, Martin's wife, Alma, encouraged him to make a career in the Navy, but Martin thought that the accident on the oiler would hold him back.

Sublett wanted to stay in the service, but he had a wife and young son, and his mother-in-law strongly encouraged him to come home. "The marriage failed anyway," Sublett later said. "I wish things had wound up differently but you can't turn back the clock."[42]

Arbor harbored similar regrets. He left the Navy after his service in Guam, figuring he could make more money as a civilian. "Had I known the potentials at the time, I would have stayed because I think I could have done more in the Navy than I did out," he said. "But knowledge only comes with age and experience."

Cooper had hurt his back when he slipped off a diving board during officer training and was given a medical discharge.[43]

Sam Barnes had had enough stevedore work in Okinawa to last a lifetime. He returned to Oberlin to care for his ailing mother.

John Reagan left the Navy in 1946 and returned to Montana State to play football and finish his degree. The "Montana Grizzly" was still a stud on the field and played professionally for the Winnipeg Blue Bombers in the Canadian Football League. His wife, Lillian, the nurse he had chased back at Hampton, didn't care much for Canada or the cold, so the couple moved back to California.[44]

Nelson was the only one of the thirteen who decided to make a career out of the Navy, and he spent much of his tenure at the Bureau of Naval Personnel pushing to make the Navy a more hospitable place for black men.

He befriended John L. Sullivan, who became secretary of the Navy in 1947 when President Harry Truman appointed Forrestal secretary of defense. That friendship provided Lieutenant Nelson uncommon access to the halls of power.

Nelson took advantage, firing off letters and memos to senior staff, seeking subtle reforms such as changing the stewards' uniform so they looked like those of regular seamen, and not-so-subtle reforms such as demanding that stewards, most of whom were black, stop being called "boy."

"This has been a constant practice in the Service and is most objectionable, is in bad taste, shows undue familiarity and pins a badge of inferiority, adding little to the dignity and pride of adults," Nelson wrote Captain E. B. Dexter, deputy director of Navy public relations.[45]

Nelson wrote that letter in August 1948, shortly after President Truman's Committee on Civil Rights noted that 80 percent of black sailors were serving as cooks, stewards, and stewards' mates, while less than 2 percent of whites served in those roles. "It is clear," the committee wrote, "that discrimination is one of the major elements which keeps the service from attaining the objectives which it has set for itself."[46]

But Nelson kept pushing.

In October 1949, he asked if Reagan might come back to active duty and help recruit other black men into the Navy. At the time, only fourteen black men were enrolled among more than 5,600 students in the Navy ROTC program, and African Americans made up just 4.3 percent of those serving in the Navy.[47]

Reagan's task was to show black men that the Navy did have a lot to offer, though he was never certain he had much success. He would travel to various cities and make the very best pitch for the Navy he could. Invariably, during the question-and-answer session, someone would raise his hand and ask the black lieutenant (junior grade), "Can [black men] be anything other than a mess cook in the Navy?"[48]

The following June, war broke out on the Korean Peninsula, and Reagan finally got to see the action he had always craved. He was ordered to serve in an amphibious boat unit that made its way from San Diego to Japan. The skipper chose Reagan—not the white lieutenant—as his executive officer, a move Reagan could not have imagined happening during World War II.

During the Korean War, Nelson, in an effort to promote the Navy, courted the black press to promote black sailors' achievements. In 1950, the *Chicago Defender* happily reported that aboard the USS *Missouri* black men "mingled in every department of the ship's crew, and taking active part in the maneuvers are many colored lads who are 'learning by doing' in the radar section, gun turrets, mechanical and engineering divisions."[49]

But Nelson understood his was an uphill climb. Black men, he told historian Lee Nichols, knew promotions came more quickly in other branches of the military, where there was "less caste and class to buck."[50]

Nelson laid it all out in his master's thesis, "The Integration of the Negro into the U.S. Navy," which the Navy published. It was, according to a reviewer, a "factual presentation of the progress to date of the Navy in its new racial policies" and included a scathing takedown of Armstrong, who died from a heart attack he suffered while playing tennis in 1947.[51]

Nelson was quite brave to publish a critique of the Navy while still in uniform. Equally impressive was the Navy's decision to publish the manuscript instead of ignoring it or even suppressing it.

Captain Fred R. Stickney decided to publish it because, he said, it was such excellent scholarship and deserved wider public attention than it would have received if it remained merely an academic work.[52]

Nelson made no attempt to sugarcoat the Navy's past prejudice or gloss over how much work still needed to be done.[53] He said current treatment of black personnel "makes fertile grounds" for Communism, writing, "The attitudes of our country toward minority groups, and those manifested and practiced by its armed forces, provide ready-made propaganda for the Communist state."

Sam Barnes later mused that Nelson's bullishness, and the pressure he put on the Navy to reform and face its failings, hampered his career. After twenty-one years in the service, Nelson retired as a lieutenant commander, even as other black officers commissioned after he was earned promotions to higher ranks.

Nelson was older than other officers who were being promoted, and he'd had no sea duty, an important consideration in Navy promotions. No doubt these factors hampered his prospects as well, but it is also true that Nelson simply wouldn't play by the Navy's rules, or act the part of the "unspoiled young Negro," the quiet, obsequious black man that the Navy had desired since it opened its messman's branch to African Americans in 1933. Nelson, sometimes at his own peril, opened doors that other men walked through.

"You have to have some tree-shakers, and then some others come along and pick up the fruit from the man who shakes it down," Arbor said. "Nelson was a tree-shaker."[54]

Among the men whom Nelson tapped for recruiting duty was Lieutenant Samuel L. Gravely. While Nelson pushed in Washington for black men to have more, Gravely proved they could handle the responsibility. He served as a communications officer aboard the USS *Iowa* during the Korean War, and took command of the *Falgout* in 1962, the first black man to command a warship. Then, on April 28, 1971, the Pentagon announced that Captain Gravely, a former railway postal clerk who had joined a segregated Navy and was then sailing home from Vietnam, would be promoted.[55]

The United States would have its first black admiral.

CHAPTER 13

"THERE IS THAT SALUTE
YOU NEVER GOT."

James Hair was home alone in his modest three-story house in Hollis, a section of Queens in New York City, when the phone rang. He got up to answer, moving a bit more gingerly than he once did. Age had stolen his agility and time had taken the spring from his step. Slowed by a triple by-pass, Hair, just shy of his sixty-seventh birthday, was no longer the athlete of his youth or the powerful man of his prime. He was a retired social worker, at the dusk of life, not quite certain what to do with himself now that he was no longer working.

Hair picked up the phone. His son was on the other end of the line, calling from work and speaking with some urgency.

Take a look at the newspaper, James Hair Jr. said.

Hair grabbed a copy of the *New York Times* and, as instructed, turned to page A18. "8 of First Black Navy Officers Hold Reunion At Sea," the headline read. Hair looked from the headline to the photo. He recognized the face. It belonged to Syl White, a man he hadn't seen in nearly forty years.

"The United States Navy brought them back to sea today," the first sentence read, describing the reunion on the USS *Kidd* off the coast of Virginia, "the eight surviving members of the Golden 13."[1]

"I'll be damned," Hair said, his eyes darting over the words again and again to be sure he hadn't made a mistake. "I know I'm still alive."

Hair pinched himself just to be sure.

"I know damn well I'm alive," he said again, having passed this all-important tactile test. "Why aren't I there?"

Hair called the *New York Times* and asked for Ben A. Franklin, the reporter who wrote the story. Franklin works in the Washington, DC, bureau, Hair was told.

Hair thought about calling, but, fearing the run-around, instead decided to call the United States Navy. He dialed Navy Intelligence and told them about the *Times* article.

"I'm not with them," he said, "but I'm a member of the Golden Thirteen."

"Huh?" came a befuddled reply.

"Yeah, I'm a member of the Golden Thirteen."

"You sure?"

Yeah, Hair was sure.

The Navy took Hair's name and address and told him to wait by the phone.

Hair did as he was told, waiting in the home that had provided a foundation for him and his wife to raise three children. The kids had grown, moved out, and started lives of their own. Hair and his wife had divorced.

Now, it was just Hair and Taja, a German shepherd for whom he had great affection. In another time and place, Taja might have served as a hunting dog, more companion than pet.

Hair had recently become involved with his church, attending services more frequently and reading the Bible. He was becoming more spiritual in his later years, though he still had not decided exactly how he would spend his retirement. So on this particular Wednesday morning in 1982, waiting for the Navy to get back to him was no problem, and he had plenty of time to talk when they did—which was good, because over the next several hours Hair received more than twenty phone calls from Navy headquarters.

Finally, a captain got on the line. "You are James Hair, aren't you?"

"I certainly am," Hair replied.

"Can you travel?"

"Oh yeah, yeah, I'm able to travel."

"Could you get ready in three hours, because we'll have somebody there to pick you up?"

Hair packed a few items, then sat and waited, a torrent of memories flooding his mind. Being one of the Golden Thirteen was a point of pride, but it was not something he thought about often. He rarely spoke about his experience, even with his own children. The war was far behind him. He had a master's degree from Fordham University. He had worked for Roman Catholic and private agencies in the Bedford-Stuyvesant section of Brooklyn, helping loving families adopt children. He had been a caseworker and supervisor for thirty-one years.

Hair waited, wondering how the Navy had forgotten about him. It turned out to be a clerical mix-up. James Hair had entered the Navy as James Hare, on the advice of the Browns, who had told him to spell his last name the "right way," the white way. Over the years, Hair reverted the spelling but had never informed the Navy. When James Hare could not be found, the Navy assumed he must be dead.

A car pulled up on schedule. Hair was driven to LaGuardia Airport, named for the beloved mayor who led New York City during the days when Hair patrolled and protected its coast. He flew south to Norfolk, Virginia, a place once referred to as the "asshole of creation," because it was so hostile toward black men. The Navy rented him a motel room and told him to rest up because tomorrow would be a big day.

The next morning Hair boarded a helicopter at Norfolk Naval Air Station and flew twenty miles out to sea, landing on the deck of the USS *Kidd*, a guided missile destroyer.

Hair leaped off the helicopter, feeling spry and young. He looked around for the captain, wanting to ask permission to come aboard, just as he had been trained to do forty years before. But Hair could not get to the captain before his old Navy buddies started pummeling him with high-fives, back slaps, and hugs.[2]

Dalton Baugh, Frank Sublett, John Reagan, Sam Barnes, George Cooper, Graham Martin, Syl White, and Jesse Arbor had not seen Hair since the end of the war. They were older, fatter, and balder than Hair remembered, but here on the ship, in this moment, they were young again—the men of Barracks 202.

They kidded Hair for missing the first few reunions, which had begun in 1977, and joked that maybe he had been posing as a white man all these years, only to rejoin the race when the ceremonies and special treatment began.[3]

Aboard the ship the now nine surviving members were served lunch by white sailors while the USS *Kidd*'s only African American officer, Lieutenant (junior grade) Bruce Martin, stood in awe of these men—the Jackie Robinsons of the Navy.

"I am so pumped up to have these guys here," Lieutenant Martin told a reporter. "These guys opened the door for us and if they hadn't it might have been another 50 years before the Navy got black officers."[4]

For more than three decades these men, who had broken one of the most intractable color barriers in the Navy, were known only as "those Negro officers" or, later, as "those black officers."

But Dennis Nelson never stopped pushing for more recognition, and by the late 1970s, a decade after the civil rights movement had forever changed the status of black people in the United States, the Navy was newly proud of their accomplishment and ready to show them off. The surviving officers were feted as a symbol of racial integration, of progress, of pride.

The first reunion, which took two years to plan, was held in Berkeley, California, in 1977.

Captain Edward Sechrest, a Vietnam veteran who was assigned to the Navy Recruiting Command, coined the term "Golden Thirteen," a bit of ingenious PR that gave the group a catchy nickname the Navy could use to tout their achievements.

Lorraine Baugh, Dalton's second wife, printed stationery for the men. In the center was "13+1," a nod to John Dille, who remained close to their hearts all those years later.

There were nine who gathered that day to mark what they had accomplished thirty-three years earlier and remember their departed comrades.

Charles Lear had been the first to pass. Navy documents show that he died on October 28, 1946, from a self-inflicted gunshot wound to the chest "while in a state of melancholia."[5] Lear's application for a transfer into the regular Navy had been rejected the previous June, and a few other members of the Golden Thirteen surmised this is what led to his depression. But on September 5, less than two months before he died, the Navy changed its mind and Lear was recommended for appointment to the regular Navy.

In January 1949 Phil Barnes entered the US Naval Hospital in Bethesda, Maryland, because of painful kidney stones. He suffered complications following a nephrolithotomy, and doctors removed his right kidney on February 24, hopeful that would save his life. His condition appeared to be improving and he was slowly regaining strength, but one week later he vomited violently and gasped for breath. The doctors tried everything they could but to no avail. At 2:05 p.m., on March 2, 1949, Phil Barnes became the second member of the Golden Thirteen to die.[6]

Reginald Goodwin had run a lucrative law practice in Chicago. He was a member of the group of traffic court defense lawyers known as "miracle workers" for their unusually high success rate in drunk-driving cases. Goodwin retired to Scottsdale, Arizona, in 1973. The next year he returned to Chicago to address a Saturday dinner gathering of the Frogs Club, an African American leadership organization. After he finished his remarks, Goodwin walked back toward his seat. His legs gave out as he approached it, and he fell, slumped over his chair. He was rushed to Mercy Hospital, where he was pronounced dead from an apparent heart attack.[7] Goodwin had turned his law practice over to a man named Bruce Campbell, who later admitted to paying $100 cash bribes to judges to fix drunk-driving cases, and accused Goodwin, long dead, of being in on the scheme.[8]

When the men gathered for this first reunion they felt as if it had been just thirty minutes since they'd last seen each other, not thirty years. They posed for pictures, gave interviews, and swapped stories about their lives and families.

They had so much to catch up on.

Baugh told them he was now living in Massachusetts and had achieved his lifelong dream when in 1956 he graduated with a master's degree in engineering from the Massachusetts Institute of Technology. He had stayed in the Naval Reserve until 1964, rising to the rank of lieutenant commander. He'd also worked for the Massachusetts public works department and was one of the first two engineers hired by Boston's traffic department. Now, he ran his own engineering firm.[9]

The year Baugh graduated MIT, Dennis Nelson was in San Diego campaigning for Adlai Stevenson, who was fighting Senator Estes Kefauver of Tennessee in the Democratic primary. Kefauver was making inroads in the black community because he favored rapid desegregation of American schools. Stevenson thought it would be a mistake to use federal troops to enforce *Brown v. Board of Education*, the landmark 1954 Supreme Court decision declaring segregated schools unconstitutional. California was a pivotal state in that year's contest, and Stevenson's position caused many influential African Americans to support Kefauver. Nelson, by then a lieutenant commander, proved an effective surrogate, telling the press that he owed his career to Stevenson.

"There has never been any question of his sincere interest in these matters," Nelson told reporters. "He fought for them long before he had any interest in a political career."[10] Stevenson won California and the nomination before losing the general election to President Dwight Eisenhower.

Nelson retired from active duty in 1963, and the next year teamed up with his son, Dennis Denmark Nelson III, and Reagan to form a public relations firm.[11] Nelson and Reagan had remained friends after the war, and both men's sons had joined the Navy. Nelson's namesake became an ensign in 1953. His younger brother, Charles A. Nelson, in 1951 became just the fourth African American ever admitted to the US Naval Academy.[12]

When John "Skip" Reagan Jr.'s Navy enlistment ended, he signed up for the Marines. His father thought maybe the boy was just trying to show up his old man—prove how tough he was, how much of a man he had become. Reagan was so proud of his son, and he hoped to bring Skip into the business as Nelson had done with his namesake.

On July 22, 1966, Skip Reagan, only twenty years old, was killed in Vietnam.

Reagan was devastated and his partnership with Nelson did not last long after that.

The next year, Nelson was appointed director of Los Angeles' nascent Human Relations Bureau—he'd been the top scorer on the civil service exam. The bureau was conceived of following the 1965 race riots, and Nelson was tasked with doing for Los Angeles what he had accomplished in the Navy—building bridges between the races.[13]

Arbor told his old Navy buddies that he had settled in Chicago, where he'd opened his own tailor shop, which he ran until retiring, in 1969.[14]

In 1970, George Cooper became Dayton, Ohio's first black director of human resources, responsible for nine hundred employees in the departments of corrections, housing, health, consumer protection, and parks and recreation.[15]

That same year, Sam Barnes was elected to the National Association of Collegiate Directors of Athletics Hall of Fame, and the year after, he became the first African American officer of the NCAA. Those were just a couple of the many honors he earned during his more than two decades at Howard University and the University of the District of Columbia.

Before the war, Barnes had hoped to coach alongside his older brother James, a role model whom he would cherish all his life. A terrible illness had robbed Barnes of that chance, but he honored his older brother's legacy for decades by instilling the principles in young athletes that he knew James stood for. Barnes coached boxing, track, and wrestling. His only experience with boxing was the brief training he received during officer candidate school, so he picked up a book on technique, stood in front of a mirror, and taught himself the maneuvers, same as he had done with badminton back at Camp Robert Smalls.

After seven years at Howard, Barnes used a sabbatical to work on his PhD thesis. Dr. Sam Barnes graduated with a PhD from Ohio State University in 1956. His thesis focused on the role of intercollegiate athletics in the realm of higher education, including its influence on student life and educational values and its effects on institutional morale and relationships with secondary schools. He returned to Howard as athletic director and head of the Department of Physical Education for Men.[16]

For much of Barnes's early career, the nation's capital remained a segregated town. One of the Navy's first black officers, and a distinguished coach and athletic director at an elite university, could not eat in most restaurants, but he could show through his own example that the world would get better.

William Sylvester White took a cabinet post with Illinois governor Otto Kerner, who had been his boss at the US attorney's office. Then, in 1968, White became only the second black man to head Cook County's Juvenile Court system. He would go on to win a seat on the state's Appellate Court and later become presiding judge for the third division of the first district.[17]

Graham Martin told his comrades that he was still working at Crispus Attucks High School, which he had attended as a teenager and where he had taught since 1947. The school that the Klan created to segregate black children employed one of the Navy's first black officers. He was there for *Brown v. Board* when the highest court in the land declared separate but equal unconstitutional. He was there for the civil rights marches of the 1960s. And he was there in the 1970s to see white students make up about one-third of the student body.[18]

Frank Sublett became the first black service manager for a GM dealership in the Chicago Metro area. Then he took up modeling, appearing in commercials for Bud Light and various other products.[19] In one, his hands broke open a hot Pillsbury biscuit. In another, his smile beamed as he modeled preacher's robes.

It was during their first reunion that the legacy of the Golden Thirteen came into focus for these men. John Reagan had never seen more than a handful of black officers in the same room, but at the get-together in Berkeley, he saw dozens of black faces—lieutenants, captains, even an admiral.[20]

Reagan wasn't the kind of man to take himself too seriously, but on that day he reflected on all that the Golden Thirteen had accomplished as other black Navy officers walked over to pay their respects and salute these trailblazers.

"We owe it all to you," one after the next said. "If it hadn't been for you guys, we wouldn't be here."[21]

Reagan just stood there—as awestruck as he'd ever been in his life.

Nelson used the occasion of the first reunion to encourage his mates to promote the Navy in black communities. He told them that the more black men entered the Navy, the more black men would rise through the ranks.

They had one more mission, he told them.

The men of Barracks 202, the Golden Thirteen, answered their country's call once more.

All became members of the Navy Recruiting District Advisory Committees in their communities.[22] Baugh was active in Boston. Sam Barnes worked around Washington, DC. Cooper was elected president of the Navy League in Dayton, Ohio.

And they weren't only interested in advancing African Americans. They celebrated women's achievements, too. And at a time when many in the United States, especially older men, looked askance at the idea of gay sailors, Cooper and White told audiences that a person's sexual orientation would have no impact on Navy efficiency, nor would it hamper morale or battle readiness. They swatted away the same arguments that were once used to keep them out of the service. "Ever since we've had a Navy, there've been gays in the Navy, and it has not ruined that Navy," Cooper told NPR's Neal Conan, nearly two decades before LGBT sailors could serve openly. "Gays are in every aspect of this society, and they operate effectively," he said. "They operate just like anybody else. They operate just as well as women do, they operate just as well as blacks do. This is a part of living in our society today, and we have to accept it, and find out ways to live with it."[23]

The reunions continued every year, always sponsored by Navy Recruiting Command. The second was in New Orleans, then Orlando, then Washington, DC, then Boston, and so on.[24]

But as the men began to pass—Nelson in 1979, Baugh in 1985, Hair in 1992, Reagan in 1994, Sam Barnes in 1997, Arbor in 2000, Cooper in 2002, White in 2004, Martin and Sublett in 2006—their story faded from most people's memories.

There would be brief mentions in local papers during Black History Month. Sublett was on hand when the first memorial for black Navy veterans in the nation was commissioned in 2005 in Illinois. That same year, in Ohio, a local diversity award was named for Cooper.[25] A park in Indianapolis was named for Martin in 2011.[26] And in 2008, a Navy press officer gave President-elect Barack Obama a copy of Paul Stillwell's *The Golden Thirteen*, an oral history.[27]

The Navy used the memory of these thirteen officers to recruit young African Americans and steadily increased the percentage of black officers. But seventy-five years after the Golden Thirteen were commissioned, although African Americans made up 19 percent of the enlisted force, only 7 percent of the officers were black. As of January 2019, there were 54,151 officers in the US Navy; 42,376 were white and 3,916 were black.[28]

And mentions of the Golden Thirteen remained few and far between.

Three years before he died, White was asked by the History Maker's Society to provide some recollections from his time in the Navy, because "not many people know of this story."

A look of alarm came over White's eighty-six-year-old face.

"They don't?" he said, raising his brows in disbelief. "I thought everybody knew it."[29]

Fifteen years later, White's daughter Marilyn confessed that she didn't know much about what her father had done. He didn't talk much about the war or the barriers he broke.

Goodwin's son didn't know much either.

Neither did James Hair Jr., who said his father talked very little about his time in the Navy. Hair's father had never let on to his son that he had been part of a special group. He didn't have any plaques on the wall or memorabilia displayed. It was just something he had done when he was younger.[30]

Even their wives knew little of their achievements. Willimeta Reagan, Lorraine Baugh, and Susan Lopez-Sublett, all of whom married their husbands decades after the war, didn't know much about those years.

Lopez-Sublett said her husband just didn't think the "kids these days" would be interested in what he had done a lifetime ago. She'd tease him and say how many things in this world are there left to be the first of, but he refused to brag about his place in history.

Sam Barnes's twenty-two-year-old daughter, Olga, was studying in the library at the University of Tennessee, Knoxville, when, bored with her own words, she decided to take a break from working on a paper and peruse the newly created African American studies section. She ran her fingers across the bindings of the books on the shelf. By chance she pulled down a book on blacks in the military and was idly thumbing through its pages when she came across a picture of thirteen men standing in Navy uniforms. The caption said these were the first black officers. The man in the front row looked an awful lot like her father. She was so excited that she could not wait for the elevator and bolted down four flights of steps to a pay phone on the first floor.

"Dad, I'm holding this book. Were you one of the first blacks commissioned in the United States Navy?"

"Yes," he matter-of-factly replied.

"Why didn't you tell me?" Olga asked incredulously.

"Well, a lot of people fought in the war."[31]

Baugh, similarly, regarded his place in history as accidental.

"Look, if I hadn't been selected, an equally qualified black man would have done the same thing as me," the MIT graduate said at the group's first reunion. "He would have demonstrated the same skills. The fact that I was one of the first is only a statistic, and statistics bore me."

———

Baugh died New Year's Day, 1985, two years before the intake center at Great Lakes Naval Training Station was named in honor of the Golden Thirteen. To this day, a large framed photograph of the nation's first thirteen black officers greets fresh boots when they arrive for basic training.

The honor came about thanks to John Dille, who never lost touch with the men he helped. Dille ran in high circles in Indiana and was friends with Dick Lugar, the longtime US senator. Dille asked Lugar to speak to John Lehman, President Ronald Reagan's Navy secretary, about naming something for the Golden Thirteen. The first idea was a ship, but that was nixed because ship names were often reserved for the dead. Then, there was talk of naming something at the Officer Candidate School in Newport, Rhode Island, but Lehman thought the Navy could do better than that. Eventually everyone settled on the intake center at Great Lakes.[32]

"It's ironic we're dedicating this building in your name," Vice Admiral Samuel L. Gravely said at the ceremony in 1987. "For you, there was no graduation ceremony, no officers' privileges."

The eight surviving members were surrounded that day by young black officers asking for autographs. Reagan signed graduation programs and a copy of that *Life* magazine photo from all those years ago.

Arbor, still cheeky and irreverent, told friends that he was only upset that all this honor and recognition came when he was too old to drink all the free whiskey on offer.

Lorraine Baugh attended the dedication ceremony at Great Lakes in her husband's stead. She was so honored to be included among those great men, she said later, as she remembered how inspired she was to hear their stories. Her husband, she said, never talked much about the war. But at those reunions, she had heard of their trials and travails, how they knew that they'd have to be twice as good to receive half as much.

"That's true with most black folk," Baugh said. "We know we have to be better than anyone else because they are going to try their damndest to keep us out."

She understood the bond the men shared. It had depth and substance. She could feel it being in their presence. They were from another time, when no one thought much of denying African Americans dignity or live-lihood, when black men could disappear or be killed, leaving behind only a community too afraid for their own lives to ask any questions. "They had to provide for each other because of their blackness," she said. "They knew they'd only survive if they had cohesiveness."

She recounted that her husband often said the two high points of his life were being accepted to engineering school at MIT and earning his naval commission. When he announced to folks in Crossett, the tiny Arkansas town of his birth, that his ambition was to attend the famed Massachusetts school, they shook their heads, bemused and slightly sorry for this young dreamer. They asked, "How are you ever going to do that?" When he later returned wearing a Navy officer's uniform, they stopped asking such questions. They all understood that Dalton Louis Baugh could do whatever he desired.

The pity was that her husband never saw the same respect and ad-miration from white men in the Navy. Lorraine Baugh recalled how her husband regretted that there had been no ceremony to mark their commissioning and how bitter he felt about the sailors who crossed the street to avoid saluting a black man.

"Nobody wanted to be proud of them," she said. "Nobody acknowledged their achievement. When you think about it, it is so heartbreaking. You just feel so disrespected and unappreciated."[33]

But Baugh and the other members of the Golden Thirteen tolerated it all because that was the world they came from, and to do otherwise would have made it that much harder to change the world for those to come.

Riding in a staff car, being driven from the ceremony to the luncheon at Great Lakes in June of 1987, Lorraine Baugh thought about all that had changed in the forty-three years since her husband had been commissioned. Through the windshield she could see the sentries dressed in perfectly pressed white uniforms, teenagers who looked barely old enough to shave, let alone fight. For them, World War II was ancient history. The battles they had heard of—Iwo Jima, Midway, Guadalcanal—were far different from the battles for respect her husband and the other black officers had waged. As she passed these fresh faces, they smartly snapped their hands to their hats. A staff car meant an officer was in sight.

"Oh, my beloved Dalton," she said softly. "I only hope the good Lord is letting you see all this. There is that salute you never got."[34]

ACKNOWLEDGMENTS

This book would not have been possible without Paul Stillwell, a retired naval officer and historian who interviewed the eight surviving members of the Golden Thirteen in the 1980s. Without these oral histories and his probing questions, patience, and foresight, this story would almost certainly have been lost.

When I first reached out to Paul in 2011, I wasn't sure how he would feel about a twenty-six-year-old health-care reporter who had never served in the military attempting to tell the story of the Navy's first black officers. I could not have asked for more. He was supportive, patient, encouraging, and helpful for nearly a decade, asking nothing in return. He corrected numerous mistakes in the draft, for which I am eternally grateful. He shared his time, his thoughts, and his unpublished works, because he, like me, thought this was an important story to tell.

I owe a special debt to Terry Golway, who immediately understood the potential of this project and was the first person to say, without reservation, that it merited book-length treatment. Terry allowed me to gush about trivia that I found in my research, to say out loud the words I wanted on the page, to test out ideas and themes. His edits of early and late drafts helped make this a much easier read. He also calmed me down when I felt anxious and assured me that crushing self-doubt was all part of the writing process. I am very fortunate to have his mentorship.

Terry introduced me to my agent, John Wright, who believed in this story from the very start and took a chance representing a never-published author. Wright kept pushing me to refine the book proposal, cut away excess material and focus my story. Many agents would have given up after the first publishers passed on the project, but Wright kept at it, believing that this book would find a home.

Rakia Clark, a senior editor at Beacon Press, pushed to make this book happen, believing that these men and this story were worthy of being shared. The team at Beacon, Helene Atwan, Susan Lumenello, Carol Chu, Haley Lynch, Beth Collins, Katherine Scott, and many others, were instrumental in helping a news reporter become an author. Their patience and effort to make this a more enjoyable read were invaluable.

I am thankful to John Sheppard, who handles public affairs at Great Lakes Naval Training Station, and Dr. Jennifer Searcy, director of the National Museum of the American Sailor, for directing me to archival material that helped me understand what life must have been like for the men at Camp Robert Smalls.

Dara Baker, at the Franklin D. Roosevelt Presidential Library and Museum, probably contributed more than she realizes. She pointed me in a dozen directions that I would not have thought of on my own, and they all proved useful.

David Tucker, a world-class editor; Patricia Cole, a world-class copyeditor; and Roosevelt "Rick" Wright Jr., PhD, Captain USNR (retired), offered advice and encouragement that kept me on track.

I never met any of the Golden Thirteen, but I was fortunate to speak with many of their friends, wives, children, and grandchildren. They were gracious with their time, corrected my errors, and provided loving details that helped bring these men to life.

My wife, Holly, was at my side for this and everything else. Her patience seems to have no limit. Her enthusiasm for this book matched my own, and she never appeared to tire of her husband droning on about another "Golden Thirteen" story. She forgave me the nights and weekends she gave up with me as I pursued this project, and offered countless helpful notes along the way. She is my best friend and my most loving critic.

Finally, this book is dedicated to the Golden Thirteen. This work has been my privilege and I have never for a moment lost sight of the special responsibility I have to these men, their times, and to do their story justice. It is my sincerest hope that I was equal to the task.

NOTES

CHAPTER 1: "WE'RE SENDING YOU UP TO GREAT LAKES."

1. Reminiscences of Jesse Walter Arbor, interviewed by Paul Stillwell, October 9, 1986, and July 20, 1988, US Naval Institute Oral History Program, Annapolis, Maryland (hereafter NIOHP), 5; see, also, Stillwell, *The Golden Thirteen*, 177.

2. Douglass Hall, "No Colored Sailors on Seagoing Vessels," *Baltimore Afro-American*, July 3, 1943.

3. Kelly, *Proudly We Served*, 53.

4. Arbor, NIOHP, 58.

5. Arbor, NIOHP, 5–6.

6. Reminiscences of John Walter Reagan, interviewed by Paul Stillwell, January 15, 1987, and April 10, 1989, NIOHP, 28.

7. Reminiscences of James Edward Hair, interviewed by Paul Stillwell, November 12, 1986, and November 10, 1988, NIOHP, 54–56.

8. Reminiscences of Samuel E. Barnes, interviewed by Paul Stillwell, November 24, 1986, January 30, 1989, and May 12,1989, NIOHP, 37–38.

9. Stillwell, "Two Black Lives," unpublished typescript.

CHAPTER 2: "DON'T PUT YOUR TIME IN NEGROES."

1. Sam Barnes, NIOHP, 44.

2. "Mess Attendants Write: 'Don't Join the Navy,'" *Pittsburgh Courier*, October 5, 1940, 1.

3. Maj. Gen. H. E. Ely, Commandant, *The Use of Negro Manpower in War* (US Army War College, November 10, 1925).

4. Lanning, *The African-American Soldier*, 139.

5. Bullard, *Personalities and Reminiscences of the War*, 295–98.

6. Selden, "Transforming Better Babies into Fitter Families."

7. Mikkelsen, "Coming from Battle to Face a War," 19–21; see, also, Chad Williams, "African-American Veterans Hoped Their Service in World War I Would Secure Their Rights at Home. It Didn't," *Time*, November 12, 2018.

8. Nalty and MacGregor, *Blacks in the Military*, 91.

9. Nalty, *Strength for the Fight*, 86.

10. Davis, "Many of Them Are Among My Best Men," 1.

11. Miller, *Messman Chronicles*, 4–8.

12. Davis, "Many of Them Are Among My Best Men," 187.

13. Davis, "Many of Them Are Among My Best Men," 56.

14. Mallison, *The Great Wildcatter*, 403.

15. Robert Lee Vann, "This Year I See Millions of Negroes Turning the Picture of Abraham Lincoln to the Wall," *Pittsburgh Courier*, September 17, 1932, 12.

16. Weber, *Don't Call Me Boss*, 50–54.

17. Bunie, *Robert L. Vann of the Pittsburgh Courier*, 179–202.

18. Brewer, "Robert Lee Vann, Democrat or Republican."

19. Gibson, *Knocking Down Barriers*, 5.

20. Myrdal, *An American Dilemma*, 909–15.

21. Logan and Winston, *Dictionary of American Negro Biography*, 614–16; Toppin, *A Biographical History of Blacks in America Since 1528*, 434.

22. Robert L. Vann, "Courier's Letter to College Presidents," *Pittsburgh Courier*, March 19, 1938, 14.

23. Robert L. Vann, "BECAUSE! Ten Cardinal Points in Courier's Campaign for Army and Navy Equality," *Pittsburgh Courier*, March 1, 1938, 1.

24. Robert L. Vann to FDR, January 19, 1939, Office File (hereafter OF) 93A, Franklin D. Roosevelt Presidential Library and Museum (hereafter FDRL).

25. Hair, NIOHP, 7.

26. For Alfred's age and race, listed as mulatto, see US Census Bureau, 1920 Census for Blackville, SC, Enumeration District 52, line 18.

27. Hair, NIOHP, 14–16.

28. Hair, NIOHP, 19–21.

CHAPTER 3: "I JUST DON'T BELIEVE YOU CAN DO THE JOB."

1. Remnick, *The Bridge*, 143–44.

2. Gibson, *Knocking Down Barriers*, 31–32.

3. Arbor, NIOHP, 8, 32–40.

4. For Arbor's résumé and college transcript, see Arbor, Jesse Walter, National Personnel Records Center, St. Louis Office of Military Personnel Files (hereafter NPRC St. Louis).

5. Goodwin, *No Ordinary Time*, 165; Garfinkle, *When Negroes March*, 20–21.

6. "Lynching and Liberty," *Crisis*, July 1940, 209.

7. Finkle, "Conservative Aims of Militant Rhetoric," 697.

8. Lee, *The Employment of Negro Troops*, 74.

9. "The U.S. Navy Is for White Men," editorial, *Crisis*, September 1940, 5.

10. O'Farrell, *She Was One of Us*, 80.

11. "Mayor Says Labor Backs Roosevelt," *New York Times*, September 17, 1940, 23.

12. Alfred A. Duckett, "Porter's Banquet Addressed by Eleanor Roosevelt," *New York Age*, September 21, 1940, 1.

13. Scott and Womack, *Double V*, 123–24.

14. Goodwin, *No Ordinary Time*, 167–68.

15. "The Choice of a Candidate," *New York Times*, September 19, 1940, 20.

16. Gibson, *Knocking Down Barriers*, 87.

17. Knox to Rear Admiral Randall Jacobs, memo, December 29, 1942, General Records of the Department of the Navy (hereafter GenRecsNav), box 37, folder 54-1.

18. Doyle, *Inside the Oval Office*, 12. The University of Virginia's Miller Center has an audio recording of the conversation.

19. Eiler, *Mobilizing America*, 132.

20. Reddick, "The Negro in the United States Navy during World War II," 202.

21. MacGregor, *Integration of the Armed Forces*, 59–60.

22. "End of a Strenuous Life," *Time*, May 8, 1944, 12.

23. "U.S. at War," *Time*, September 7, 1942, 25.

24. Lobdell, "Frank Knox," 682.

25. Jack Alexander, "Secretary Knox," *Life*, March 10, 1941, 60.

26. For a description of Knox, see "In Line of Duty," *Newsweek*, May 8, 1944, 31, and Stevenson, *The Papers of Adlai Stevenson*, 77.

27. "U.S. at War," 25.

28. Beasley, *Frank Knox, American*, 153.

29. For a description of Charles Edison, see Ickes, *Lowering Clouds, 1939–1941*, 202.

30. Alexander, "Secretary Knox," 63.

31. Knox to Robert G. Simmons, September 16, 1942, Frank Knox Papers, box 4, Library of Congress (hereafter cited as Knox Papers).

32. Ketchum, *The Borrowed Years*, 725.

33. Alexander, "Secretary Knox," 58.

34. Knox to FDR, December 15, 1939, President's Secretary's Files, box 62, FDRL.

35. Tully, *FDR: My Boss*, 243.

36. Lobdell, "Frank Knox," 692.

37. Lobdell, "Frank Knox," 687.

38. Reminiscences of George Clinton Cooper, interviewed by Paul Stillwell, October, 15, 1986, and July 18, 1988, NIOHP, 14–17.

39. Cooper, NIOHP, 88.

40. Loy and Worthy, *Washington and the Pamlico*, 86, 474.

41. Peggy Cooper Davis, interview with author, February 6, 2019.

42. Cooper, NIOHP, 80.

43. Cooper, NIOHP, 74.

44. Cooper, NIOHP, 90.

45. Peggy Cooper Davis, interviewed by author, March 11, 2019.

46. Cooper, NIOHP, 102.

47. Finkle, "'The Conservative Aims of Militant Rhetoric," 694.

48. Miller, *The Messman Chronicles*, 121–22.

49. Logan and Winston, *Dictionary of American Negro Biography*, 616.

50. "Mess Attendants Write:'Don't Join the Navy.'"

51. "'Those Brave Colored Sailors," *Pittsburgh Courier*, October 12, 1940, 6.

52. Weiss, *Farewell to the Party of Lincoln*, 282.

53. "'The Negro Vote," *Pittsburgh Courier*, November 2, 1940, 3.

54. George Schuyler, "Views and Reviews," *Pittsburgh Courier*, December 21, 1940, 6.

55. "Navy Messmen, in Prison, Cry Out for Help from Readers," *Pittsburgh Courier*, November 9, 1940, 1.

56. "Navy Messmen, in Prison, Cry Out for Help from Readers."

57. "Navy Fires Mess Attendants," *Pittsburgh Courier*, December 7, 1940, 1.

58. "Judge William H. Hastie, Oral History Interview," interviewed by Jerry N. Hess, January 5, 1972, transcript, Harry S. Truman Presidential Library, Independence, MO, https://www.trumanlibrary.org/oralhist/hastie.htm#note.

CHAPTER 4: "WE ARE DISCRIMINATED AGAINST IN EVERY WAY."

1. Grossman, Keating, and Reiff, *Encyclopedia of Chicago*, 269.

2. W. E. B. Du Bois, "Close Ranks," *Crisis*, July 1918.

3. "Prep Mat Champion Johnny Reagan Graduates in June," *Chicago Defender*, March 25, 1939, 8. See, also, "Enrolled at Montana U.," *Chicago Defender*, December 2, 1939, 2.

4. Reagan, NIOHP, 3–25, 92–125.

5. "A Montana Grizzly," *Pittsburgh Courier*, October 19, 1940, 18.

6. John T. Campbell, "Reagan Is First the Goat, Then Real Hero," *Chicago Defender*, November 9, 1940, 24.

7. Moye, "The Tuskegee Airmen Oral History Project."

8. Gibson, *Knocking Down Barriers*, 7.

9. Perry, "It's Time to Force a Change."

10. Gibson, *Knocking Down Barriers*, 80.

11. Sullivan, *Days of Hope*, 136.

12. Alexa Mills, "A Lynching Kept Out of Sight," *Washington Post*, September 2, 2016, A1.

13. Gibson, *Knocking Down Barriers*, 80–84.

14. Lee, *The Employment of Negro Troops*, 141.

15. Lee, *The Employment of Negro Troops*, 142.

16. Dalfiume, "The 'Forgotten Years' of the Negro Revolution," 90–106.

17. "Now Is the Time Not to Be Silent," editorial, *Crisis*, January 1942, 7.

18. "The Negro in the United States Army," *Crisis*, February 1942, 47.

19. Finkle, *Forum for Protest*, 102–3.

20. Edward T. Folliard, "All Fleet Flags at Half-Staff; Full Military Rites to Be Held Monday," *Washington Post*, April 29, 1944, 1.

21. US Navy, Bureau of Naval Personnel, "The Negro in the Navy in World War II (1947)" (hereafter cited as "The Negro in the Navy"), 3.

22. Addison Walker, memo, December 6, 1941, GenRecsNav, 131-N, box 1.

23. "FDR Is Asked for Order on Navy Bias," *Chicago Defender*, December 27, 1941, 2.

24. "Mark F. Ethridge, Journalist, Dies at 84," *New York Times*, April 7, 1981, B1.

25. Schneller, *Breaking the Color Barrier*, 142.

26. Marie Baker to Lieut. Edward Hayes, January 4, 1942; Hayes to Baker, January 7, 1942, GenRecsNav, box 37, folder 54-1.

27. James E. Boyack, "Army Gets World's Most Famous Bomber," *Pittsburgh Courier*, January 24, 1942, 16.

28. Ernest E. Johnson, "Leaders Discuss Momentous War Problems: Correction of Evils Is Aim," Associated Negro Press, January 14, 1942.

29. "Judge William Hastie, 71, of Federal Court, Dies," *New York Times*, April 15, 1976, 36.

30. "Race Support of War Effort Is Lukewarm Say Conferees," *Pittsburgh Courier*, January 17, 1942, 1.

31. "Reveal Race War Apathy," *New York Amsterdam News*, January 17, 1942, 1.

32. "Judge Hastie Takes Message to 'Garcia,'" *Chicago Defender*, January 24, 1942, 14; "Leaders Find Negroes' War Effort Wanting," *New York Herald Tribune*, January 11, 1942, 23; "Reveal Race War Apathy."

33. "Attack Query on Loyalty of U.S. Negroes," *Chicago Defender*, January 31, 1942, 3.

34. "Mrs. Roosevelt Scores Prejudice as Obstacle to Country's Defense," *New York Amsterdam News*, January 17, 1942, 2; "Mrs. Roosevelt Warns Group Against Prejudice," *Pittsburgh Courier*, January 17, 1942, 8.

35. Sitkoff, *Toward Freedom Land*, 34.

36. Goodwin, *No Ordinary Time*, 328.

37. "Negroes Learn Navy Cannot Take Them Yet," *New York Herald Tribune*, April 9, 1942, 10.

38. Reddick, "The Negro in the United States Navy During World War II," 207.

39. FDR to Knox, January 9, 1942, President's Secretary's Files, box 7, FDRL; "The Negro in the Navy," 4–5.

40. MacGregor, *Integration of the Armed Forces*, 63–64.

41. Leonard L. Farber to Knox, January 19, 1942, and Knox to Farber, January 23, 1942, both GenRecsNav, box 37, folder 54-1.

CHAPTER 5: "WOULD IT BE DEMANDING TOO MUCH
TO DEMAND FULL CITIZENSHIP?"

1. Douglas Martin, "Doris E. Travis, Last of the Ziegfeld Girls, Dies at 106," *New York Times*, May 12, 2010, B12.

2. "Glorified by Ziegfeld," *Norfolk Journal and Guide*, July 25, 1931, 12.

3. "Deny Marital Troubles," *New York Amsterdam News*, October 14, 1939, 1.

4. "Emmita Due Back without Her Reginald," *New York Amsterdam News*, May 30, 1942, 1.

5. Sam Barnes, NIOHP, 165.

6. Sam Barnes, NIOHP, 21.

7. Olga Lash Barnes, interview with author, August 12, 2012.

8. Sam Barnes, NIOHP, 21, 149.

9. Sam Barnes, NIOHP, 196.

10. Sam Barnes, NIOHP, 164.

11. Sam Barnes, NIOHP, 6.

12. Sam Barnes, NIOHP, 171.

13. Sam Barnes, NIOHP, 9–10, 158.

14. Sam Barnes, NIOHP, 14–15, 27.

15. Sam Barnes, NIOHP, 133–34.

16. "Sunny Jim Barnes, Va. State Coach, Dies Suddenly," *Baltimore Afro-American*, April 6, 1935, 21.

17. Sam Barnes, NIOHP, 300.

18. Sam Barnes, NIOHP, 149–50.

19. William G. Nunn, "Race Leaders Demand Government End Discrimination At OFF Meet," *Pittsburgh Courier* March 28, 1942, 1; "U.S. Asked to Take Firm Stand," *Norfolk Journal and Guide*, March 28, 1942, 1; "Leaders Demand that U.S. Clean Own House," *Baltimore Afro-American*, March 28, 1942, 1; Roy Wilkins, "The Watchtower," *New York Amsterdam News*, March 28, 1942, 7.

20. Dalfiume, *Desegregation of the U.S. Armed Forces*, 126.

21. James G. Thompson, "Should I Sacrifice to Live 'Half-American'?," *Pittsburgh Courier*, January 31, 1942, 3.

22. "Enlistment of Men of Colored Race in Other Than the Messman Branch," February 3, 1942, President's Secretary's Files, box 7, FDRL.

23. Knox to FDR, February 5, 1942, President's Secretary's Files, box 7, FDRL.

24. FDR to Knox, February 9, 1942, President's Secretary's Files, box 7, FDRL.

25. Knox to FDR, December 19, 1941, President's Secretary's Files, box 62, FDRL.

26. Nalty, *Strength for the Fight*, 187; Nalty and MacGregor, *Blacks in the Military*, 138.

27. Gifford Pinchot to Knox, January 17, 1942; Knox to Pinchot, January 19; Pinchot to Knox, January 22, 1942, all in GenRecsNav, box 37, folder 54-1.

CHAPTER 6: "A CORDIAL SPIRIT OF EXPERIMENTATION"

1. Washburn, "*Pittsburgh Courier's* Double V Campaign in 1942," 5.

2. Johnson, *To Stem This Tide*, 102.

3. "'Double V' Clubs Unite, Fight for Abolition of Poll-Tax," *Pittsburgh Courier*, July 18, 1942, 15.

4. Washburn, *A Question of Sedition*, 107.

5. Finkle, "The Conservative Aims of Militant Rhetoric," 696.

6. Reed, *Seedtime for the Modern Civil Rights Movement*, 95.

7. Johnson, *To Stem This Tide*, 71.

8. Johnson, *To Stem This Tide*, 66.

9. Blum, *V Was for Victory*, 193–94.

10. Westbrook Pegler, "Fair Enough," *Atlanta Constitution*, April 29, 1942, 8. Pegler's syndicated column ran in many papers.

11. "Westbrook Pegler," *Chicago Defender* May 23, 1942, 14.

12. Washburn, *A Question of Sedition*, 115.

13. Washburn, "*Pittsburgh Courier's* Double V Campaign in 1942," 22–23.

14. Washburn, *A Question of Sedition*, 89–90.

15. J. E. Branham to Sen. Robert Taft, March 27, 1942, GenRecsNav, 131-N, box 1, folder B.

16. Martin L. Sweeney to Frank Knox, March 27, 1942; Addison Walker to Sweeney, March 30, 1942, GenRecsNav, 131-N, box 1.

17. Lorna R. F. Birtwell to FDR, March 31, 1942, GenRecsNav, 131-O, box 1.

18. Lobdell, "Frank Knox," 712.

19. "Along the NAACP Battlefront," *Crisis*, April, 1942, 139.

20. "Willkie Says Navy Jim Crow Is Mockery of Fine Words," *Baltimore Afro-American*, March 28, 1942, 3.

21. Ollie Stewart, "Willkie Says He'd End Navy Jim Crow: Roosevelt or Secretary Knox Could Dispose of Question with Snap of the Finger," *Baltimore Afro-American*, April 4, 1942, 1.

22. Knox to Paul Scott Mowrer, May 1, 1942, Knox Papers, box 4.

23. For "least disadvantages:" "Enlistment of Men of the Colored Race in Other Than the Messman Branch"; for "unwise": The Negro in the Navy," 90.

24. "Enlistment of Men of the Colored Race in Other Than the Messman Branch."

25. FDR to Knox, March 31, 1942, President's Secretary's Files, box 7, FDRL.

26. "The Negro in the Navy," 7.

27. Buell, *Master of Sea Power*, 343.

28. "Enlistment of Men of the Colored Race in Other Than the Messman Branch."

29. Goodwin, *No Ordinary Time*, 366.

30. Stillwell, *The Golden Thirteen*, xx.

31. Knox to Sen. David I. Walsh, May 21, 1942, GenRecsNav, box 37, folder 54-1.

32. Knox to Sen. William H. Smathers, February 7, 1942, GenRecsNav, box 37, folder 54-1.

33. Enoc Waters, "New Navy Policy No Gain for Race: Assail NAACP and NNC for Approving Jim Crow," *Chicago Defender*, April 18, 1942, 1.

34. "Knox's Pronouncement Insults 13,000,000 Colored Citizens," *Philadelphia Tribune*, April 18, 1942, 4.

35. "The Navy: Where Do We Stand?," *Pittsburgh Courier*, April 18, 1942, 6.

36. Alvin White, "Washington Leaders Ask Knox [to] Resign over New Navy Policy," *Cleveland Call and Post*, April 18, 1942, 13.

37. "The Navy and the Negro," *Opportunity: A Journal of Negro Life* 20, no. 5 (May 1942): 130.

38. "The Navy: Where Do We Stand?," 6.

39. "The Negro and the Navy," *New York Times*, April 9, 1942, 18.

40. "The Navy: Where Do We Stand?," 6.

41. Waters, "New Navy Policy No Gain for Race."

42. Letter to Knox, May 24, 1942, GenRecsNav, 131-O, box 1.

43. Martin J. Keefe to Sen. Francis Maloney, April 8, 1942, and Knox to Maloney (undated), GenRecsNav, 131-O, box 1.

44. Knox to Algernon D. Black, April 23,1943, GenRecsNav, box 37, folder 54-1.

45. William H. Jernagin to Addison Walker, April 23, 1942, GenRecsNav, 131-O, box 1.

46. Trip File, OF 200, box 61, FDRL.

47. "First Negroes for Combat Duty at Great Lakes: They'll Be Trained in New School," *Chicago Daily Tribune*, June 6, 1942, 21.

48. "The Negro in the Navy," 54.

49. Nelson, *The Integration of the Negro into the U.S. Navy*, 103.

50. "9th Courier Poll Shows Citizens' Disgust at Navy Discrimination," *Pittsburgh Courier*, November 21, 1942, 4.

51. Nelson, *The Integration of the Negro into the U.S. Navy*, 135.

52. "Nashville Has a Fine Crack Boy Scout Group," *Atlanta Daily World*, August 27, 1934, 2; "Origin of Negro Scouting in Nashville," *Baltimore Afro-American*, December 7, 1935, 19; "Dennis Nelson Promoted to Lt. Commander," *Norfolk Journal and Guide*, August 15, 1953, A1.

53. "Seven Knox Boys Join U.S. Navy," *Atlanta Daily World*, September 1, 1943, 6.

54. "Navy Urged to Train Colored Officers," *Baltimore Afro-American*, July 25, 1942, 12.

55. "Protest Exclusion of Negro College Students from Navy's V-1 Program," *Cleveland Call and Post*, July 11, 1943, 13.

56. "Students Excluded at Present: Land-Grant College Heads Confer with Navy Dept. Officials," *Norfolk Journal and Guide*, July 11, 1942, A1.

57. "The Negro in the Navy," 29–30.

58. John Wilhelm, "Negro Makes Quality Sailor, Navy Discovers: 1,000 Eager Recruits at Great Lakes," *Chicago Daily Tribune*, August 16, 1942, N1.

CHAPTER 7: "AS GOOD AS ANY FIGHTING MEN THE US NAVY HAS"

1. Reminiscences of Graham Edward Martin, interviewed by Paul Stillwell, October, 10, 1986, and July 19, 1988, NIOHP, 45–46.

2. Martin, NIOHP, 15.

3. Liebowitz, *My Indiana*. 189–90.

4. Hoose, *Hoosiers*, 57–58.

5. Bodenhamer and Barrows, *The Encyclopedia of Indianapolis*, 7–9.

6. Martin, NIOHP, 79.

7. A. H. Maloney, "The Negro of Indianapolis," *Indianapolis Recorder*, March 24, 1928, 1.

8. Martin, NIOHP, 79.

9. Martin, NIOHP, 8.

10. "'Jim Crow' School Is Legal: Indiana Supreme Court Places 'OK' on Segregated High School," *Pittsburgh Courier*, April 10, 1926, 1.

11. Hoose, *Hoosiers*, 59–61.

12. Martin, NIOHP, 21, 133.

13. Martin, NIOHP, 12. See, also, program for funeral of Dr. Russell Adrien Lane, May 1, 1986.

14. Martin, NIOHP, 13.

15. Martin, NIOHP, 29–40, 146.

16. Chief of Naval Personnel, "U.S. Naval Training Center, Great Lakes, Illinois" (hereafter cited as "Great Lakes"), 28.

17. Trip File, OF 200, box 61, FDRL.

18. John W. Fountain, "Men and Music of Another Time and Another War," *New York Times*, April 9, 2003, A12.

19. Newton, *Better Than Good*, 17.

20. Reminiscences of William Sylvester White, interviewed by Paul Stillwell, October 6, 1986, and July 22, 1988, NIOHP, 24.

21. Reminiscences of Frank Ellis Sublett, interviewed by Paul Stillwell, October 8, 1986, and July 21, 1988, NIOHP, 14–16.

22. "The Negro in the Navy," 62.

23. Sam Barnes, NIOHP, 298.

24. Reagan, NIOHP, 19, 27–31.

25. Hair, NIOHP, 136–38.

26. Hair, NIOHP, 136–38, 29.

27. Hair, NIOHP, 31–32.

28. Hare, NIOHP, 37.

29. Newton, *Better Than Good*, 12.

30. Stevenson, *The Papers of Adlai Stevenson*, 25.

31. Trip File, OF 200, box 61, FDRL.

32. "Great Lakes," 28–33, 152.

33. "Great Lakes," 33–34.

34. "Great Lakes," 34.

35. "Naval Reservists Learning How to Become Seagoing Fighters at Great Lakes Naval Training Station," *Norfolk Journal and Guide*, August 15, 1942, A11.

36. "Toughened Navy 'Boots' Now Ready for Action on Seas: Youths Gaining Weight, Begin Maturing Mentally," *Atlanta Daily World*, September 25, 1942, 1; Lt. Comm. Daniel W. Armstrong, "The Navy Needs Men . . . Yes, Negro Men," *Chicago Defender*, September 26, 1942, A16.

37. "Great Lakes," 129–30.

38. Reminiscences of Paul Deming Richmond, interviewed by Paul Stillwell, January, 14, 1990, NIOHP, 5.

39. "Navy's Colored Commandos Complete Tough Routine: Tough, Alert, Keen, Gallant Negro Naval Recruits First to Finish Commando Course at Great Lakes," *Pittsburgh Courier*, August 8, 1942, 14. See, also, "Negro Makes Quality Sailor, Navy Discovers: 1,000 Eager Recruits at Great Lakes," *Chicago Daily Tribune*, August 16, 1942, N1.

40. Trip File, OF 200, box 61, FDRL.

41. "Negro Sailors Maintain Excellent Naval Record," *Pittsburgh Courier*, August 1, 1942, 3.

42. "War Training Class at Howard U.," *Baltimore Afro-American*, October 3, 1942, 8.

43. "Great Lakes," 28–34, 80–81, 96, 150–52, 214.

44. Hair, NIOHP, 181.

45. Wilhelm, "Negro Makes Quality Sailor, Navy Discovers," N1.

46. Newton, *Better Than Good*, 17.

47. Martin, NIOHP, 154.

48. Reminiscences of John Flint Dille, interviewed by Paul Stillwell, October, 9, 1986, and August 25, 1989, NIOHP, 16.

49. Richmond, NIOHP, 27.

50. Floyd, "The Great Lakes Experience: 1942–45," 19–21.

51. Richmond, NIOHP, 8.

52. Hair, NIOHP, 41.

53. "Name Naval Camp in Honor of Negro Civil War Hero," *Norfolk Journal and Guide*, August 15, 1942, 2.

54. Knox to Sexton, memo, March 7, 1942, GenRecsNav, box 37, folder 54-1.

55. Daniel W. Armstrong to Ralph A. Bard, March 4, 1942, GenRecsNav, 131-N, box 1.

56. Richmond, NIOHP, 12.

57. Martin, NIOHP, 91; see, also, Arbor, NIOHP, 119.

58. Nelson, *The Integration of the Negro into the U.S. Navy*, 97–98.

59. "Great Lakes," 268.

60. Hatch and Hill, *A History of African American Theatre*, 337; "Owen Dodson to Sign for Navy; Leaves Hampton: Young Playwright Formerly Taught at Spelman College," *Atlanta Daily World*, November 5, 1942, 2.

61. Arbor, NIOHP, 121.

62. Wilhelm, "Negro Makes Quality Sailor, Navy Discovers," N1.

63. Nelson, *The Integration of the Negro into the U.S. Navy*, 102.

64. MacGregor, *Integration of the Armed Forces*, 67.

65. Van Ness, NIOHP, 7–9.

66. For a look at discipline, see Newton, *Better Than Good*, 16; "Great Lakes," 264–65; "The Negro in the Navy," 63.

67. Dille, NIOHP. See, also, "Great Lakes," 273.

68. Van Ness, NIOHP, 11–12.

69. Wilhelm, "Negro Makes Quality Sailor, Navy Discovers."

70. "Great Lakes," 263.

71. "Black Sailors," *Time*, August 17, 1942, 56.

72. Arbor, NIOHP, 1.

73. Trip File, OF 200, box 61, FDRL.

74. Medical report in "Arbor, Jesse Walter" (military personnel file).

75. Arbor, NIOHP, 53–54.

76. "Great Lakes," 136.

77. Trip File, OF 200, box 61, FDRL.

78. Goodwin, *No Ordinary Time*, 366; Trip File, OF 200, box 61, FDRL.

79. "First Sailors End Basic Navy Training," *Pittsburgh Courier*, August 15, 1942, 4.

80. US Copyright Office, *Catalog of Copyright Entries, 1942*, 41905.

81. Grace Tully Papers, box 7, logs of the President's trips, 10 FDRL.

82. Newton, *Better Than Good*, 18–19.

83. "The Negro in the Navy," 36.

84. Richmond, NIOHP, 13.

85. For a discussion on the literacy program at Camp Robert Smalls, see "The Negro in the Navy," 88–89; Martin, NIOHP, 50.

86. Martin, NIOHP, 1–5, 55.

87. Martin, NIOHP, 49–50.

88. Martin, NIOHP, 53–54.

89. Richmond, NIOHP, 21–22.

90. Richmond, NIOHP, 30.

CHAPTER 8: "YOU ARE NOW MEN OF HAMPTON."

1. "Lt. Commander Downes and Staff Welcome First of Naval Selectees," *Chicago Defender*, September 19, 1942, 12.

2. On the arrival of the first class at Hampton, see Bernard P. Young Jr., "A Report on History in Making: First Recruits Open Navy School," *Norfolk Journal and Guide*, September 19, 1942, 1; John Jordan, "The Ghosts of Great Naval Heroes Smiled on Hampton," *Norfolk Journal and Guide*, September 19, 1942, A12; "Hampton Base Gets First Apprentice Seamen: 128 Selectees Start Training for U.S. Navy," *Chicago Defender*, September 19, 1942, 12; "128 Seamen Begin Training at Hampton," *Baltimore Afro-American*, September 19, 1942, 3; "Commander Dubs Navy Seamen 'Men of Hampton,'" *Baltimore Afro-American*, September 19, 1942, 3.

3. "Hampton Ready to Receive Advanced Naval Recruits," *Philadelphia Tribune*, August 29, 1942, 5.

4. L. Baynard Whitney, "Who's Nutty Now?" *Philadelphia Tribune*, December 5, 1940, 4.

5. Walter White, "Why MacLean Resigned," *Chicago Defender*, January 23, 1943, 1.

6. Shetterly, *Hidden Figures*, 45–46.

7. Vic Stone, letter, *Oberlin Alumni Magazine* (Winter 1998), http://www2.oberlin.edu/alummag/oampast/oam_winter/Letters/oamwinter98_letters.html.

8. Clarence Toliver, "The Point Is This," *Baltimore Afro-American*, August 8, 1942, 5.

9. Sublett, NIOHP, 111.

10. "Efficiency Is Objective of Hampton Naval School: First Class to Graduate in January Commander Cites Aptitude of Men Now in Training," *Norfolk Journal and Guide*, November 21, 1942, A5.

11. Newton, *Better Than Good*, 24–25.

12. S. A. Haynes, "Navy School Building Men of Skills and Character," *Norfolk Journal and Guide*, September 25, 1943, A16.

13. Reagan, NIOHP, 164–65.

14. Newton, *Better Than Good*, 25–26.

15. Sublett, Frank Ellis, NPRC St. Louis.

16. Sublett, NIOHP, 11–17, 84–92.

17. On Reagan and Sublett working together, see Reagan, NIOHP, 31, 56, 144; "Naval Cadets Work Out with Hampton," *Norfolk Journal and Guide*, October 3, 1942. 14; "Back to Hampton in Navy Togs," *Chicago Defender*, October 31, 1942, 24.

18. Reagan, NIOHP, 169.

19. S. A. Haynes, "Navy Officials Praise Work at Hampton Naval Training Station, First of Its Kind," *Norfolk Journal and Guide*, September 11, 1943, B6.

20. Marion L. Starkey, "Contralto Is Fine Trooper as Well as Talented Artist," *Norfolk Journal and Guide*, October 24, 1942. 13.

21. Sublett, NIOHP, 26.

22. Sublett, NIOHP, 114.

23. "The Negro in the Navy," 74.

24. Haynes, "Navy Officials Praise Work at Hampton Naval Training Station."

25. Frank Sublett, NIOHP, 116.

26. Young, "A Report on History in Making"; "There's Plenty of Evidence That Negroes Are 'Doing Fine' in Navy," *Cleveland Call and Post*, July 24, 1943, 10.

27. Cooper, NIOHP, 5, 17–18, 111.

28. "Strike Mars Hampton Graduation," *Chicago Defender*, June 3, 1939, 1; "Howe Quits at Hampton," *Baltimore Afro-American*, March 2, 1940, 1.

29. "Hampton Students Protest Effects of Economy Program: Commencement Comes Off as Scheduled," *Norfolk Journal and Guide*, June 3, 1939, 1; "Hampton Goes 'Radical'— Students Strike," *Pittsburgh Courier*, June 3, 1939, 1.

30. "Hampton Seeks a New President," *Baltimore Afro-American*, March 2, 1940, 1.

31. "Strike Mars Hampton Graduation" ; "Hampton Students Protest Effects of Economy Program."

32. Peggy Cooper Davis, interview with author, January 19, 2019.

33. For the Coopers' wedding and marriage, see Cooper, NIOHP, 55; "Ohio Beauty to Wed," *Chicago Defender*, December 9, 1939, 18.

34. Cooper, NIOHP, 100; Peggy Cooper Davis, interviewed by author, May 11, 2012; Stillwell, "The Navy Years."

35. Reagan, NIOHP, 167.

36. Frank E. Bolden, "Democracy in Command Performance at Hampton," *Baltimore Afro-American*, May 13, 1944, 7.

37. Sublett, NIOHP, 117.

38. Kelly, *Proudly We Served*, 45; Astor, *The Right to Fight*, 215.

39. Reagan, NIOHP, 168.

40. Reagan, NIOHP, 114.

41. Reagan, NIOHP, 169–70.

42. Sitkoff, "Racial Militancy and Interracial Violence in the Second World War," 667.

43. Klinkner, *The Unsteady March*, 171.

44. Marjorie McKenzie, "Pursuit of Democracy: Army Unable to Protect Soldiers in South Because of Inadequate U.S. Laws," *Pittsburgh Courier*, December 19, 1942, 7.

45. "Negro Soldiers Shot, Beaten in Louisiana Riot," *New York Herald Tribune*, January 12, 1942, 13; Klinkner, *The Unsteady March*, 166–71.

46. McGuire, *Taps for a Jim Crow Army*, 11.

47. "Lynch Victim's Body Burned in Mo. Street," *Baltimore Afro-American*, January 31, 1942, 1; Capeci, "The Lynching of Cleo Wright," 863.

48. Gibson, *Knocking Down Barriers*, 11.

49. Baldwin, *Notes of a Native Son*, 101.

50. Enoc Waters, "One Man's Journal," *Chicago Defender*, September 26, 1942, 14.

51. Lloyd L. Brown, "Brown v. Salina, Kansas," *New York Times*, February 26, 1973, 31.

52. Flynn, "Selective Service and American Blacks During World War II," 19.

53. Sidney Walker, "Navy Abolishes Messman Branch; May Enlist Negro," *Pittsburgh Courier*, March 20, 1943, 1.

54. Nalty and MacGregor, *Blacks in the Military*, 145.

55. FDR to Knox, memo, February 22, 1943, President's Secretary's Files, box 7, FDRL.

56. "The Negro in the Navy," 13.

57. Lanning, *The African-American Soldier*, 200–201.

58. Walker, "Navy Abolishes Messman Branch; May Enlist Negro," 1.

59. FDR to Knox, memo, February 22, 1943.

60. "The Negro in the Navy," 32.

61. Johnston, "*And One Was a Priest*, 63.

62. Lanning, *The African-American Soldier*, 207–8.

63. "Navy Jim Crow Irks Hampton Institute," *Baltimore Afro-American*, April 10, 1943, 1.

64. Davis, "The Negro in the United States Navy, Marine Corps and Coast Guard," 347.

65. "Hampton Institute and the Navy during the Second World War, Part II: The Compromise."

66. Baugh, Dalton Louis, NPRC St. Louis.

67. Cooper, NIOHP, 19, 133.

CHAPTER 9: "I FEEL VERY EMPHATICALLY THAT WE SHOULD COMMISSION A FEW NEGROES."

1. Sam Barnes, NIOHP, 54.

2. Olga Lash Barnes, interviewed by author, August 7, 2012.

3. Sam Barnes, NIOHP, 33.

4. Sam Barnes, NIOHP, 16–17.

5. Davis, "The Negro in the United States Navy, Marine Corps and Coast Guard," 347.

6. See Sam Barnes, NIOHP, 8, 33–35, 54, 257, 291–98.

7. Klinkner, *The Unsteady March*, 171.

8. Reynolds, *From World War to Cold War*, 301.

9. Willkie, *One World*, 191.

10. "Sailors Protest Chores at Base," *Baltimore Afro-American*, May 29, 1943, 1.

11. Douglass Hall, "No Colored Sailors on Seagoing Vessels," *Baltimore Afro-American*, July 3, 1943, 1.

12. Nelson, *The Integration of the Negro into the U.S. Navy*, 99.

13. "Hampton Naval Trainees Say Skills Wasted on Menial Jobs," *Baltimore Afro-American*, July 24, 1939, 9.

14. "Hawaii Hate! Navy Braid Messes Knox Policy on Race Sailors," *Chicago Defender*, January 9, 1943, 1.

15. "Army Race Riots Grow!," *Chicago Defender*, June 19, 1943, 1.

16. Burran, "Racial Violence in the South during World War II," 161.

17. Bergman, *The Chronological History of the Negro in America*, 114.

18. Burran, "Racial Violence in the South during World War II," 133.

19. Perni, *A Heritage of Hypocrisy*, 65. The sergeant and a local sheriff later testified that Walker had started the scuffle.

20. "3 Slain at Miss. Camp," *Chicago Defender*, June 12, 1943, 1.

21. Burran, "Racial Violence in the South during World War II," 136.

22. "3 Slain at Miss. Camp."

23. Blum, *V Was for Victory*, 191; Burran, "Racial Violence in the South during World War II," 165.

24. Johnson, "Gender, Race, and Rumours," 258.

25. For the story of the Beaumont riot, see Burran, "Racial Violence in the South during World War II," 170–76; "Beaumont Race Riot Put Down, *Austin Statesman*, June 16, 1943, 1; "Court of Inquiry Begins Hearings on Race Rioting," *Austin Statesman*, June 17, 1943, 1.

26. Burran, "Racial Violence in the South during World War II," 184–85.

27. Bergman, *The Chronological History of the Negro in America*, 500.

28. Johnson, "Gender, Race, and Rumours," 264.

29. On the Detroit riots, see John H. Witherspoon, commissioner of police, report, June 28, 1943, and FBI to Attorney General, memo, July 8, 1943, both in Office File 93C, "Colored Matters," Container 8, "Detroit Race Riots, 1943–45," FDRL (henceforth cited as "Detroit Race Riots, 1943–45"). See, also, Blum, *V Was for Victory*, 203.

30. Vito Marcantonio to FDR, June 16, 1943, "Detroit Race Riots, 1943–45."

31. Sylvia Velkoff to FDR, August 6, 1943, "Detroit Race Riots, 1943–45."

32. "Defeat at Detroit," *Nation*, July 3, 1943, 4.

33. Walter White to FDR, telegram, June 21, 1943, "Detroit Race Riots, 1943–45."

34. John F. Lang to FDR, July 29, 1943, "Detroit Race Riots, 1943–45."

35. Blum, *V Was for Victory*, 204.

36. Eleanor Roosevelt, My Day, June 23, 1943, Eleanor Roosevelt Papers, Digital Edition, https://www2.gwu.edu/~erpapers/myday/displaydoc.cfm?_y=1943&_f=md056528b.

37. "The Negro in the Navy," 75–79.

38. Eleanor Roosevelt, My Day, July 14, 1943, Eleanor Roosevelt Papers, Digital Edition, https://www2.gwu.edu/~erpapers/myday/displaydoc.cfm?_y=1943&_f=md056544b.

39. John Sengstacke to FDR, June 29, 1943, OF 93C, FDRL.

40. White to FDR, telegram, June 21, 1943, and Jonathan Daniels to Rev. Francis J. Haas, memo, June 29, 1943, both in "Detroit Race Riots, 1943–45."

41. Lee, *Race Riot, Detroit 1943*, 60–62.

42. Wynn, *The Afro-American and the Second World War*, 108.

43. Klinkner, *The Unsteady March*, 184, 199.

44. Russell B. Porter, "Harlem Unrest Traced to Long-Standing Ills," *New York Times*, August 8, 1943, E10.

45. Polenberg, *One Nation Divisible*, 77.

46. MacGregor, *Integration of the Armed Forces*, 76–77.

47. Nichols, *Breakthrough on the Color Front*, 57.

48. Lanning, *The African-American Soldier*, 201–2.

49. MacGregor, *Integration of the Armed Forces*, 77.

50. Hall, "No Colored Sailors on Seagoing Vessels," 1.

51. MacGregor, *Integration of the Armed Forces*, 77.

52. Ernest Johnson, "Navy Boss Knox Bars Mixed Crews in Navy," *Chicago Defender*, November 20, 1943, 1.

53. "Our Boys to Man Navy Ships: 22 Officers and Crews Will Fight Enemy," *Pittsburgh Courier*, February 26, 1944, 1.

54. "Navy Day for Whom," *Baltimore Afro-American*, October 23, 1943, 4.

55. Cochran, *Adlai Stevenson*, 135–38; Lobdell, "Frank Knox," 693.

56. Stevenson, *The Papers of Adlai Stevenson*, 77, 79, 90, 105.

57. MacGregor, *Integration of the Armed Forces*, 80.

58. Nelson, *The Integration of the Negro into the U.S. Navy*, 63.

59. Adlai Stevenson to Knox, memo, September 29, 1943, Adlai E. Stevenson Papers, MC124, box 387, folder 6.

60. "The Honorable William Sylvester White," interview (video), History Makers (website), September 5, 2000, https://www.thehistorymakers.org/biography/honorable-william-sylvester-white.

61. "Gets 3 Years in Jail for Praising Japs as Hope of Negroes," *Chicago Tribune*, April 20, 1943, 12; "Newby Gets Three Years for Sedition," *Chicago Defender*, April 24, 1943, 1.

62. White, NIOHP, 16.

63. White, NIOHP, 27.

64. White, NIOHP, 1–18.

65. White, NIOHP, 26

66. "Attorney in Navy," *Chicago Defender*, November 6, 1943, 6.

67. White, NIOHP, 53.

68. Martin, NIOHP, 159.

69. Reddick, "The Negro in the United States Navy during World War II," 209.

70. Nelson, *The Integration of the Negro into the US Navy*, 29.

71. Gogan, *By Air, Ground, and Sea*, 134.

72. Martin, NIOHP, 29, 40.

73. Gogan, *By Air, Ground, and Sea*, 144.

74. Emmet replaced Admiral John Downes as commandant of the Great Lakes Naval Training Center in 1943 and served in that post until 1945, when he retired. See Werner Bamberger, "Adm. Emmet, 89, Dies; Served in Two Wars," *New York Times*, July 8, 1977, 13; Dave Hoff, "Hawks Soften Irish: Bluejackets Apply Finishing Touch," *Daily Illini*, November 28, 1943, 4.

75. "The Negro in the Navy," 32.

76. "Commander Armstrong on Navy Officers," *Norfolk Journal and Guide*, November 27, 1943, 6.

77. "The Negro in the Navy," 32.

78. Martin, NIOHP, 56.

79. Sam Barnes, NIOHP, 41–42, 72, 73.

80. "Letters to Naval Training Commander Reveal Race Youths Are 'Doing Fine,'" *Atlanta Daily World*, July 18, 1943, 4.

81. Newton, *Better Than Good*, 28–29.

82. Jeff Smith, "The Douglas Hotel: The Harlem of the West," *San Diego Reader*, August 5, 1999.

83. Ron Grossman, "Breaking a Naval Blockade," *Chicago Tribune*, July 8, 1987, 1.

84. Reagan, NIOHP, 114–15.

CHAPTER 10: "YOU CAN MAKE ME AN OFFICER, BUT MY PARENTS MADE ME A GENTLEMAN."

1. Arbor, NIOHP, 129; Sam Barnes, NIOHP, 203.

2. Cooper, NIOHP, 22.

3. John Brindley, Glenn R. Amato, and Ralf H. R. Edle, "Getting Back Together after All These Years," *All Hands*, October, 1977, 11.

4. Brindley, Amato, and Edle, "Getting Back Together after All These Years," 8.

5. White, NIOHP, 30.

6. Sam Barnes, NIOHP, 203.

7. Cooper, NIOHP, 140.

8. Lear, Charles Byrd, NPRC St. Louis.

9. Sam Barnes, NIOHP, 44, 201.

10. Sam Barnes, NIOHP, 329.

11. Sam Barnes, NIOHP, 216, 319, 329.

12. Sam Barnes, NIOHP, 221.

13. White, NIOHP, 90; Arbor, NIOHP, 22.

14. Lloyd Wendt, "The Navy's Debt to the Negro," *Chicago Tribune*, May 29, 1949, C5.

15. Dille, NIOHP, 38; Cooper, NIOHP, 48.

16. Cooper, NIOHP, 42.

17. Martin, NIOHP, 69.

18. Martin, NIOHP, 164; White, NIOHP, 74–75.

19. Hair, NIOHP, 43.

20. Cooper, NIOHP, 38; Sam Barnes, NIOHP, 212–13; Sublett, NIOHP, 135; Reagan, NIOHP, 43.

21. Martin, NIOHP, 67.

22. Barnes, Phillip George, NPRC St. Louis.

23. Sublett, NIOHP, 33; Martin, NIOHP, 67; Cooper, NIOHP, 39, 144.

24. Cooper, NIOHP, 46, 48; Arbor, NIOHP, 135; Martin, NIOHP, 64.

25. Hair, NIOHP, 51–53, 189–95; White, NIOHP, 68. Cooper, NIOHP, 45.

26. Martin, NIOHP, 58, Arbor, NIOHP, 60.

27. Cooper, NIOHP, 50–52; Martin, NIOHP, 77.

28. Cooper, NIOHP, 53.

29. Sublett, NIOHP, 35; Cooper, NIOHP, 45; "Pearl Harbor Gets 1st Naval Officers," *Baltimore Afro-American*, July 29, 1944, 1.

30. Lorraine Baugh, interviewed by author, March 11, 2019.

31. Cooper, NIOHP, 143–44.

32. Sublett, NIOHP, 142.

33. Sublett, NIOHP, 29; Richmond, NIOHP, 26.

34. Sublett, NIOHP, 30; Martin, NIOHP, 170–71.

35. The syllabus is found in the George Cooper Collection, National Museum of the American Sailor, Great Lakes, IL.

36. Sublett, NIOHP, 137.

37. Nelson, *The Integration of the Negro into the U.S. Navy*, 154–55.

38. For more on their curriculum, see the George Cooper collection.

39. Brindley, Amato, and Edle, "Getting Back Together after All These Years," 8.

40. White, NIOHP, 72; Sam Barnes, NIOHP, 207; Martin, NIOHP, 163.

41. Hair, NIOHP, 59.

42. Brindley, Amato, and Edle, "Getting Back Together after All These Years," 8.

43. Cooper, NOIHP, 26.

44. Stillwell, "The Navy Years," 5–8.

45. Peggy Cooper Davis, interview with author, May 11, 2012.

46. Cooper, NIOHP, 167.

47. For the story of Phillip Barnes and his sister, see Martin, NIOHP, 58; White, NIOHP, 37; Arbor, NIOHP, 9.

48. For descriptions of the ruler and pharmacist's mate, see Martin, NIOHP, 167; Hair, NIOHP, 64-65, 225.

49. Richmond, NIOHP, 31.

50. Schneller, *Breaking the Color Barrier*, 157.

51. Reagan, NIOHP, 43; Arbor, NIOHP, 132.

52. White, NIOHP, 107.

53. John Dille III, interviewed by author, April 16, 2018.

54. Ron Grossman, "Breaking a Naval Blockade," *Chicago Tribune*, July 8, 1987, 1.
55. Dille, NIOHP, 1–10.
56. Ostewig, *The Sage of Sinnissippi*, 300.
57. Dille, NIOHP, 25.
58. Dille, NIOHP, 11, 14, 21–25, 47; Sam Barnes, NIOHP, 228–29, 247–49, 254; Richmond, NIOHP, 4, 20.
59. Sam Barnes, NIOHP, 204.
60. Author interview with Paul Richmond, a cousin of Lieutenant Paul Richmond, June 5, 2019.
61. For Richmond's relationship to the men, see Sam Barnes, NIOHP, 204, 318; Richmond, NIOHP, 26.
62. Grossman, "Breaking a Naval Blockade," 1.
63. "The Negro in the Navy," 33.
64. Nelson, *The Integration of the Negro into the U.S. Navy*, 54–55.
65. Arbor, NIOHP, 13.
66. Reagan, NIOHP, 58.
67. Sam Barnes, NIOHP, 236
68. Cooper, NIOHP, 27.
69. White, NIOHP, 56.
70. Cooper, NIOHP, 153–54.
71. "Powell Is Second of Race Made a Warrant Officer," *Norfolk Journal and Guide*, June 17, 1944, 16.
72. Reagan, NIOHP, 191.
73. Hair, NIOHP, 53.
74. "Another 'First' in Navy," *Baltimore Afro-American*, January 27, 1945, 7.
75. Reagan, NIOHP, 131.
76. Arbor, NIOHP, 59–60.
77. White, NIOHP, 112; Nelson, *The Integration of the Negro into the U.S. Navy*, 155.
78. "Navy Appoints 12 Ensigns; See[s] Color Line Fade," *Chicago Defender*, March 25, 1944, 1.
79. White, William Sylvester, NPRC St. Louis.
80. "First Negro Ensigns," *Life*, April 24, 1944, 44.
81. "First Negro Ensigns," *Life*, May 15, 1944, 2; "Negro Ensigns," and "First Negro Ensigns," *Life*, June 5, 1944, 2.
82. Cooper, NIOHP, 28, 168.
83. Arbor, NIOHP, 148–49.
84. Cooper, NIOHP, 28.
85. White, NIOHP, 20.
86. Arbor, NIOHP, 13.
87. Arbor, NIOHP, 55.

CHAPTER 11: "HIS INTELLIGENCE AND JUDGMENT ARE EXCEPTIONAL."
1. "End of a Strenuous Life," *Time*, May 8, 1944, 12. See, also, Navy Department, "Secretary of the Navy Frank Knox Dies," press release, April 28, 1944, Adlai E. Stevenson Papers, MC124, Box 387, Folder 7, Princeton University
2. Sidney Shalett, "Knox Dies in Home of Heart Attack; Navy in Mourning" *New York Times*, April 29, 1944, 1.

3. Lobdell, "Frank Knox," 721.

4. Navy Department, "Secretary of the Navy Frank Knox Dies"; "Knox, Navy Secretary, Dies of Heart Attack at 70 in Washington," *Washington Post*, April 29, 1944, 1.

5. FDR to Annie Reid Knox, April 26, 1944, President's Secretary's Files, box 62, FDRL.

6. Sam Barnes, NIOHP, 77.

7. "The Negro in the Navy," 85.

8. John H. Sengstacke to Randall Jacobs, March 16, 1944, GenRecsNav, box 37, folder 54-1.

9. Leland P. Lovette to Knox, memo, March 31, 1944, GenRecsNav, box 37, folder 54-1.

10. White, William Sylvester, NPRC St. Louis.

11. White, NIOHP, 31–36.

12. M. Collins, performance report for William White, March 8, 1945, in White, William Sylvester.

13. Edward Downs, performance report for Frank Sublett, July 4, 1944, in Sublett, Frank, NPRC St. Louis.

14. William Turek, performance report for Jesse Arbor, July 26, 1944, in Arbor, Jesse Walter, NPRC St. Louis.

15. LeRoy F. Moore Jr., performance report for George Cooper, May 28, 1945, in Cooper, George, NPRC St. Louis.

16. "Navy Commissions Negro Lieutenant; Staff Officers Next," *Cleveland Call and Post*, May 20, 1944, A1.

17. "The Negro in the Navy," 85.

18. Chief of Naval Personnel, "Negro Training," in "Great Lakes," 179.

19. William Turek, performance report for Reginald Goodwin, August 14, 1944, in Goodwin, Reginald, NPRC St. Louis.

20. "Ready to Fight V-D at Naval Training Station," *Baltimore Afro-American*, June 30, 1945, 10.

21. "Navy Remedial Schools Lower Illiteracy Ratios," *Pittsburgh Courier*, August 5, 1944, 3.

22. White, NIOHP, 45.

23. "The Negro in the Navy," 30; Nelson, *The Integration of the Negro into the U.S. Navy*, 105, 136.

24. Reagan, NIOHP, 146.

25. Nelson, *The Integration of the Negro into the U.S. Navy*, 159.

26. Sam Barnes, NIOHP, 237.

27. Richmond, NIOHP, 31.

28. Nelson, *The Integration of the Negro into the U.S. Navy*, 160.

29. Chief of Naval Personnel, "Negro Training," in "Great Lakes," 268.

30. MacGregor, *Integration of the Armed Forces*, 82.

31. Nelson, *The Integration of the Negro into the U.S. Navy*, 161.

32. Brindley, Amato, and Edle, "Getting Back Together after All These Years," 8.

33. Martin, NIOHP, 93.

34. Reagan, NIOHP, 146.

35. Sam Barnes, NIOHP, 72, 79.

36. Al Monroe, "Swinging in the News," *Chicago Defender*, August 26, 1944, 6.

37. Buckley, *American Patriots*, 307. See also Ted Sherman, "Lena Horne at 100: WW2 Memories of Meeting Her," *90isthenewblack* (blog), June 30, 2017, https://90isthenewblack.wordpress.com/2017/06/30/lena-horne-at-100-ww2-memories-of-meeting-her/comment-page-1/#comment-951.

38. Cooper, NIOHP, 31–35.

39. Sublett, NIOHP, 44, 150.

40. Hair, NIOHP, 69.

41. Cooper, NIOHP, 30.

42. Schneller, *Breaking the Color Barrier*, 158.

43. MacGregor, *Integration of the Armed Forces*, 85.

44. MacGregor, *Integration of the Armed Forces*, 85.

45. Reminiscences of Lester B. Granger, interviewed by William T. Ingersoll, November 1, 1960, and Ed Edwin, May 8, 1961, Columbia Center for Oral History, Columbia University, New York (hereafter cited as Granger reminiscences), 159–60.

46. Jacobs to Commanding Officers, August, 9, 1944, GenRecsNav, box 37, folder 54–1.

47. MacGregor, *Integration of the Armed Forces*, 85–86.

48. Nelson, *The Integration of the Negro into the U.S. Navy*, 46.

49. Nelson, *The Integration of the Negro into the U.S. Navy*, 49.

50. MacGregor, *Integration of the Armed Forces*, 87.

51. White, *A Man Called White*, 272–75.

52. Nelson, *The Integration of the Negro into the U.S. Navy*, 160–61.

53. Chief of Naval Personnel, "Negro Training," in "Great Lakes," 281–82.

CHAPTER 12: "YOU FORGET THE COLOR AND YOU REMEMBER THE RANK."

1. White, *A Man Called White*, 278–85.

2. Arbor, NIOHP, 16, 63.

3. Arbor, NIOHP, 14.

4. Sam Barnes, NIOHP, 83.

5. Sam Barnes, NIOHP, 74–75.

6. Sublett, NIOHP, 47–48, 161; Reagan, NIOHP, 58.

7. Martin, NIOHP, 95–96.

8. Martin, NIOHP, 100–101.

9. Sublett, NIOHP, 50.

10. Martin, NIOHP, 97, 187.

11. Brindley, Amato, and Edle, "Getting Back Together after All These Years," 8.

12. R. A. Wolverton to Forrestal, February 13, 1946, in Martin, Graham, NPRC St. Louis.

13. Levin, *The Negro Sailor*, 1945.

14. Hair, NIOHP, 83–84.

15. Reagan, NIOHP, 60–61.

16. Hair, NIOHP, 80–81.

17. James E. Smith, "Negro Ensign Now Skipper of U.S. Navy Combat Ship," *Pittsburgh Courier*, September 16, 1944, 1.

18. Kelly, *Proudly We Served*, 150.

19. Hair, NIOHP, 156.

20. Reagan, NIOHP, 158–59.

21. Reagan, NIOHP, 194.

22. Reminiscences of Commander Norman Harry Meyer, interviewed by Paul Stillwell, November 6, 1986, NIOHP, 8, 15.

23. Hair, NIOHP, 87; Meyer, NIOHP, 17–20.

24. Hair, NIOHP, 85–86.

25. Meyer, NIOHP, 24.

26. Granger reminiscences, 146.

27. White, NIOHP, 42.

28. "Navy's Mixed Plan Praised," *Norfolk Journal and Guide*, July 21, 1945, 1.

29. Sublett, NIOHP, 163.

30. Sublett, NIOHP, 40.

31. Martin, NIOHP, 190.

32. Sublett, NIOHP, 147.

33. White, NIOHP, 88.

34. "Extra! Naval Racial Practice Lagging behind Policy, Granger Reports," *Baltimore Afro-American*, November 10, 1945, 1.

35. H. B. Miller, performance report for William White, June 30, 1946, in White, William Sylvester, NPRC St. Louis.

36. White, NIOHP, 115.

37. Chief of Naval Personnel, "Negro Training," in "Great Lakes," 276–77, 280.

38. MacGregor, *Integration of the Armed Forces*, 144.

39. "Last All-Colored Class Graduated at Great Lakes," *Baltimore Afro-American*, September 8, 1945, 8.

40. Chief of Naval Personnel, "Negro Training," in "Great Lakes," 279–82.

41. White, NIOHP, 84.

42. Stillwell, *The Golden Thirteen*, 162.

43. Cooper, NIOHP, 36.

44. Reagan, NIOHP, 205

45. MacGregor, *Integration of the Armed Forces*, 242–43.

46. Nelson, *The Integration of the Negro into the U.S. Navy*, 159.

47. Nelson, *The Integration of the Negro into the U.S. Navy*, 93; MacGregor, *Integration of the Armed Forces*, 246.

48. Reagan, NIOHP, 208.

49. "Dustin' Off the News," *Chicago Defender*, August 20, 1949, 4.

50. MacGregor, *Integration of the Armed Forces*, 243.

51. Gertrude Martin, "Book Reviews," review of *The Integration of the Negro into the U.S. Navy*, by Dennis Nelson, *Chicago Defender*, September 1, 1951, 7.

52. "Negro Officer Assails Navy's Treatment but Praises Its Attempt at Improvement," *New York Times*, February 2, 1948, 3.

53. Lester B. Granger, "Our Newer Navy," *New York Amsterdam News*, September 1, 1951, 6.

54. Stillwell, *The Golden Thirteen*, 190; Sam Barnes, NIOHP, 306–8; Cooper, NIOHP, 50.

55. "US Navy Will Appoint First Black as Admiral," Associated Press, April 28, 1971.

CHAPTER 13: "THERE IS THAT SALUTE YOU NEVER GOT."

1. Ben A. Franklin, "8 of First Black Navy Officers Hold Reunion at Sea," *New York Times*, April 14, 1982, A18.

2. Hair, NIOHP, 109–11; James Hair Jr. interviewed by author, April 15, 2011.

3. Sam Barnes, NIOHP, 130–31.

4. For the story of the reunion on the USS *Kidd*, see "Reunion of First Black Navy Officers," *Baltimore Afro-American*, April 24, 1982, 6.

5. Navy death notice, November 21, 1947, in Lear, Charles, NPRC St. Louis.

6. Navy death notice, May 4, 1949, in Barnes, Phillip George, NPRC St. Louis.

7. "Attorney Drops Dead after Talk," *Chicago Defender*, November 9, 1974, 1.

8. Maurice Possley, "Attorney Says He Paid Bribes to Judge," *Chicago Tribune*, April 23, 1987, 7.

9. "Lt. Cmdr. Dalton L. Baugh Sr., 72; One of the First Black Naval Officers," *Boston Globe*, January 5, 1985, 31.

10. "Naval Officer Pays Tribute to Work of Former Governor," *Atlanta Daily World*, February 16, 1956, 2.

11. "First 2 Negro Naval Officers Form Firm," *Atlanta Daily World*, January 5, 1964, A4.

12. "Howard Student, 19, Becomes 4th Negro Admitted to Naval Academy," *Chicago Defender*, July 7, 1951, 3; "Family Tradition," *Norfolk Journal and Guide*, August 15, 1953, 1.

13. "Ex-Navy Integration Advisor Will Head Relations Bureau," *Los Angeles Times*, September 7, 1966, A1.

14. John Flink, "Jesse Arbor of 'Golden Thirteen,'" *Chicago Tribune*, January 14, 2000, 2C11.

15. Cooper, NIOHP, 63.

16. "Dr. Samuel Barnes Named Howard Athletic Director," *Atlanta Daily World*, September 19, 1956, 5; "Sam Barnes Receives Fame Award," *Cleveland Call and Post*, July 11, 1970, 9B

17. White, NIOHP, 116–18.

18. Reginald Stuart, "Indianapolis Black School Preserves 50-Year Identity," *New York Times*, January 29, 1977, 9.

19. Sublett, NIOHP, 59.

20. Bert Mann, "Tide Turns: Black Navy Man Recall[s] Early Bias," *Los Angeles Times*, August 7, 1977, SG1.

21. Reagan, NIOHP, 36, Stillwell, *Golden Thirteen*, 143.

22. Franklin, "8 of First Black Navy Officers Hold Reunion at Sea," A18.

23. Conan, "Two of the Golden Thirteen Interviewed."

24. Barnes, NIOHP, 125.

25. Adele Koehnen, "Centerville Manager, Library Honored for Diversity Leadership," *Dayton Daily News*, July 28, 2005, Z2–1.

26. Brandon A. Perry, "Martin Honored for Making a Difference," *Indianapolis Recorder*, August 26, 2011, A1.

27. Carol. E. Lee, "Obama Waves, Salutes," *Politico*, December 23, 2008.

28. "U.S. Navy Demographic Data," https://www.navy.mil/strategic/Navy_Demographics_Report.pdf.

29. "The Honorable William Sylvester White," interview (video), History Makers (website), September 5, 2000,

30. James Hair Jr., interviewed by author, April 15, 2011.

31. Olga Welch, interview with author, May 20, 2019.

32. Reagan, NIOHP, 217.

33. Lorraine Baugh, interviewed by author, March 11, 2019.

34. Grossman, "Breaking a Naval Blockade," 1.

BIBLIOGRAPHY

A NOTE ON SOURCING: Much of the material in this book comes from oral histories taken roughly forty years after the war. In some cases, men remember the same event differently, reflecting their own perceptions and the passage of time. This is particularly true of their first and last days of officer training. In all instances, I endeavored to present what I believe to be the most accurate account, based on primary sources such as military personnel records and contemporaneous newspapers.

ARCHIVES AND MANUSCRIPT COLLECTIONS
Franklin D. Roosevelt Library and Museum, Hyde Park, NY: President's Secretary's Files; Office Files; Trip File, OF 93, 200; Colored Matters 93C; Committee on Fair Container Employment Practices 4245-G.
General Records of the Department of the Navy, 1798–1947, Records of the Bureau of Naval Personnel College Park, MD.
National Museum of the American Sailor, US Naval Training Station, Great Lakes, IL: George Cooper Collection.
Princeton University Library, Princeton, NJ: Adlai E. Stevenson Papers, MC124, Public Policy Papers, Department of Rare Books and Special Collections.

ORAL HISTORIES
Columbia Center for Oral History, Columbia University, NY: Reminiscences of Lester B. Granger
US Naval Institute Oral History Program, Annapolis, MD: Reminiscences of Jesse W. Arbor, Samuel E. Barnes, George C. Cooper, John F. Dille Jr., James E. Hair, Graham E. Martin, Norman H. Meyer, John W. Reagan, Paul D. Richmond, Frank E. Sublett Jr., Donald O. Van Ness, William Sylvester White.

MILITARY PERSONNEL RECORDS
National Personnel Records Center, St. Louis, MO: Jesse Arbor, Phil Barnes, Dalton Baugh, George Cooper, Reginald Goodwin, Charles Lear, Graham Martin, John Reagan, Frank Sublett, William White.

GOVERNMENT PUBLICATIONS
US Copyright Office. *Catalog of Copyright Entries, 1942.* "Music New Series," vol. 37, pt. 3. Washington, DC: Government Printing Office, 1942, https://archive .org/details/catalogofcopyri373lib/page/1536.
"Command of Negro Troops." Found in President's Secretary's Files, Box 4245-G, Franklin D. Roosevelt Library, Hyde Park, NY.

BOOKS
Allen, Robert L. *The Port Chicago Mutiny.* New York: Warner Books, 1989.
Astor, Gerald. *The Right to Fight: A History of African Americans in the Military.* Novato, CA: Presidio, 1998.
Baldwin, James. *Notes of a Native Son.* Boston: Beacon Press, 1955.
Beasley, Norman. *Frank Knox, American: A Short Biography.* Garden City: Doubleday, Doran & Co., 1936.
Bellush, Bernard. *He Walked Alone: A Biography of John Gilbert Winant.* The Hague, Netherlands: Mouton, 1968.
Bergman, Peter M. *The Chronological History of the Negro in America.* New York: Harper & Row, 1969.
Blum, John Morton. *V Was for Victory: Politics and American Culture During World War II.* New York: Harcourt Brace Jovanovich, 1976.
Bodenhamer, David J., and Robert G. Barrows. *The Encyclopedia of Indianapolis.* Bloomington: University of Indiana Press, 1994.
Brownlow, Louis. *A Passion for Anonymity: The Autobiography of Louis Brownlow.* Chicago: University of Chicago Press, 1958.
Buckley, Gail Lumet. *American Patriots: The Story of Blacks in the Military from the Revolution to Desert Storm.* New York: Random House, 2001.
Buell, Thomas. *Master of Sea Power: A Biography of Fleet Admiral Ernest J. King.* Boston: Little, Brown, 1980.
Bullard, Robert L. *Personalities and Reminiscences of the War.* New York: Doubleday, 1925.
Bunie, Andrew. *Robert L. Vann of the Pittsburgh Courier: Politics and Black Journalism.* Pittsburgh: University of Pittsburgh Press, 1974.
Cannadine, David. *Mellon: An American Life.* New York: Knopf, 2006.
Chen, Anthony S. *The Fifth Freedom: Jobs, Politics, and Civil Rights in the United States, 1941–1972.* Princeton, NJ: Princeton University Press, 2009.

Cochran, Bert. *Adlai Stevenson: Patrician among the Politicians.* New York: Funk & Wagnalls, 1969.

Dalfiume, Richard M. *Desegregation of the U.S. Armed Forces: Fighting on Two Fronts, 1939–1953.* Columbia: University of Missouri Press, 1969.

Doyle, William. *Inside the Oval Office: The White House Tapes from FDR to Clinton.* New York: Kodansha International, 1999

Eiler, Keith. *Mobilizing America: Robert P. Patterson and the War Effort, 1940–1945.* Ithaca, NY: Cornell University Press, 1997.

Finkle, Lee. *Forum for Protest: The Black Press During World War II.* Rutherford, NJ: Fairleigh Dickinson University Press, 1975.

Fisher, Donald M. *Lacrosse: A History of the Game.* Baltimore: Johns Hopkins University Press, 2002.

Freidel, Frank. *FDR and the South.* Baton Rouge: Louisiana State University Press, 1965.

Garfinkle, Herbert. *When Negroes March: The March on Washington Movement in the Organizational Politics for FEPC.* Glencoe, IL: Free Press, 1959.

Gibson, Truman K. *Knocking Down Barriers: My Fight for Black America.* Evanston, IL: Northwestern University Press, 2005.

Gogan, Roger. *By Air, Ground, and Sea: The History of Great Lakes Navy Football.* Gurnee, IL: Great Lakes Sports Publishing, 2013.

Goodwin, Doris Kearns. *No Ordinary Time: Franklin and Eleanor Roosevelt; The Home Front in World War II.* New York: Simon & Schuster, 1994.

Graves, John Temple. *The Fighting South.* New York: G. P. Putnam's Sons, 1943.

Grossman, James R., Ann Durkin Keating, and Janice L. Reiff, editors. *Encyclopedia of Chicago.* Chicago: University of Chicago Press, 2004.

Hagan, Kenneth J. *The People's Navy: The Making of American Sea Power.* New York: Freedom Press, 1991.

Hatch, James V. *Sorrow Is the Only Faithful One: The Life of Owen Dodson.* Urbana: University of Illinois Press, 1993.

Hatch, James V., and Errol G. Hill. *A History of African American Theatre.* New York: Cambridge University Press, 2003.

Haynes, Richard F. *The Awesome Power: Harry S. Truman as Commander in Chief.* Baton Rouge: Louisiana State University Press, 1973.

Hoops, Townsend. *Driven Patriot: The Life and Times of James Forrestal.* New York: Knopf, 1992.

Hoose, Phillip M. *Hoosiers: The Fabulous Basketball Life of Indiana.* 3rd ed. Bloomington: Indiana University Press, 2016.

Hull, Cordell. *The Memoirs of Cordell Hull.* New York: Macmillan, 1948.

Ickes, Harold L. *The Inside Struggle, 1936–1939.* Vol. 2 of *The Secret Diaries of Harold L. Ickes.* New York: Simon & Schuster, 1953.

Ickes, Harold L. *The Lowering Clouds, 1939–1941.* Vol. 3 of *The Secret Diaries of Harold L. Ickes.* New York: Simon & Schuster, 1954.

Ingham, John N. *Biographical Dictionary of American Business Leaders,* Vol. 4. Westport, CT: Greenwood Press, 1983.

Johnson, Charles S. *To Stem This Tide: A Survey of Racial Tension Areas in the United States.* Boston: Pilgrim Press, 1943.

Johnston, Araminta Stone. *And One Was a Priest: The Life and Times of Duncan M. Gray Jr.* Jackson: University of Mississippi Press, 2010.

Kelly, Mary Pat. *Proudly We Served: The Men of the USS* Mason. Annapolis: Naval Institute Press/Bluejacket Books, 1995.

Kempton, Murray. *Part of Our Time: Some Ruins and Monuments of the Thirties.* New York: Simon & Schuster, 1955.

Ketchum, Richard M. *The Borrowed Years, 1938–1941: America on the Way to War.* New York: Random House, 1989.

Kimball, Warren F., editor. *Churchill & Roosevelt: The Complete Correspondence Volume 1.* Princeton, NJ: Princeton University Press, 1984.

Klinkner, Philip A. *The Unsteady March: The Rise and Decline of Racial Equality in America.* Chicago: University of Chicago Press, 1999.

Kryder, Daniel. *Divided Arsenal: Race and the American State during World War II.* Cambridge, UK: Cambridge University Press, 2000.

Lanning, Michael Lee, *The African-American Soldier: From Crispus Attucks to Colin Powell.* Secaucus, NJ: Carol Publishing Group, 1997.

Lash, Joseph P., *Eleanor and Franklin: The Story of Their Relationship.* New York: Norton, 1971.

Lee, Alfred McClung. *Race Riot, Detroit 1943.* New York: Octagon Books, 1968.

Lee, Ulysses. *The Employment of Negro Troops: United States Army in World War II.* Washington: Government Printing Office, 1966.

Liebowitz, Irving. *My Indiana.* Upper Saddle River, NJ: Prentice-Hall, 1964.

Lobdell, George. "Frank Knox." In *American Secretaries of the Navy.* Edited by Paolo E. Coletta. Annapolis, MD: Naval Institute Press, 1980.

Logan, Rayford W., and Michael R. Winston, editors. *Dictionary of American Negro Biography.* New York: W. W. Norton, 1982.

Loy, Ursula Fogleman, and Pauline Marion Worthy. *Washington and the Pamlico.* Raleigh, NC: Edwards & Broughton, 1976.

MacGregor, Morris J. *Integration of the Armed Forces.* Washington, DC: Government Printing Office, 1981.

Mallison, Sam Thomas. *The Great Wildcatter.* Charleston: Education Foundation of West Virginia, 1953.

McGuire, Phillip. *Taps for a Jim Crow Army: Letters from Black Soldiers in World War II.* Santa Barbara: ABC-Clio, 1983.

McNeil, Genna Rae. *Groundwork: Charles Hamilton Houston and the Struggle for Civil Rights*. Philadelphia: University of Pennsylvania Press, 1983.

Miller, Richard E. *Messman Chronicles: African Americans in the U.S. Navy, 1932–1943*. Annapolis, MD: Naval Institute Press, 2004.

Myrdal, Gunnar. *An American Dilemma: The Negro Problem and Modern Democracy*. New York: Harper & Row, 1944.

Nalty, Bernard C. *Strength for the Fight: A History of Black Americans in the Military*. New York: Free Press, 1986.

Nalty, Bernard C., and Morris J. MacGregor. *Blacks in the Military: Essential Documents*. Wilmington, DE: Scholarly Resources, 1981.

Nelson, Dennis D. *The Integration of the Negro into the U.S. Navy*. New York: Farrar, Straus, and Young, 1951.

Newton, Adolph W. *Better Than Good: A Black Sailor's War, 1943–1945*. Annapolis: Naval Institute Press, 1999.

Newton, Michael. *Unsolved Civil Rights Murder Cases, 1934–1970*. Jefferson, NC: McFarland & Company, 2016.

Nichols, Lee. *Breakthrough on the Color Front*. New York: Random House, 1954.

O'Farrell, Brigid. *She Was One of Us: Eleanor Roosevelt and the American Worker*. Ithaca, NY: ILR Press, 2010.

Olson, Lynne. *Citizens of London: The Americans Who Stood with Britain in Its Darkest, Finest Hour*. New York: Random House, 2010.

Ostewig, Kinnie A. *The Sage of Sinnissippi*. Shabbona, IL: Press of J. A. Noel, 1907.

Perkins, Frances. *The Roosevelt I Knew*. New York: Viking Press, 1946.

Perni, Holliston. *A Heritage of Hypocrisy: Why 'They' Hate Us*. Uniondale, PA: Pleasant Mount Press, 2005.

Polenberg, Richard. *One Nation Divisible: Class, Race, and Ethnicity in the United States Since 1938*. New York: Viking Press, 1980.

Rawn, James. *The Double V: How Wars, Protest, and Harry Truman Desegregated America's Military*. New York: BloomsburyUSA, 2013.

Reed, Merl Elwy. *Seedtime for the Modern Civil Rights Movement: The President's Committee on Fair Employment Practice, 1941–1946*. Baton Rouge: Louisiana State University Press, 1991.

Remnick, David. *The Bridge: The Life and Rise of Barack Obama*. New York: Knopf, 2010.

Reynolds, David. *From World War to Cold War: Churchill, Roosevelt, and the International History of the 1940s*. Oxford, UK: Oxford University Press, 2006.

Roper, Scott C. *When Baseball Met Big Bill Haywood: The Battle for Manchester, New Hampshire, 1912–1916*. Jefferson, NC: McFarland & Company, 2018.

Rosenman, Samuel I. *Working with Roosevelt*. New York: Harper, 1952.

Rosenman, Samuel I., and Dorothy Rosenman. *Presidential Style: Some Giants and a Pygmy in the White House*. New York: Harper, 1952.

Rustin, Bayard. *Strategies for Freedom: The Changing Patterns of Black Protest*. New York: Columbia University Press, 1976.

Schneller, Robert, Jr. *Breaking the Color Barrier: The U.S. Naval Academy's First Black Midshipmen*. New York: New York University Press, 2005.

Scott, Lawrence P., and William M. Womack. *Double V: The Civil Rights Struggle of the Tuskegee Airmen*. East Lansing: Michigan State University Press, 1998.

Shapiro, Herbert. *White Violence and Black Response: From Reconstruction to Montgomery*. Amherst: University of Massachusetts Press, 1988.

Sherwood, John Darrell. *Black Sailor, White Navy: Racial Unrest in the Fleet during the Vietnam War Era*. New York: New York University Press, 2007.

Sherwood, Robert E. *Roosevelt and Hopkins: An Intimate History*. New York: Harper, 1948.

Shetterly, Margot Lee. *Hidden Figures: The American Dream and the Untold Story of the Black Women Mathematicians Who Helped Win the Space Race*. New York: William Morrow, 2016.

Sitkoff, Harvard. *Toward Freedom Land: The Long Stuggle for Racial Equality in America*. Lexington, KY: University Press of Kentucky, 2010.

Stevenson, Adlai Ewing. *The Papers of Adlai Stevenson*. Vol. 2, *Washington to Springfield, 1941–1948*. Boston: Little, Brown, 1972.

Stillwell, Paul. *The Golden Thirteen: Recollections of the First Black Naval Officers*. Annapolis, MD: Naval Institute Press, 1993.

Sullivan, Patricia. *Days of Hope: Race and Democracy in the New Deal Era*. Chapel Hill: University of North Carolina Press, 1996.

Tindall, George Brown. *The Emergence of the New South, 1913–1945*. Baton Rouge: Louisiana State University Press, 1967.

Toppin, Edgar A. *A Biographical History of Blacks in America Since 1528*. New York: David McKay, 1971.

Tully, Grace. *FDR: My Boss*. New York: Charles Scribner's Sons, 1949.

Ware, Gilbert. *William Hastie: Grace Under Pressure*. New York: Oxford University Press, 1984.

Washburn, Patrick S. *A Question of Sedition: The Federal Government's Investigation of the Black Press During World War II*. New York: Oxford University Press, 1986.

Weber, Michael. *Don't Call Me Boss: David L. Lawrence, Pittsburgh's Renaissance Mayor*. Pittsburgh: University of Pittsburgh Press, 1988.

Weiss, Nancy. *Farewell to the Party of Lincoln: Black Politics in the Age of FDR*. Princeton, NJ: Princeton University Press, 1983.

White, Walter. *A Man Called White: The Autobiography of Walter White*. New York: Viking, 1948.

Willkie, Wendell L. *One World*. New York: Simon & Schuster, 1943.
Wynn, Neil, A. *The Afro-American and the Second World War*. New York: Holmes & Meier, 1975.

SOURCES ACCESSED ONLINE

Hampton Roads Naval Museum. "Hampton Institute and the Navy during the Second World War, Part II: The Compromise." March 28, 2018. http:// hamptonroadsnavalmuseum.blogspot.com/2018/03/hampton-institute-and -navy-during.html.

Hampton Roads Naval Museum. "A Legendary Name Is Reborn," April 13, 2018. http://hamptonroadsnavalmuseum.blogspot.com/2018/04/seventy-five-years -ago-legendary-name.html.

Hardy, Rob. "Thank You, Robert Hardy!" Letter to the editor. *Oberlin Alumni Magazine* (Winter 1998). http://www2.oberlin.edu/alummag/oampast/oam _winter/Letters/oamwinter98_letters.html.

Sherman, Ted. "Lena Horne at 100: WW2 Memories of Meeting Her." *90isthenew black* (blog), September 22, 2018. https://90isthenewblack.wordpress.com /2017/06/ 30/lena-horne-at-100-ww2-memories-of-meeting-her/comment -page-1/#comment-951.

JOURNAL ARTICLES

Brewer, James H. "Robert Lee Vann, Democrat or Republican: An Exponent of Loose Leaf Politics." *Negro History Bulletin* 21, no. 5 (1958): 100–103.

Capeci, Dominic J. "The Lynching of Cleo Wright: Federal Protection of Constitutional Rights During World War II." *Journal of American History* 72, no. 4 (1986): 859–87.

Dalfiume, Richard M. "Military Segregation and the 1940 Presidential Election." *Phylon* 30, no. 1 (1969): 42–55.

———. "The 'Forgotten Years' of the Negro Revolution." *Journal of American History* 55, no. 1 (1968): 90–106.

Davis, John W. "The Negro in the United States Navy, Marine Corps and Coast Guard." *Journal of Negro Education* 12, no. 3 (1943): 345–49.

Finkle, Lee. "The Conservative Aims of Militant Rhetoric: Black Protest during World War II." *Journal of American History* 60, no. 3 (1973): 692–713.

Floyd, Samuel A. "The Great Lakes Experience: 1942–45." *Black Perspective in Music* 3, no. 1 (1975): 17–24.

Flynn, George Q. "Selective Service and American Blacks During World War II." *Journal of Negro History* 69, no. 1 (1984): 14–25.

Johnson, Marilynn S. "Gender, Race, and Rumours: Re-examining the 1943 Race Riots." *Gender & History* 10, no. 2 (August 1998): 252–77.

Moye, J. Todd. "The Tuskegee Airmen Oral History Project and Oral History in the National Park Service." *Journal of American History* 89, no. 2 (2002): 584.

Murray, Paul T. "Blacks and the Draft: A History of Institutional Racism." *Journal of Black Studies* 2, no. 1 (1971): 57–76.

"The Navy and the Negro." Editorial. *Opportunity: A Journal of Negro Life* 20, no. 5 (May 1942): 130.

Perry, Earnest L. "It's Time to Force a Change: The African American Press' Campaign for a True Democracy During World War II." *Journalism History* 28, no. 2 (2002): 85–95.

Reddick, L. D. "The Negro in the United States Navy during World War II." *Journal of Negro History* 32, no. 2 (1947): 201–19.

Selden, Steven. "Transforming Better Babies into Fitter Families: Archival Resources and the History of the American Eugenics Movement, 1908–1930." *Proceedings of the American Philosophical Society* 149, no. 2 (2005): 204.

Sitkoff, Harvard. "Racial Militancy and Interracial Violence in the Second World War." *Journal of American History* 58, no. 3 (1971): 661–81.

Washburn, Patrick S. "The *Pittsburgh Courier's* Double V Campaign in 1942." *American Journalism* 3, no. 2 (1986): 73–86. Paper presented at the Annual Meeting of the Association for Education in Journalism (August 8–11, 1981).

DOCUMENTARY FILMS AND RADIO BROADCASTS

Conan, Neal. "Two of the Golden Thirteen Interviewed." *Morning Edition*, National Public Radio. February 24,1993.

Levin, Henry, director. *The Negro Sailor*. Documentary. US Navy, 1945.

"The Honorable William Sylvester White." The History Makers (website), September 5, 2000, https://www.thehistorymakers.org/biography/honorable-william -sylvester-white.

DISSERTATIONS

Burran, James Albert. "Racial Violence in the South During World War II." University of Tennessee, Knoxville, 1977.

Davis, Michael Shawn. "Many of Them Are Among My Best Men: The United States Navy Looks at Its African American Crewmen, 1755–1955." Kansas State University, 2011.

Mikkelsen, Vincent. "Coming from Battle to Face a War: The Lynching of Black Soldiers in the World War I Era." Florida State University, 2007.

Woods, Louis Lee, II. "Messmen No More: African-American Sailors on the USS *Mason* in World War II." Howard University, 2006.

UNPUBLISHED DOCUMENTS

Chief of Naval Personnel. "U.S. Naval Training Center, Great Lakes, Illinois."
 Bound original typescript, December 28, 1945. Archival Collection, National
 Museum of the American Sailor, Naval Station Great Lakes, Great Lakes, IL.

Stillwell, Paul. "The Navy Years." Chapter 8 of unpublished work, "Two Black Lives."

US Navy, Bureau of Naval Personnel. "The Negro in the Navy: United States Naval
 Administrative History of World War II #84." Washington: US Navy, Bureau
 of Naval Personnel, 1947. Unpublished multivolume administrative history
 of World War II. Available online at https://www.history.navy.mil/research
 /library/online-reading-room/title-list-alphabetically/n/negro-navy-1947
 -adminhist84.html.

INDEX